RESTORING THE RIGHT TO LIFE

Volume One

of the

Horatio R. Storer Series in Ethics, Law, and Medicine

RESTORING THE RIGHT TO LIFE

The Human Life Amendment

Edited by James Bopp, Jr.
Brigham Young University Press

ISBN 0-8425-2100-3

Brigham Young University Press, Provo, Utah 84602

Printed in the United States of America

84 69143

CONTENTS

INTRODUCTION

Since abortion was legalized by the Supreme Court in 1973, considerable momentum has grown in favor of a human life amendment. As a result of elections since 1978, the support in Congress for such an amendment has grown substantially and the prospects for passage have similarly increased.*

With public attention continuing to be focused on abortion, we deem it appropriate to examine professionally the need for and probable effects of a human life amendment. To this end, St. Louis University Center for Health Care Ethics sponsored the conference from whence these papers come, and the Horatio R. Storer Foundation has chosen to publish them as the first in their series on ethics, law, and medicine. While the authors of the papers herein share respect for the inherent value of all innocent human life, each is an expert in his field and has sought to examine the human life amendment critically with respect to his area of interest and expertise. While not every opinion expressed herein is embraced by the directors of the Horatio R. Storer Foundation or the St. Louis University Center for Health Care Ethics, we feel that the positions presented are fairly drawn.

The primary focus of this volume is on the Garn and National Right to Life Committee (NRLC) amendments, both of which are designed to provide full legal protection under the Constitution to the unborn. Also examined are the Hatch Federalism and Hatch-Eagleton amendments, both of which have been designed (and presented to Congress as such) merely to reverse *Roe v. Wade* by declaring that abortions are not protected by the Constitution, thereby returning the authority to Congress and/or the state legislatures to provide, or not provide, legal protection to the unborn. Additionally, there are several references to the Human Life Bill, a bill designed to employ the power of the U.S. Congress, under Section 5 of the 14th Amendment, to extend protection of personhood to the unborn. The several proposed amendments are

---

*In the U.S. Senate, for instance, support for abortion restrictions have steadily grown. In 1976, the Senate voted for the first time on a human life amendment, the Helm Amendment. It was defeated on a tabling motion by a vote of forty-seven to forty [122 CONG. REC. 11580 (1976)]. In 1983, forty-nine senators voted in favor of the Hatch-Eagleton Amendment [129 CONG. REC. S 9310 (daily ed. June 28, 1983)]. In the first year after *Roe v. Wade,* only twenty-seven senators could be mustered to vote to restrict federal funding of abortion [120 CONG. REC. 18730 (1974)].

cited in full in Chapter 1. The Human Life Bill is cited in Appendix A.

The volume opens with an in-depth historical and legal analysis of the development of the ongoing effort to provide protection for the unborn through the constitutional amendment process. The editor examines the historical development of the several proposals for a human life amendment, explains their strengths and weaknesses, and concludes that the NRLC Amendment (drafted in 1981) meets all of the goals of the right-to-life movement and would provide fullest legal protection to the unborn.

Lynn Wardle follows with an examination of the effect on federal and state law of a human life amendment providing full protection to the unborn. Professor Wardle focuses primarily on the Garn Amendment, his opinion being that the Garn Amendment rather than the NRLC Amendment will be the amendment ultimately passed by Congress and presented for ratification. He first reviews the impact of *Roe v. Wade* and its progeny, then goes on to project the probable consequences of the Garn Amendment on property, tort, criminal, and constitutional law.

Part Two analyzes legal abortions from the perspectives of philosophy and morality. John P. Doyle argues that the unborn are properly considered as persons and, scientifically as well as logically, should be so considered from the moment of conception because, from the moment the zygote is formed, "an incipient embodied human person . . . is embarked upon a historical career in space and time." Robert J. Henle analyzes the basis of a pluralistic society and concludes that respect for human life is part of the consensus within American pluralism. As a result, restrictive abortion legislation is justified as a matter of natural and legal justice. He argues, however, that the pro-life movement may need to accept abortion in the rare instances of rape, incest, and fetal deformity.

In Part Three, Professor Rue provides a comprehensive analysis of the devastating impact of abortion on the family. He particularly examines the effect of abortion on the putative father, a person often ignored in the abortion debate.

Part Four examines the consequences of a human life amendment, such as the Garn and NRLC amendments, that would provide legal protection for the unborn. The effect of such an amendment on medical treatment for pregnant women is examined by Denis Cavanagh. Dr. Cavanagh examines, comprehensively and in depth, virtually every medical condition which might afflict a pregnant woman in order to determine whether the proper course of medical treatment would be impeded by a human life amendment. Additionally, he explains those circumstances when an abortion would be necessary to prevent the death of the mother. He concludes that a human life amendment would not adversely affect the health of pregnant women and would allow for abortion in those few instances where it is necessary.

Birth control drugs and devices are examined in two papers. First, James D. Madden explains the function and action of such drugs and devices. Dennis J. Horan follows with an examination of the impact of a human life amendment on these same drugs and devices. Mr. Horan concludes that the human life amendment will only affect those birth control drugs and devices which are used after positive proof of pregnancy. While subsequent federal or state laws may regulate abortifacients, a human life amendment would not restrict their use until there is positive evidence of pregnancy.

Pregnancy due to rape and incest is explored by Basile J. Uddo. Finding that such pregnancies are extremely rare, Professor Uddo concludes that proper treatment and care of the incest and rape victim does not include abortion.

In the final paper, the effect of a human life amendment beyond abortion—in the areas of infanticide, euthanasia, in vitro fertilization, and fetal experimentation—is explored. Professor Rosenblum concludes that a human life amendment would protect life across the spectrum and would have an impact in each of these areas.

Neither this volume nor the conference from which its contents issued would have been possible without the sponsorship of the St. Louis University Center for Health Care Ethics. The center cosponsored the seminar with the National Right to Life Foundation, Incorporated; and Kevin O'Rourke, S.J., its director, was invaluable in assisting in its development. Father O'Rourke played a critical role in the development of topics for the papers and selection of speakers. Additionally, John Grellner of the St. Louis University Medical Center Continuing Education administered the seminar. His expertise and professionalism insured its success.

Many other individuals volunteered their time with the St. Louis seminar. Kathy Edwards of Kansas City, Missouri, cochaired the seminar with the editor. Her selfless efforts and competent judgment insured the seminar's success. Ann O'Donnell of St. Louis, Missouri, mobilized many local volunteers to staff the seminar. Her support of the project is highly appreciated.

The seminar also received substantial financial support from the National Right to Life Educational Trust Fund and the Missouri Citizens for Life Educational Foundation. Additionally, the seminar received a major grant from the Pallottine Center for

Apostolic Causes. Without these grants, the seminar and this volume would not have been attempted.

Additionally, I express appreciation to my loyal and competent secretary, Mary Winn, without whose skill, judgment, and hard work this volume would have been impossible. Larry Liggett of Terre Haute, Indiana, served as editorial consultant and assumed the arduous task of compiling the papers. Howard Christy of Brigham Young University provided invaluable direction and assistance. Finally, special thanks are extended to Professor Robert Byrn of Fordham University Law School. Professor Byrn provided invaluable critical analysis and advice: his insight guided this work.

James Bopp, Jr.

1

DEVELOPMENT AND LEGAL EFFECTS OF A HUMAN LIFE AMENDMENT

Chapter One

AN EXAMINATION OF PROPOSALS FOR A HUMAN LIFE AMENDMENT

James Bopp, Jr.

Since the Supreme Court's decision in *Roe v. Wade*[1] and *Doe v. Bolton*[2] legalizing abortion by a woman's choice, numerous proposals for a constitutional amendment reversing these decisions have been offered. Some of these amendments have been introduced in Congress and others have been circulated within the right-to-life movement. The intent of this chapter is to analyze these suggested constitutional amendments against the goal of the right-to-life movement to restore full legal protection to the unborn.

The Holdings of *Roe v. Wade*

In *Roe v. Wade* the Supreme Court declared that the right of privacy "encompasses a woman's decision whether or not to terminate her pregnancy" and thus was protected against state infringement by the 14th Amendment.[3] Finding this to be a "fundamental" constitutional right, the Court declared that state laws infringing upon this right cannot be sustained unless they are necessary to effectuate a compelling state interest.

Having clarified the standard of judicial review, the Court then proceeded to determine whether the state had a "compelling" state interest to support abortion restrictions. The first argument it considered was that the unborn were "persons" and that states had a compelling interest in protecting their lives. The Court rejected that argument and concluded that the unborn are not "persons." In reaching this conclusion, Justice Blackmun, who wrote the opinion for the Court, (1) analyzed the text of the Constitution and the usage of the word "person" therein,[4] (2) referred to the history of less restrictive abortion practices throughout the major portion of the nineteenth century (when the 14th Amendment was enacted),[5] and (3) noted that the Court's conclusion that the unborn are not constitutional "persons" was in accord with

James Bopp, Jr., J.D., is general counsel to the National Right to Life Committee and chairman of the NRLC Human Life Amendment Committee. He is editor of HUMAN LIFE AND HEALTH CARE ETHICS (1984).

the results reached by state courts and lower federal courts that had addressed the issue.[6]

The Court went on to consider whether there were any other potentially "compelling" state interests that would justify criminal abortion prohibitions. The Court examined two primary arguments: (1) that the state's interest in protecting maternal health is a compelling justification for abortion restrictions,[7] and (2) that, even if the unborn are not persons, they are at least human beings and the state interest in protecting the life of human beings is compelling.[8] The Court concluded that the unborn possessed only "potential life" and that interest in potential life was not compelling throughout pregnancy, but only after viability.[9]

There are, therefore, two distinct holdings of the Court: (1) a woman's right to privacy included her decision of whether or not to terminate her pregnancy, and (2) states' interest in unborn life is not sufficiently compelling to permit regulation of abortion before viability. The holding which resulted in unfettered abortion is the finding of a constitutional right in the woman. Without it, states could still protect unborn life since it is a legitimate state interest even under *Roe v. Wade,* albeit not a compelling one. By illustration, a government may protect eagle eggs from destruction even though it does not have a compelling interest to do so.[10] After all, an eagle does not have a constitutional right to destroy its egg, nor does anyone else.

The Supreme Court decision in *Roe v. Wade* has been subject to severe criticism by legal scholars. Even those who support legalized abortion have criticized its serious jurisprudential and logical flaws. In his dissent in *Roe v. Wade* and its companion, *Doe v. Bolton,* for instance, Justice White observed:

> I find nothing in the language or history of the Constitution to support the Court's judgment. The Court simply fashions and announces a new constitutional right for pregnant mothers and, with scarcely any reason or authority for its action, invests that right with sufficient substance to override most existing State abortion statutes.[11]

Justice Rehnquist added in his accompanying dissent:

> The decision here to break the term of pregnancy into three distinct terms and to outline the permissible restrictions the State may impose in each one, for example, partakes more of judicial legislation than it does of a determination of the intent of the drafters of the Fourteenth Amendment . . . To reach its result the Court necessarily has had to find within the scope of the Fourteenth Amendment a right that was apparently completely unknown to the drafters of the Amendment.[12]

Constitutional scholars, regardless of their views on abortion, have also criticized the Court. Professor Archibald Cox, the former solicitor general of the United States, remarked of the *Roe v. Wade* decision:

The failure to confront the issue in principled terms leaves the opinion to read like a set of hospital rules and regulations*** Neither historian, nor layman, nor lawyer will be persuaded that all the prescriptions of Justice Blackmun are part of the Constitution.[13]

Professor John Hart Ely of the Harvard Law School, while taking care to divorce himself from critics of the substantive policy expressed in *Roe,* concluded:

It is, nevertheless, a very bad decision. . . . It is bad because it is bad constitutional law or rather because it is not constitutional law and gives almost no sense of an obligation to try to be.[14]

Alexander Bickel, professor at the Yale Law School, described the decision as akin to a "model statute" and expressed bewilderment at how such a responsibility had come to be vested in the Court:

One is left to ask why. The Court never said. It refused the discipline to which its function is properly subject. . . . Roe is derived not from Herbert Spencer's Social Statics, but from fashionable notions of progress . . . this will not do.[15]

Professor Charles Rice of the Notre Dame Law School described the decision as "the most outrageous decision ever handed down by the Court in its entire history;"[16] Professor Richard Epstein of the University of Chicago Law School referred to *Roe* as "comprehensive legislation . . . (without) principled grounds;"[17] Professor Robert Byrn of the Fordham Law School attacked the decision as resting upon "multiple and profound misapprehension of law and history;"[18] and Dean Harry Wellington of the Yale Law School viewed *Roe* as "Pickwickian" and "without mandate."[19] Professor John Noonan concluded his analysis of the abortion case by stating:

The liberty established has no foundation in the Constitution of the United States. It was established by an act of raw judicial power. Its establishment was illegitimate and unprincipled, the imposition of the personal beliefs of seven justices on the men and women of fifty States. The continuation of the liberty is a continuing affront to constitutional government in this country.[20]

The criticism of *Roe v. Wade* has been almost unanimous from a principled constitutional law approach,[21] while those who have defended it have done so on the basis of reasons not mentioned by the Court.[22]

The decision in *Roe v. Wade* is also subject to a series of logical criticisms, pointed out by Senator Hatch at the opening of the 1983 Senate hearings:[23]

—The question of when life begins, according to the Court, is beyond the competency of the Judiciary to answer. Nevertheless the Court effectively answers the question for the legislatures and citizens of all 50 states by declaring that states can protect unborn life only after "viability."

—The Court conceded that if the unborn were "persons" they would be afforded 14th Amendment protections. Yet both reasons the Court offers for rejecting the "personhood" of the unborn were wholly inadequate. In the first place, the Court suggests that none of the other uses of the term "person" in the Constitution appear to apply to the unborn. As a matter of fact, however, none of the other uses of the term appear to apply to anyone under the age of 24. All other uses of the term apply to adults. Surely adolescents could not thus be stripped of personhood. The second reason given by the Court is the absence of case law indicating the unborn should be persons. This only proves a well-known fact: This question was before the Court for the first time. It is unseemly that an issue which could have disposed of the case was given such shallow consideration.

—Although the Court maintained that it could not determine when life begins, it nonetheless divided a pregnancy into three separate trimesters with different legal implications for each subdivision. One looks in vain for any reasoning from constitutional, legal or scientific sources for a guiding principle underlying this division process.

—When finding a right to privacy, the Court employed imagination and innovation to find a never-before-identified right to abortion within the due process clause of the 14th Amendment; when finding "person" does not include the unborn, the Court was literalistic to a fault. Without reaching the merits of appropriate judicial construction techniques, vacillating between two extremes inspires little confidence that the decision was based solely upon purely neutral criteria of constitutional interpretation.

—Even if the unborn have no rights under the 14th Amendment, this is irrelevant to the question of whether a state may restrict abortion. Professor Ely uses a particularly enlightening analogy to illustrate this point:

> Dogs are not "persons in the whole sense" nor have they constitutional rights, but that does not mean the state cannot prohibit killing them: It does not even mean the state cannot prohibit killing them in the exercise of the First Amendment right of political protest.[24]

In 1983, the Supreme Court reaffirmed *Roe v. Wade* in one of its most wide-ranging decisions since 1973. In *City of Akron v. Akron Center for Reproductive Health,*[25] the Supreme Court substantially eroded available government protection of pregnant women by severely limiting the circumstances in which a state might regulate abortion on behalf of maternal health. As a result, the Court restricted the circumstances under which a state may regulate abortion in the exercise of its interest in maternal health.

In the *Akron* case, the Supreme Court was faced with a series of regulations which had their justification in the advancement of the state's interest in maternal health in order to protect pregnant women from the hazards of abortion. By requiring informed consent and a waiting period, the City of Akron sought to insure that a woman's consent to abortion was knowing and voluntary. The second trimester hospitalization requirement insured that abortions, which were more risky than childbirth at this time, were performed in circumstances insuring their greatest safety. Minors under fifteen were required to receive parental or court consent based on the assumption that minors this young were not mature enough to make the decision themselves. In expanding *Roe v. Wade* and further limiting the state's right to protect women, the Court struck down these regulations.

The state's interest in maternal health, found by the Court in 1973 to be compelling after the first trimester, was substantially limited by this decision. The Court found that the exercise of this compelling interest may not "depart from acceptable medical practice"[26] and must be limited "to the period in the trimester"[27] during which this health interest would be secured. In determining acceptable medical practice, the Court looked to standards adopted by the American College of Obstetricians and Gynecologists[28] and the American Public Health Association,[29] both of which have called for abortion on demand since the 1960s. Additionally, the Court cited the National Abortion Federation guidelines,[30] which are the guidelines adopted by the abortion industry itself. Thus, the Court has set itself up as "the nation's ex officio medical board,"[31] according to the dissent by Justice Sandra O'Connor. Thus, a compelling interest in maternal health during this period is not sufficient if the physicians who perform abortions would not regulate themselves in the same manner thought best by the legislature.

Further, the Court has apparently conferred heightened status to physicians in the abortion decision by striking down regulations which do not allow "her physician (to) be given the room he needs to make his best medical judgment."[32] This conferral on the physician of the exercise of his medical judgment is despite the fact that a physician normally would not see an abortion patient until she is on the operating table.[33] Paradoxically, in the same decision, the Court found that the physician himself need not counsel the woman,[34] thus allowing him to delegate to nonphysicians his protected "medical judgment."[35] In this context, the Court would not allow the state "to influence the woman's informed choice between abortion or child birth."[36]

In addition to these restrictions in the area of the state's interest in maternal health, the Court has also apparently resolved an issue left unresolved in *Roe v. Wade.* In that case, the Justices found that they could not decide when life began, leaving this question to philosophers and theologians.[37] In the *Akron* case, they have apparently made that determination. Their decision struck down the requirement that the physician inform his patient that "the unborn child is a human life from the moment of conception"[38] on the basis that it was not consistent with the Court's holding in *Roe v. Wade* "that a state may not adopt one theory of when life begins to justify its regulation of abortion."[39] Thus, the Court has apparently declared that it is unconstitutional for a legislature to decide that human life begins at conception.

In light of the extreme nature of the Court's majority opinion, the dissent, made up of Justices O'Connor, Rehnquist, and White, calls for the reversal of *Roe v. Wade.*[40] Justice O'Connor, writing the dissenting opinion, found that the "trimester approach is a completely unworkable method."[41] Additionally, she repudiated the Court's declaration of "potential life" and its alleged compelling nature only after viability by stating that "potential life is no less potential in the first weeks of pregnancy than it is at viability or afterwards. At any stage in pregnancy there is the potential for human life."[42] According to the dissent, the state's interest in protecting human life and maternal health are compelling interests throughout pregnancy and thus are available to restrict or even prohibit abortion.[43]

This dissent marks the first time since *Roe v. Wade* where three Justices of the Supreme Court have called for its reversal. The Court, therefore, appears to be strongly polarized, one side rigidly in favor of abortion on demand throughout pregnancy and the other as rigidly opposed to it.[44]

The widespread criticism of *Roe v. Wade* has led, in part, to the considerable effort to overturn it, particularly since the majority of the Court has continued to be adamant regarding the 1973 decisions. The effort to overturn a Supreme Court decision by constitutional amendment is not unprecedented. For example, the 11th Amendment of the Constitution, prohibiting the federal judicial power to be exercised in suits by citizens of one state against another state, came in direct response to the action of the Supreme Court in accepting jurisdiction over such a case.[45] Additionally, the 14th Amendment to the Constitution was proposed following the infamous decision of the Supreme Court in *Dred Scott v. Sanford*[46] which also found that certain individuals—in that case blacks—were nonpersons under the Constitution. The 16th Amendment, permitting the imposition of a federal income tax, was enacted in response to a Supreme Court decision[47] finding an unapportioned—by state—tax to be a violation of the Constitution. Finally, the 26th Amendment, according eighteen-year-olds the right to vote in federal and state elections, was proposed following the Court's decision[48] that Congress lacked authority to impose such an obligation statutorily upon the states. Similar serious, but unsuccessful, efforts have been made in response to Court decisions on the subject of child labor laws[49] and state legislative apportionment requirements.[50]

Constitutional Standards For Abortion Restrictions

In framing a constitutional amendment to restore full legal protection to the unborn, traditional constitutional standards must be examined to determine how the court will deal with challenges to abortion legislation after the adoption of the amendment. Additionally, it must be kept in mind that it is a constitutional amendment that is being drafted. As a result, several principles and their consequences, enunciated by Professor John Noonan of the University of California at Berkeley, are evident:

> First, the Constitution is not a criminal code. Therefore, neither the detail nor the preciseness appropriate to a criminal code are appropriate to it. Second, the Constitution is not addressed to persons of bad will, but to persons—judges, legislators, officeholders, citizens—who want to abide by its provisions. Therefore, it is neither necessary nor desirable to draft with an eye to silly, sophistical, or evasive interpretations. No language can be made foolproof. No language cannot be distorted by evil men. The Constitution is not addressed to the foolish or the wicked, but to the people and their representatives; it assumes good faith on the part of those interpreting it. Third, the Constitution is not self-executing. It sets a framework in which power may be exercised. Therefore, it is wrong to suppose that any controversy is settled by the Constitution because the Constitution must be executed by the government, observed by legislators, interpreted by judges, and responded to by the people.[51]

In this examination, therefore, it is assumed that the courts will, in good faith, attempt to interpret and apply any constitutional amendment consistent with its intent to extend legal protection to the unborn.

No constitutional right is absolute. The constitutional rights guaranteed by the United States Constitution are each subject to infringement or devestment by balancing one constitutional right against another competing constitutional right or by the exercise of a state's compelling interest.[52] The potential hazard to restoring full legal protection to the unborn, by the employment of these tests, are many and must be anticipated in drafting a constitutional amendment.

Balancing the Woman's Right to Privacy Versus the Unborn's Right to Life

If a proposed constitutional amendment would restore to the unborn the constitutionally protected right to life while not abrogating the woman's right to privacy to decide whether or not to have an abortion, the courts, in examining a statute restricting abortion, would have to balance the conflict between the constitutional rights of the woman and the unborn. The Supreme Court has traditionally given some discretion to a legislature in adjusting conflicting rights between groups of people, each of whom has a claim to constitutional protection.[53] In the context of abortion, the Supreme Court has previously sought to balance competing constitutional rights. In *Planned Parenthood v. Danforth,*[54] the Supreme Court was faced with the requirement of parental consent for a minor to have an abortion. This legislative requirement was based upon the constitutional right of parents to supervise the upbringing and education of their children.[55] The Missouri legislature, therefore, was seeking to balance the constitutional right of parents versus the constitutional right of minor women to decide whether or not to seek an abortion. In that case, the Supreme Court found that the constitutional rights of a parent were not sufficient to justify requiring their consent to their minor child's abortion, and that the state did not have a compelling interest in requiring parental consent and could not grant to parents a right that the state itself did not possess.[56] The Court, therefore, weighed the minor woman's right to privacy as greater than her parent's competing constitutional rights.

The *Planned Parenthood* case was foreshadowed by pre-1973 cases considering these matters. In *Abele v. Markle,*[57] the District Court, in striking down Connecticut's criminal abortion statute, declared that a woman's right to privacy had a "far greater degree of significance" than parental rights protected in *Pierce v. Society of Sisters.*[58] Additionally in *Babbitz v. McCann,*[59] the Court balanced the right to privacy of the woman against the right to life of the unborn and found that "the mother's right transcends that of an embryo [of four months or less]." This attitude has been carried over into post-1973 cases.[60] The abortion right, therefore, has been elevated above most other constitutional rights by the courts.

In the nonabortion context, several courts weighed the right to life of the unborn against competing rights of the parents and have held that the unborn's right to life must prevail. In *Raleigh Fitkin-Paul Memorial Hospital v. Anderson,*[61] a pregnant woman refused a blood transfusion for her unborn child based upon her right to practice her religious beliefs as a Jehovah's Witness, a faith which prohibits blood transfusions. The New Jersey court ordered the transfusion, despite the parent's religious objection, by preferring the life of the child over a constitutional right which was less than life.[62] Most later cases in the abortion context, however, have not followed this value preference.

If the courts are permitted, therefore, to balance these constitutional rights, the results for the unborn are not clear. To insure maximum legal protection to the unborn, therefore, the doctrines established in *Roe v. Wade* and its antecedents and progeny must be reversed.

Balancing a State's Compelling Interest in Unborn Life Against the Woman's Right to Privacy

Where a fundamental right is involved, the Supreme Court has held that regulations limiting those rights may be justified only by a compelling state interest.[63] If the Supreme Court holding that a woman had a constitutional right to decide whether or not to have an abortion (found in *Roe v. Wade*) was unreversed by a constitutional amendment, a state would have to rely upon a compelling state interest in unborn life in order to restrict the woman's right to privacy. This compelling interest could be established by restoring personhood under the Constitution to the unborn or by a constitutional declaration of such a compelling interest.[64]

Courts have previously sought to analyze the extent to which a state may assert a compelling interest in protecting unborn life against the woman's right to privacy. In *Roe v. Wade,* of course, the court determined that the state's interest in unborn life did not become compelling until viability, and even then abortions could not be prohibited if necessary to preserve the woman's health.[65] Arguably, with the adoption of a constitutional amendment giving the states a compelling interest in protecting unborn life, this ruling would have to be reexamined and the nature of the state's compelling interest in unborn lives redetermined. Unfortunately, it is not obvious that the courts would find a compelling interest in unborn life from conception sufficient to abrogate the woman's right to privacy to decide whether or not to have an abortion.

Once again, cases before 1973 are instructive on how courts might interpret this compelling interest. While some courts upheld restrictive abortion statutes in the face of a recognized woman's right to privacy because of the state's compelling interest in unborn lives,[66] most upheld the statutes on the ground that no such constitutional right in a woman existed.[67] Most courts, however, struck down restrictive abortion statutes because of the insufficiency of the states' interest in unborn life in the face of a woman's right to privacy.[68] Most of these cases weighed the nature and extent of the states' compelling interest in unborn life. As a result of this analysis, courts found that the states' interest in unborn life was not sufficiently compelling to abrogate a woman's right to privacy during the first trimester,[69] when the unborn child may be deformed or crippled,[70] when the unborn child is unwanted,[71] or when the pregnancy is a result of rape or incest.[72] Additionally, in the recent case of *Committee to Defend Reproductive Rights v. Myers,*[73] the California Supreme Court found that the state's interest in unborn life was not sufficiently compelling to justify the denial of state funds for medically necessary abortions because of the overriding state interest in maternal health.

Thus, the courts would still have the opportunity to shape the nature of the states' compelling interest in unborn life after it is restored. The nature of this interest would be weighed against and in the face of the woman's constitutional right to privacy to decide whether or not to have an abortion. Cases prior to 1973 disclose the danger to the unborn in leaving this matter to the courts for resolution.

The State's Compelling Interest in Maternal Health

Despite the adoption of any constitutional amendment, some states can be expected to pass statutes permitting abortion for health reasons. If the constitutional amendment restored constitutional personhood to the unborn, these laws would be subject to equal protection attacks on the grounds that they did not extend effective protection to the unborn and thereby denied the unborn, as persons, the equal protection of the laws.[74] The outcome of such challenges is not clear.

Permitting abortions for reasons of health, under prevailing Supreme Court decisions, amounts to abortion in all circumstances. Health has been defined by the Supreme Court to include "mental health."[75] Additionally, the Supreme Court has held that factors such as "physical, emotional, psychological, familial, and the woman's age" are all relevant to the well-being of a patient and are thus factors which relate to health.[76] The Supreme Court, therefore, has apparently adopted the 1960 World Health Organization's definition of health as "a state of complete physical, mental and social well-being, not simply the absence of illness and disease."[77] Thus, health abortions are, in fact, abortions on demand if a physician is willing to perform the operation.

This definition of health has been broadly interpreted by doctors who support abortion. Dr. David Zbaraz, for instance, declared that all first-trimester and most second-trimester abortions were medically necessary since, during that time, abortion was medically safer than childbirth.[78] Some pro-abortion physicians feel that there is a medical indication to abort a pregnancy if it "is not wanted by the patient"[79] or if the woman says, "I can't cope with this pregnancy."[80] In fact, no more than 2 percent of induced abortions are performed "for clinically identifiable reasons," and no more than 1 percent are performed to save the life of the mother—or for any other purpose related to physical health.[81]

The notion that abortion is safer than childbirth, at least in the first trimester, first received acceptance by the United States Supreme Court in *Roe v. Wade.* There, the Court noted that "[m]ortality rates for women undergoing early abortion, where the procedure is legal, appear to be as low or lower than the rates for normal childbirth."[82] As a result, the Court concluded that the state may not regulate the abortion procedure in the interest of maternal health until the second trimester where that interest becomes compelling due to abortion becoming as dangerous as childbirth at this late stage.

This notion has come under considerable attack recently on the grounds that the tendered comparison of childbirth and abortion was "seriously flawed by comparing uncomparable data."[83] The Hilgers analysis[84] concludes that, in comparing the relative risks of natural pregnancy versus those of legal abortion, "natural pregnancy was found to be safer in both the first and second 20 weeks of pregnancy."[85]

Additionally, the claim that abortion is safer than childbirth also ignores the morbidity associated with abortion. In recent years there has been an explosion of knowledge about the devastating long-term health consequences of abortion. A recent study in New York,[86] comparing the relative risk of low-birth-weight infants and prematurities in subsequent pregnancies, found an increased risk of 36 to 67 percent for low-birth-weight infants and 61 to 120 percent for premature infants in women ending their first pregnancy in abortion rather than live birth. These risks increase with repeated abortions.[87] Even the Supreme Court has now come to recognize that "the medical, emotional, and psychological consequences of an abortion are serious and can be long lasting."[88]

Some authorities, however, continue to claim that the scientific literature does not support the "firm conclusion" that induced abortion causes any long-term complications.[89] Unfortunately, it is not clear that the courts would accept this new data and conclude that abortion is more dangerous than childbirth. In a challenge by right-to-life advocates against a statute permitting health abortions after the ratification of a constitutional amendment, the courts should recognize the unborn child's constitutional right to life but then would determine if there are any counterbalancing, compelling state interests justifying the health exception. In this instance, the court need look no further than the Supreme Court's decision in *Roe v. Wade,* wherein the court found a compelling interest in maternal health sufficient even to restrict a woman's right to privacy. The compelling interest of maternal health permitting regulation of abortions was even superior to the state's compelling interest in protecting potential life after viability. In analyzing the nature of this compelling interest, a court could find that the compelling interest in maternal health is sufficient to justify abortions for "health" reasons. Under such a ruling, the statutes permitting health abortions could be upheld.

The Woman's Right to Life

Proposals to restore legal protection to the unborn all seek to protect unborn life from abortion. Most do so by restoring the constitutional protection of the unborn's right to life. Women are considered persons under the 14th Amendment[90] and, therein, their right to life is constitutionally guaranteed. These proposals for a human life amendment seek, not to abrogate the woman's right to life, but to guarantee to the unborn a right to life comparable to the pregnant woman's.

Thus, the woman's right to life must be considered in any proposal to prohibit abortion. The woman's right to life needs to be considered because childbirth involves a risk of death.[91] In recognition of the woman's right to life, all but four of the state statutes regulating abortion before 1965 explicitly permitted abortion to save the life of the mother.[92] Of the four providing no specific exception to the general prohibition against abortion, only two—Massachusetts and New Jersey—have reported cases interpreting their statutes, and both were interpreted to permit lifesaving abortions.[93] These statutes were so interpreted because their object was "not only the protection of the unborn child, but to protect the life and health of the mother as well."[94] This recognition of the woman's right to life has led some courts, even though not directly faced with the issue, to declare that the woman's right to life prevents a state from forbidding a woman to procure an abortion where her death would result from childbirth.[95]

The exception for lifesaving abortions, found in state statutes, also appears to have its roots in the general rationale of self-defense.[96] The states have "always recognized that where a choice must be made between the life of the mother and the life of the child, it falls within the general rationale of self-defense if the mother seeks an abortion to preserve her own life."[97]

Additionally, the exception for lifesaving procedures is grounded in the doctrine of legal necessity.[98] The doctrine of legal necessity excuses conduct from criminality under these conditions:

> (1) [T]he harm, to be justified, must have been committed under pressure of physical forces; (2) it must have made possible the preservation of at least an equal value; and (3) the commission of the harm must have been the only means of conserving that value.[99]

On this basis, therefore, maternal lifesaving exceptions coexisted in state statutes with judicial condemnation of abortion as a violation of the sacred and inalienable right to life of the unborn child.[100] Since the unborn was considered a person in the whole sense under the laws of these states,[101] the exclusion is explainable as an application of the broader doctrine of legal necessity.

In a few cases, courts have interpreted state statutes more broadly to include health abortions. Two of these cases involved laws which had no express exceptions for the life of the mother.[102] Only one of the state statutes permitting maternal lifesaving abortions has been so interpreted.[103]

The woman's right to life, therefore, must be considered in drafting a constitutional amendment restoring full legal protection to the unborn. While no court has directly faced the issue, the woman's right to life probably prevents a state from prohibiting lifesaving abortions. In addition, principles of the common law support a maternal lifesaving provision. In those rare circumstances where abortion is necessary to save the life of the mother,[104] states have consistently and necessarily allowed it.

Private Killing

The deprivation of the lives of unborn children by abortion, which is the primary concern of the right-to-life movement, is an act of private killing. Only a relatively few abortions are performed in state or municipal hospitals. The vast majority of abortions take place between private parties in private facilities. The effect of *Roe v. Wade* has been to prevent state regulation of their private conduct. As a result, to restore full legal protection to the unborn, private conduct must be affected.

In an analogous context, Congress saw a need to deal with private conduct whereby an oppressed group was suffering a loss of its civil rights. The response to slavery was, in part, the 13th Amendment, which affected private conduct.

13th Amendment, U.S. Constitution

SECTION 1. Neither slavery nor involuntary servitude, except as a punishment for crime whereof the party shall have been duly convicted, shall exist within the United States, or any place subject to their jurisdiction.

SECTION 2. Congress shall have power to enforce this article by appropriate legislation.

This amendment, therefore, permitted Congress to enact laws "directly and primarily operating upon the acts of individuals."[105] Congress was empowered to reach "the unofficial acts of private individuals, whether or not sanctioned by state law."[106] Any conduct which seeks to restore full legal protection to the unborn, therefore, must affect private parties.

While constitutional provisions are not normally self-executing, the federal courts have recognized a private cause of action, under the Constitution, to enforce constitutional rights.[107] As a result, "a citizen suffering a compensable injury to a constitutionally protected interest could invoke the general federal question jurisdiction of the [federal] district courts to obtain an award of monetary damage against the responsible federal officials."[108] The courts have recognized such a private cause of action under the 5th Amendment, which provides that "[n]o person shall be . . . deprived of life, liberty, or property, without due process of law."[109] Since some state or federal laws may be insufficient to protect the unborn, a properly drafted amendment, therefore, should provide the basis for a private cause of action under this doctrine to protect the unborn.

Objectives of a Human Life Amendment

The goal of a human life amendment should be to restore full legal protection to the unborn. There are, however, limitations to the protection which can be afforded the unborn under a constitutional amendment. As a result, subsequent state and federal laws will be necessary to fashion remedies and criminal and civil actions against abortion. There is, however, much that can be done by a constitutional amendment. In order to maximize the protection afforded by a human life amendment, the following objectives should guide its drafting:[110]

1. Restoration to unborn children of human parents of the constitutional status and protection of persons, with respect to their right to life, under the 5th and 14th amendments, which right was specifically destroyed by the Supreme Court decisions in *Roe v. Wade* and *Doe v. Bolton*
2. Specific protection for all persons of the fundamental right to life
3. Assurance for all human beings, irrespective of their age, health, function, or condition of dependency, of the constitutional status and protection of persons, with respect to their right to life under the 5th and 14th amendments, which right was seriously jeopardized for at least some of these human beings by the principles enunciated by the Supreme Court on January 22, 1973
4. Assurance that the lives of unborn children are protected against aggression at every stage of their biological development from the first state of fertilization of the female ovum by the male sperm through all subsequent stages
5. Protection of the lives of unborn children not only against action of the state and federal governments but also against the action of private individuals, particularly pregnant women and their physicians, upon whom the Supreme Court conferred the constitutional right to obtain and perform abortions, respectively
6. Establishment of the precept that the right to life of persons is the paramount and most fundamental right protected by the Constitution and is superior to all other constitutional rights, such as the right to privacy
7. Provision of the basis for a private cause of action to protect the lives of unborn children in those states and localities where federal, state, or local governments will not act to insure their protection
8. Permission for use of the medical procedures necessary to treat a cancerous uterus, ectopic pregnancy, and severely traumatized uterus in a pregnant woman when the treatment is necessary to prevent the death of the woman, even if the treatment results in the termination of the pregnancy, these operations not being abortions in the legal sense
9. Preservation and protection to the same extent of the life of each human being regardless of state of health or condition of dependency
10. When two or more human beings are in the situation in which their lives are mutually endangered during a pregnancy, assurance that all ordinary means and reasonable

efforts are used to preserve and protect the life of each and every human being so endangered

11. Empowerment of both the Congress and the several States to enforce the amendment by appropriate legislation.

Proposals for a Human Life Amendment

In response to this complex legal problem, many proposals for a human life amendment have been introduced in Congress. In the 97th Congress, for example, seventeen resolutions were introduced, cosponsored, in all, by thirty senators and seventy representatives, which contained different versions of a human life amendment. Additionally, several versions of a human life amendment have been proposed by various lawyers and law professors which have yet to be introduced in Congress.

These versions of a human life amendment can be divided into six types: (1) legislative authorization, (2) reversal, (3) restoration of personhood, (4) prohibition, (5) paramount, and (6) life protective. Each seeks, in one form or another, to restore legal protection to the unborn. In principle, the legislative authorization type differs most from the rest. It would affirm the principle that the states and/or Congress should have the power to protect unborn life. The reversal type would simply reverse *Roe v. Wade* and restore to the states and Congress the power they possessed before 1973 to restrict or prohibit abortion. The other types do not leave legal protection of the unborn to the discretion of the legislature but specifically affirm the principle that the unborn's right to life is protected by the Constitution.

Legislative Authorization

The legislative authorization type of human life amendment can itself be subdivided into two types, the state-rights approach and the federal-rights approach. Each approach, however, affirms the same general principle: that the regulation of abortion should be returned to the control of the states and/or Congress and leave the particulars to legislative wisdom.[111] Thus, the legislative authorization type does not purport to recognize any right to life in the unborn child; it merely removes a federal constitutional inhibition, announced in *Roe v. Wade* and *Doe v. Bolton,* from certain governmental conduct.[112]

Several different versions of a states-rights approach have been introduced in previous sessions of Congress. In the 94th Congress, for example, Congressman Whitehurst introduced H.R.J. Res. 261, which provided that:

Whitehurst Amendment

SECTION 1. Nothing in this Constitution shall bar any State or territory or the District of Columbia, with regard to any area over which it has jurisdiction, from allowing, regulating, or prohibiting the practice of abortion.

Congresswoman Eleanor Sullivan introduced H.R.J. Res. 681, authored by Professor John T. Noonan, providing that:

Noonan Amendment

The Congress within Federal jurisdiction and the several States within their jurisdictions shall have power to protect life including the unborn at every stage of biological development irrespective of age, health, or condition of physical dependency.

Additionally, Professor Noonan has proposed a federal rights approach which provides as follows:

Federal Rights Amendment

SECTION 1. The United States shall have power to protect life, including the unborn, at every stage of biological development, irrespective of age, health, or condition of dependency.

SECTION 2. Subject to the paramount authority of the United States to establish minimal standards of protection, the States shall have the power to protect life, including the unborn, at every stage of biological development, irrespective of age, health, or condition of dependency.[113]

In the 98th Congress, Senator Orrin Hatch introduced S.J. Res. 3, a federal-rights approach, which provided that:

Hatch Federalism Amendment

A right to abortion is not secured by this Constitution. The Congress and the several states shall have concurrent power to restrict and prohibit abortion: Provided, that a provision of a law of a state which is more restrictive than a conflicting provision of a law of Congress shall govern.[114]

The intent of a legislative authorization type of amendment is to "return to the individual states full authority to make laws governing abortion."[115] As a result of the adoption of such an amendment,

> there would be no barrier to the actions which States might take with respect to abortion. Conceivably, the laws in many States could be even more permissive than the standards set by the Supreme Court. But, in our democratic system, the people should have the authority to decide issues as fundamentally important as what constitutes protectable humanity. The decision of the Court has left the authority to make

human life and death decisions with private individuals. In my view, society as a whole has an overriding interest in establishing the outer limits of the human community.[116]

The supporters of the states-rights Noonan Amendment would argue that it accomplishes the following:

1. The amendment negates the holdings of the Supreme Court of the United States in *Roe v. Wade* and *Doe v. Bolton* that the Constitution of the United States is violated by law which penalizes the killing of unborn life. Under the amendment, Congress in all places particularly governed by federal law, and the states within their own borders, are empowered by the Constitution to protect life, born or unborn.
2. The amendment negates the teaching of the Supreme Court in *Roe v. Wade* that life in the womb, prior to viability, is no more than "a theory of life," incapable of protection of law. Under the amendment, Congress and the states within their respective jurisdictions may protect life from the beginning of new life.
3. The amendment negates the teaching of the Supreme Court in *Doe v. Bolton* that the law must always prefer a physician's prescription for the well-being of a mother to the life itself of her child. Under the amendment, the law may protect the child, although he or she is within the womb and physically dependent on the mother.
4. The amendment negates the teaching of the Supreme Court in *Roe v. Wade* that "capability of meaningful life" is a criterion by which the protectability of life is to be determined. The amendment assures that federal or state legislation protecting the life of the aged, the mentally afflicted, or the chronically ill cannot be declared unconstitutional by application of such a criterion. Under the amendment, life may be protected irrespective of the health, physical or psychological, of the life being protected.[117]

A states-rights amendment, however, does not attempt to do the following:

1. The amendment does not make abortion murder. In Anglo-American legal tradition, discrimination has always been made between the crime of murder and the crime of abortion. No good reason exists to end the traditional distinction.
2. The amendment does not outlaw any particular acts of abortion. In the federal structure of the United States, it has been the responsibility of the states to design the protection of life within their borders, and the responsibility of Congress to protect life in federal areas. No good reason exists to alter the traditional allocation of responsibilities.

3. The amendment does not mandate a particular or uniform degree, level, or kind of protection. A Constitution is not a criminal statute. If an amendment is to act at a constitutional level, it is not the appropriate place to incorporate the details and qualifications of a specific criminal law.
4. The amendment does not make contraception an act which Congress or the states may prohibit under the amendment; it does not overturn *Griswold v. Connecticut.* Contraception is directed to the prevention of life. The amendment authorizes the law to act from the beginning of new life.[118]

The intent of the federal-rights Hatch Federalism Amendment is to "restore to the representative branches of government the authority to legislate with respect to the practice of abortion."[119] Thus, the federal-rights approach varies from the state-rights approach inasmuch as it would permit Congress as well as state legislatures to legislate on abortion. Additionally, the amendment would "remov[e] the abortion controversy from the Federal judicial branch"[120] "without dictating particular legislative outcomes or policies."[121]

The first sentence of the Hatch Federalism Amendment refers to the "right to abortion" as not being secured by the Constitution. This right to abortion is intended to refer to the right to abortion created in *Roe v. Wade* and *Doe v. Bolton* but ambiguously placed in either the 14th or 9th amendments. The purpose of this reference is "to preclude reliance upon any provision of the Constitution as authority for recognition of any right to abortion."[122] As a result, this sentence is intended to "foreclose any potential constitutional recognition of such a right, regardless of how it might be formulated, regardless of how it might be articulated, and regardless of what constitutional provision might be involved as authority for it."[123]

In the second sentence, the amendment gives the "concurrent" power to both Congress and the states to "restrict and prohibit abortion." This sentence is intended to restore to Congress and the states "the power to enact and enforce any laws rationally related to restricting abortion which they may, in their judgment, deem appropriate."[124] As a result, "[e]ach sovereign would have independent power to enact laws prohibiting abortion and an act in violation of both of these laws would be in violation of the legislative will of each sovereign,"[125] except that "the law of Congress would 'preempt' the less restrictive state law to the extent of the conflict."[126]

This form of a federal-rights amendment varies in several respects from the Federal Rights Amendment drafted by Professor Noonan. Specifically, the Hatch Federalism Amendment speaks of the power "to restrict and prohibit abortion" rather than the power "to protect life" as in the Federal Rights Amendment. Additionally, the first sentence in the Hatch Federalism Amendment reverses one of the holdings of *Roe v. Wade,* the woman's right to privacy to decide to have an abortion, while the Federal Rights Amendment does not attempt to do so. Further, the Federal Rights Amendment specifically includes "the unborn, at every stage of biological development, irrespective of age, health, or condition of dependency," while the Hatch Federalism Amendment has no comparable term. In intent and effect, they are otherwise the same.

Most versions of a legislative authorization type of amendment would only accomplish one of the objectives for restoring full legal protection to the unborn; that is, to give to Congress and/or the several states the power to limit abortions by appropriate legislation (Objective 11). These amendments, except for the Hatch Federalism Amendment, would not reverse the holdings of *Roe v. Wade,* since they do not restore personhood to the unborn or remove a woman's right of privacy to have an abortion. They would only permit the states to regulate abortion, if they wished, subject to a possible federal minimum. Under the proposals, therefore, the states would be free to grant as much or as little protection to the unborn as political pressure and popular sentiment in a given locale dictate. Such amendments, therefore, do not necessarily portend the demise of legal abortion.

As a result of the failure of most versions of a legislative authorization type of amendment to reverse one of the principal holdings of *Roe v. Wade,* the legislative protection enacted by the states or federal government could be subject to constitutional challenge or limitation in the face of the woman's constitutionally guaranteed right of privacy to decide whether or not to seek an abortion. In examining the Federal Rights Amendment, which would give Congress and the states the "power to protect life," Morton Rosenberg of the American Law Division of the Library of Congress's Legislative Research Service has adopted this analysis:

> On its face, the proposed amendment does not disturb the precise constitutional conclusion of *Roe v. Wade* that government cannot intervene to protect the pre-viable fetus if its mother objects. The amendment simply authorizes Congress and the state legislatures to enact laws protective of fetal life; it does not empower them to enact laws which violate any other person's constitutional rights in the course of providing such protection. Thus it may be argued that the most that would be established by allowing legislatures to protect the unborn is to create a situation of conflict between two constitutional rights without telling us which must prevail.[127]

The legislative memo goes on to point out that it is highly speculative how such a conflict would be resolved by the Supreme Court. How, for example, should the Court interpret the absence from the amendment of any direction to the legislatures to enact "protective legislation"? Moreover, as the legislative memorandum points out, "[t]he amendment does not recognize a universal legal claim to protection by a non-viable fetus."[128] Thus, these versions of a proposed amendment might result in no real alteration of the Supreme Court's decisions.

The Hatch Federalism Amendment, however, is intended to reverse one of the holdings of *Roe v. Wade*: the woman's right of privacy to decide to have an abortion. If effective, it would not suffer from the disability described above. Some have argued, however, that it does not reverse this finding.[129] In *Roe v. Wade* the court found that the constitutional right of privacy "is broad enough to encompass a woman's decision on whether or not to terminate her pregnancy."[130] This right, however, "is not unqualified,"[131] since the pregnant woman does not have "an absolute constitutional right to an abortion on her demand."[132] As the Supreme Court noted in *Maher v. Roe,*[133] the decision in *Roe v. Wade* "did not declare an unqualified 'constitutional right to an abortion'.... Rather, the right protects the woman from unduly burdensome interference with her freedom to decide whether to terminate her pregnancy."[134] As a result, it is argued that the Court might, in good faith, find that the first sentence of the Hatch Federalism Amendment does not reverse the holding of *Roe v. Wade* that a woman's right to privacy includes her decision on whether or not to terminate her pregnancy.[135]

Others, however, argue that the provision of the Hatch Federalism Amendment that "a right to abortion is not secured by the Constitution" will, in fact, accomplish this reversal.[136] This clause is modeled on the 13th Amendment in the sense that it applies to abortion as an institution.[137] This same language or similar language is used in at least eighty-four federal court cases since *Roe v. Wade,* and it is well understood.[138] Thus, the words are used in their broadest sense and are intended to eliminate any such right to abortion, whether found in the right of privacy or in any other right.[139] This phrase, therefore, would disestablish the woman's constitutional right to decide whether or not to terminate her pregnancy.

The ability of the first sentence of the Hatch Federalism Amendment to reverse *Roe v. Wade,* however, does not really affect the scope and authority granted the state and federal governments by the amendment. The second sentence grants to Congress and the states a plenary[140] power to restrict or prohibit abortion and is thus not subject to balancing against the woman's right to privacy. As a result, even if the right to abortion is not reversed and the woman still has the constitutional right to decide whether or not to have an abortion, it is of no effect. The constitutional right would be unenforceable in the face of a state or federal statute passed pursuant to this grant of authority. The state's power to regulate and prohibit abortions would be absolute.

This plenary power to restrict and prohibit abortion is given by the amendment concurrently to both Congress and the several states. The meaning of concurrent is well established by the Supreme Court as a result of cases interpreting an identical phrase in the 18th Amendment.[141] The fullest explanation is in *United States v. Lanza,*[142] which explained that the expression *concurrent power* "means that power to take legislative measures . . . shall exist in Congress in respect of the territorial limits of the United States and at the same time the like power of the several States within their territorial limits shall not cease to exist. Each state, as also Congress, may exercise an independent judgment in selecting and shaping measures. . . . Such as are adopted by Congress become laws of the United States and such as are adopted by a state become laws of that state. They may vary in many particulars, including the penalties prescribed, but this is an inseparable incident of independent legislative action in distinct jurisdictions." As a result, the preemption doctrine has no application.[143] Both Congress and the several states would have full power, independent of each other, to restrict and prohibit abortion.[144]

The Hatch Federalism Amendment also includes a provision insuring that a more restrictive state law shall govern in the face of a conflicting law of Congress. This provision is meant to insure that the supremacy clause of the Constitution[145] would not apply to invalidate state laws on the grounds that they were stricter than, and thus inconsistent with, "supreme" federal law.[146] A subcommittee's modification of this section clarified that the provision operates only in the face of a conflicting provision of a federal law.

During the 1981 Senate Hearings on the Hatch Federalism Amendment, it was suggested that the proviso clause was not necessary since no conflict between federal and state law is possible under the amendment.[147] This rationale is based on the nature of the power granted them under the amendment. The Hatch Federalism Amendment permits Congress and the states merely to "restrict and prohibit abortion," not simply to regulate it. Thus, according to Professor Richard Stith of Valparaiso University School of Law, "there is no power granted to Congress and to the States to decide affirmatively which, if any, abortions should take place and to protect, facilitate, promote, or require them. In other words, only the negative aspect of regulation—the elimination or restriction of abortion—is validated by this amendment. Only by an absence of restriction or prohibition would some abortions continue."[148] Thus, those abortions prohibited by state law may be penalized by state prosecution and those prohibited by federal law may be penalized by federal prosecution. Only those not prohibited by both federal and state law would be legal.

Thus, there is a serious question whether the proviso clause is necessary. Additionally, it provides the courts an opportunity to reanalyze what "concurrent power" means and interpret it in a way not intended by the authors of the amendment. As a result, some have urged its deletion.[149]

By using the term "abortion," the Hatch Federalism Amendment has also given the courts some opportunity to affect the scope of the amendment. This potential flaw arises due to the fact that there is no universally accepted definition of abortion. The currently accepted medical definition of abortion is limited to the expulsion of a fetus "before the 20th completed week of gestation."[150] Expulsion of the unborn child after the twentieth week is referred to as premature delivery. The courts have in fact used considerably different definitions of abortion. For instance, some courts have defined abortion as "the performance of an operation with intent on part of accused to produce or procure a miscarriage."[151] Other courts, however, have defined abortion as "committed when an instrument is used unlawfully on the body of a woman with intent to procure an abortion,"[152] "the expulsion of a fetus from the uterus before it is capable of carrying on its own life,"[153] and "the expulsion of the ovum or embryo from the uterus more than 6 weeks after conception, but less than 6 months thereafter."[154] As a result, the courts will have to interpret the definition of abortion and will thereby have an opportunity to limit this grant of power.[155] Obviously, the drafters of the Hatch Federalism Amendment intend for abortion to refer to expulsion of the fetus at any time during pregnancy, from fertilization to natural birth;[156] and this intent can be manifested in the legislative intent of the amendment.[157] Consistent with this legislative intent, the courts should define this power to apply to the entire gestational period of the unborn child.

Further, a legislative authorization type of amendment would not override state constitutional provisions which were interpreted to protect a woman's right to privacy to decide whether or not to seek an abortion.[158] Several state courts have found this right under their state constitutions.[159] State legislation prohibiting abortion in these states could be declared unconstitutional under the state constitution.[160] In this instance, the Hatch Federalism Amendment is superior. By granting a plenary power to the states to regulate and prohibit abortion by a federal constitutional amendment which is the supreme law of the land, the states would be free legislatively to overcome the effect of any prior finding by the state courts of an abortional right of privacy under the state constitution.[161] Also, if Congress enacted a federal statute providing for protection for the unborn, such a congressional act would be effective nationwide, including in those states where state legislatures failed to act. In this instance, there would be no abortion havens.

A legislative authorization type of amendment, therefore, is limited in scope. Such an amendment would grant the power to government to restrict and prohibit abortion but not impose the obligation to do so.[162] In this regard, therefore, the National Right to Life Committee is pursuing a two-amendment strategy where the power to protect unborn life will be granted by one amendment followed by another amendment imposing the obligation to protect unborn life.[163] The Hatch Federalism Amendment is clearly the best formulation of a legislative authorization amendment, since it grants full power to Congress and the several states to protect unborn life from abortion.

Reversal

A second type of amendment, the reversal type, is similar in effect to a legislative authorization amendment but quite different in principle. Such an amendment, the Hatch-Eagleton Amendment, S.J. Res. 3, was voted on in the Senate on June 28, 1983. The amendment, defeated by a vote of forty-nine to fifty, provides as follows:[164]

Hatch-Eagleton Amendment

A right to abortion is not secured by this Constitution.

The Hatch-Eagleton Amendment, while similar in wording to the Hatch Federalism Amendment, is fundamentally different from its antecedent. This amendment is intended to "wipe out the legal status afforded to the 'abortion right' by *Roe v. Wade* and return us to a legal *status quo ante*."[165] Thus, there would be no constitutionally protected right to abortion—which provides the most substantial impediment to regulation of abortion by the states and Congress—and the power to regulate it would return to the states and Congress.

This formulation for a reversal type of amendment was originally suggested by Senator Thomas Eagleton in a speech to the annual Pro-Life Convention of the Archdiocese of St. Louis, Missouri, on October 3, 1982.[166] This amendment is the first sentence of the Hatch Federalism Amendment. It deletes the second sentence of that amendment, which specifically provides that Congress and the several states shall have concurrent power to restrict and prohibit abortion and that a provision of a law of a state which is more restrictive than a conflicting provision of a law of Congress shall govern. In his testimony of February 28, 1983, before the Subcommittee on the Constitution, Senator Eagleton recommended that this formulation be adopted.[167] The testimony of other witnesses before the subcommittee on February 28, 1983, and on March 7, 1983, was directed at a careful examination of the effect of this proposed amendment. As a result of this testimony, the Subcommittee on the Constitution reported out the Hatch-Eagleton Amendment in accord with Senator Eagleton's suggestion.[168]

A reversal type of amendment is specifically designed to abolish the constitutionally protected right to abortion found originally in *Roe v. Wade* and *Doe v. Bolton* and subsequently expanded in its progeny. This constitutionally protected right, found in the constitutional right of privacy, prevents effective state or federal regulation of abortion. While a reversal type of amendment would not restore to the unborn the status of person under the 14th Amendment, it would remove the constitutional impediment to effective protection of the unborn. A follow-up amendment restoring personhood is necessary to accomplish this second result. A reversal type of amendment, therefore, does not imply or suggest that there is no obligation in another part of the Constitution requiring protection for the unborn. Indeed, it invites one to examine other parts of the Constitution to determine if such protection is mandated.

In this way, the Hatch-Eagleton Amendment is philosophically quite different from the original formulation of the Hatch Federalism Amendment. By its second sentence, the Hatch Federalism Amendment has been criticized by some as implying that the question of the regulation of abortion is settled—that it is within the discretion of the state legislatures and Congress. A follow-up amendment after the Hatch Federalism Amendment would then seem to contradict it by creating an obligation to protect. The Hatch-Eagleton Amendment, as the first amendment in a two-step strategy, however, creates no possible contradiction and is thus more suitable for a first-step amendment.

A legislative authorization type of amendment grants power to the state and/or Congress to regulate abortion specifically, and thus reverses *Roe v. Wade* only as a practical effect, but not in principle. Thus, a legislative authorization type of amendment leaves *Roe v. Wade* intact but renders it ineffective by granting power to the states and Congress to act. A reversal type of amendment, however, specifically reverses *Roe v. Wade* in principle, with the practical effect of restoring to Congress and the states the power to protect unborn life.

The intent of the Hatch-Eagleton Amendment, therefore, is to reverse the Supreme Court decisions of *Roe v. Wade*[169] and *Doe v. Bolton*[170] in finding a constitutionally protected right to abortion. The amendment is intended to preclude reliance upon any provision of the Constitution as authority for recognition of such a right, whatever its alleged constitutional basis.[171] By effectually doing so,[172] it restores to the states and Congress the residual powers they have to restrict or prohibit abortion.

The effect of the Hatch-Eagleton Amendment was subjected to considerable testimony during the 1983 Senate hearings. Professor Lynn Wardle of Brigham Young University School of Law carefully delineated ten things that the amendment would accomplish:

1. It would repeal the rule that the Constitution protects a woman's rights to abortion. In *Roe v. Wade,* the Court held that a woman's decision whether or not to terminate her pregnancy is a fundamental right protected by the Constitution. This amendment directly repeals that.
2. It uses the phrase "a right to abortion." That phrase has been used in over 80 federal court decisions as shorthand for the constitutional right created in *Roe v. Wade* and its progeny, *i.e.,* the right of a woman to choose whether or not to have an abortion without undue state interference.
3. It would prevent the creation of any other right to abortion in the harbor of any other provision of the Constitution. The article "a" makes the scope of the repeal broader than if the article "the" were used. "The" might be construed as limiting the repealer as to "the" particular doctrine of law that has developed in *Roe v. Wade* and its progeny. Use of the article "a" makes it declare that no other "right to abortion" is sheltered by the Constitution.
4. It would avoid the unnecessary repudiation of the doctrine of privacy. The use of the careful phrase "right to abortion" makes it clear that the amendment repeals only the abortion decisions. Other extensions of the right of privacy, such as in the contraception cases and the family privacy cases, would not be repealed.
5. It would mean that laws impinging upon the abortion decision will be examined under the ordinary standard of judicial review (unless they infringe other constitutional rights which do not constitute a "right to abortion," *e.g.,* a law prohibiting only black women from

obtaining abortions would still be examined under a strict scrutiny test because of the racial discrimination). Inasmuch as the Supreme Court has repeatedly acknowledged that states have a strong legitimate interest in protecting potential life throughout pregnancy, laws protecting the right to life of the unborn would necessarily be upheld as rationally related to those profound interests.

6. It would repudiate implicitly all of the bag and baggage of *Roe v. Wade* and its progeny. A ludicrous statement that the law does not recognize the personhood of the unborn as well as subsequent holdings such as those prohibiting parental and spousal participation in the abortion decision and post-viability abortion restrictions would become dead letters in the law.
7. It would restore to the states their general police power to restrict and prohibit abortion. The states could enact legislation to the same extent that they could prior to *Roe v. Wade.*
8. It would restore Congress's limited power to restrict and prohibit abortion (mostly through indirect means) as necessary and appropriate to perform its constitutional responsibilities to control interstate commerce, federal lands, federal taxation, spending, etc.
9. It would disestablish a class or type of constitutional rights. It would not establish any new constitutional rights. In essence, the Amendment does not attempt to say what balance between the interests of the unborn and the interests of the pregnant woman is established by the Constitution, if any, but it makes clear what balance is not established, *i.e.,* there is no right to abortion.
10. It would restore the constitutional balance of power between the states and the federal government and between the legislative and judicial branches of government. In sum, it would restore the *status quo ante Roe v. Wade* insofar as the power and responsibility to resolve abortion issues is concerned.[173]

In addition, Professor Wardle specified the things that the amendment would *not* do.

1. It would not establish any new constitutional right. It would only reestablish constitutional rights that existed before *Roe v. Wade.*
2. It would not prohibit the Supreme Court from interpreting the Fourteenth Amendment to protect all humans, including the unborn. The only right that could *not* be distilled from the Constitution would be a "right to abortion."
3. It would not compel or prohibit the adoption by any state legislature or by Congress of any legislation restricting abortion.
4. It would not preclude judicial review of abortion laws. It would not prohibit a court from holding proabortion laws unconstitutional.
5. It would not prevent a court from holding some abortion restriction unconstitutional if it violated other constitutional provisions, unless that would effectively create any "right to abortion." Thus, racially discriminatory abortion laws could be invalidated, but not ordinary abortion restrictions.

6. It would not affect state constitutions. It would not prohibit the citizens in any state from adopting (or, for that matter, any state supreme court from creating in *Roe*-fashion) a right to abortion under the state constitution.
7. It would not give Congress any power directly to restrict or prohibit abortion.
8. It would not deprive Congress of its limited constitutional authority to regulate abortion (mostly by indirect means) under its authority to regulate interstate commerce, control federal lands, to tax, to spend, etc.
9. It would not give the states any new authority to regulate abortion, either. Their general police powers to regulate abortion would be restored, but would not be enhanced.
10. In short, it would not alter the constitutional allocation of power between the federal and state governments, or between the legislative and judicial branches.[174]

Most importantly, the Hatch-Eagleton Amendment is directed at the institution of abortion. Thus, the amendment is not formulated just to reverse the right of privacy to decide whether or not to have an abortion; rather it eliminates any basis for the court determining that a right to abortion exists. Thus, as pointed out by the Senate Judiciary Committee in its report on the Hatch-Eagleton Amendment:

S.J. Res. 3, which states, "A right to abortion is not secured by this Constitution," is intended to preclude reliance upon any provision of the Constitution as authority for recognition of any right to abortion. In particular, S.J. Res. 3 is intended to reverse *Roe v. Wade* and its companion *Doe v. Bolton*, insofar as these cases hold that the Constitution protects an abortion liberty. In addition, any holding in any subsequent Federal or State court decision relying, as a matter of law or public policy, upon the *Roe* or *Doe* decisions, or upon the existence of a constitutionally-founded "right to abortion" would be reversed to the extent that the existence of such a "right" was a predicate to that holding.

S.J. Res. 3 does not employ the specific phraseology of the abortion liberty adopted by the Supreme Court in *Roe v. Wade*—the "right to privacy" which includes the right to decide "whether or not to terminate a pregnancy." Instead, the proposed amendment employs the more general phrase "right to abortion" in order to emphasize that the amendment is intended to foreclose any potential constitutional recognition of such a right, regardless of how it might be formulated, regardless of how it might be articulated, and regardless of what constitutional provision might be invoked as authority for it. For example, S.J. Res. 3 is intended to foreclose potential use of the Ninth or Tenth Amendments to recognize abortion as a reserved right, as much as it is intended to foreclose use of the Fourteenth Amendment to protect abortion as a "privacy right." Under S.J. Res. 3, there would exist no constitutional authority for any right to abortion.

As Professor Wardle has observed, the term "right to abortion" (or "right to an abortion" or "right of abortion") has been used in at least 84 Federal court decisions since the *Roe* and *Doe* cases were decided, including at least one decision by the Supreme Court. As he notes,

> The phrase "right to abortion" is used as shorthand for the constitutional right created in *Roe* and its progeny, the right of a woman to choose whether or not to have an abortion free from State restrictions.

The modifier "a" rather than "the" is intended to clarify, however, that the "right to abortion" referred to in the first sentence does not simply refer to the precise "right" as originally introduced in *Roe* but any alternative concept of such a right emanating from the Fourteenth Amendment or any other provision of the Constitution.

Since there would exist no constitutional basis whatsoever for the abortion liberty following the passage of S.J. Res. 3, it follows that there would be no "qualified" constitutional right to abortion in any particular circumstance, under any unusual conditions, during any stage of pregnancy or fetal development or as an incident or adjunct to some other recognized and protected right. Thus, for example, it could not be claimed that a putative "right to health" would immunize abortions from legislative restriction. There would be no case in which any abortion would be the object of any special constitutional protection.[175]

The importance of this formulation was highlighted by the testimony of Rhonda Copeland of the Center for Constitutional Rights before the 1983 Senate hearings. In her testimony,[176] she identified a series of constitutional bases for a right to abortion, including "the right of bodily integrity"; "the constitutional right of association," which "embraces the right to form a family, to choose our most intimate associates and guide the raising of children"; the 1st Amendment, which protects the right of women to "speak" with their bodies in childbearing and which protects "the right to follow religious and conscientious convictions"; and the 13th Amendment, which prevents involuntary servitude and which entitles women "to say no to the unparalleled labor demanded by pregnancy, childbirth and child-rearing and to the expropriation of her body and services for the sake of another." The Hatch-Eagleton Amendment would prevent reliance upon any of these bases for a constitutional right to abortion.[177]

Removal of a specifically granted power to the states or Congress, however, raises the question of the power that would exist in Congress and the states to regulate abortion after the adoption of the Hatch-Eagleton Amendment. As pointed out by Professor

Victor Rosenblum, "the slate would be wiped clean: as far as judicial precedent is concerned, it would be as if *Roe* and its progeny had never existed."[178]

With regard to state legislation, according to Professor Rosenblum, "the nullification of '[a] right to abortion' accomplished by the [Hatch-Eagleton] Amendment would allow legislative proscription of abortion."[179] States, acting within the traditional spheres of jurisdiction, could "legally proscribe or regulate abortion practices on behalf of their continuing, already judicially recognized, legitimate interest in protection of fetal life. This means that those laws that proscribe abortion which remain codified could be revived, and that new laws could be enacted . . . to proscribe or to restrict abortion."[180] The states, in exercise of their police power, could certainly prohibit abortion except to save the life of the mother.

A more substantial concern is the effect of the Hatch-Eagleton Amendment on the scope of federal powers that could be brought to bear to restrict or prohibit abortion. In this respect, the Hatch-Eagleton Amendment, according to Professor Rosenblum, "would not so fully effectuate the opportunity to protect the unborn on a national basis as would the Hatch [Federalism] Amendment's grant to the Congress of full plenary to restrict and prohibit abortion."[181] It would, however, restore to Congress those powers it had prior to *Roe v. Wade* to do so.

In this respect, other parts of the Constitution must be examined to determine whether or not there is power there to directly or indirectly restrict or prohibit abortion. This power may not now be exercised due to the constitutional right to abortion found by the Supreme Court in *Roe v. Wade.* After the adoption of the Hatch-Eagleton Amendment, however, this right would be removed and the residual powers of Congress could be exercised.

There exists in the Constitution both direct and indirect powers which may be brought to bear on abortion. Any direct power that Congress might have to regulate abortion—that is, private killing—could be found in Section 5 of the 14th Amendment.[182] This section, activated on behalf of the unborn by the adoption of a human life bill, would define the unborn as a human being for the purpose of protecting the right to life under the 14th Amendment; that is, it would bring to bear the 14th Amendment's protections of persons for the unborn.[183] A human life bill's constitutionality is jeopardized by the Supreme Court holding of a right to abortion. Once this holding is reversed, a court upholding its constitutionality is more likely.[184] Such a bill, properly drafted, could include the power to restrict or prohibit private abortions in addition to limiting state involvement in abortion.[185] Such a bill is a logical second step after the adoption of the Hatch-Eagleton Amendment.

Other, indirect ways by which abortion may be regulated are as follows:[186]

1. Under the commerce clause of the United States Constitution,[187] Congress has the power to protect interstate and foreign commerce and to regulate it.[188] The practice of abortion has many potential impacts on interstate commerce; and, indeed, some abortion clinics have been found to have the sufficient effect on interstate commerce that the Sherman Act has applied to them.[189] Thus, Congress would have full power under the commerce clause to ban all abortifacients and all equipment specifically designed to aid in the performance of abortion, to make it criminal to use interstate facilities to advertise or promote abortion or for an abortionist to travel interstate to perform an abortion, or for abortion devices to be imported.
2. Under the 16th Amendment, Congress has plenary power to tax income. Congress could, therefore: (a) deny tax exemption to a hospital or clinic performing abortions as regular business; (b) deny tax deductions to other than lifesaving abortions; and (c) tax at high rates the abortion-related income of clinics, hospitals, and abortionists. "The power to tax involves the power to destroy," in John Marshall's famous words.[190]
3. Congress could define abortion as an illegal act under an existing federal criminal statute, the Racketeer Influenced Corrupt Organization Act (RICO) of 1970.[191] In this way, it would be a federal felony under RICO to engage in a pattern (two or more acts) of a variety of specified crimes defined under state law.[192] Thus, an abortionist could be prosecuted under federal law if he had been previously convicted under state law for two prior illegal abortions.
4. Also under Congress's power of the purse, the federal government possesses a carrot as well as several sticks. In this regard, Congress could condition the grant of money to states upon the adoption by the state of numerous restrictions on abortion, even including the adoption of state criminal prohibitions against abortion. Congress has already exercised this power in many areas; for example, the requirement of each state to adopt the 55-miles-per-hour speed limit, to impose state criminal sanctions for its violation,[193] and to certify that it is being enforced.[194]

Congress, then, has considerable potential direct and indirect power to restrict and prohibit abortions, and this power can be brought to bear to insure that abortion havens do not arise in some states. While the Hatch-Eagleton Amendment's grant of power to Congress is not as clear and absolute as found in the Hatch Federalism Amendment, sufficient powers exist to allow Congress to make a national standard for abortion.

The Hatch-Eagleton Amendment, therefore, is a newly formulated and novel approach directed at abortion. This amendment is the first of the reversal amendments to be offered in Congress. Its adoption would clearly repudiate the Supreme Court's finding of the constitutional right to abortion and prevent its re-creation in any other portion of the Constitution. The full plenary powers of the state and considerable federal power would be restored to restrict and prohibit abortion. With the adoption of the second step, either a life-protective amendment or a human life bill, the obligation to protect unborn life would be fully restored.

Restoration of Personhood

Proposals for a human life amendment which would restore personhood to the unborn were introduced soon after the Supreme Court decision in *Roe v. Wade.* The Hogan Amendment was first introduced on January 30, 1973, as H.R.J. Res. 261, which provided as follows:

Hogan Amendment

SECTION 1. Neither the United States nor any State shall deprive any human being, from the moment of conception, of life without due process of law, nor deny to any human being, from the moment of conception, within its jurisdiction, the equal protection of the laws.
SECTION 2. Neither the United States nor any State shall deprive any human being of life on account of illness, age, or incapacity.
SECTION 3. Congress and the several States shall have the power to enforce this article by appropriate legislation.

The Buckley Amendment,[195] S.J. Res. 119, was introduced on May 31, 1973. It provided that:

Buckley Amendment

SECTION 1. With respect to the right to life, the word "person", as used in this article and in the fifth and fourteenth articles of amendment to the Constitution of the United States, applies to all human beings, including their unborn offspring at every stage of their biological development, irrespective of age, health, function, or condition of dependency.
SECTION 2. This article shall not apply in any emergency when a reasonable medical certainty exists that continuation of the pregnancy will cause the death of the mother.

SECTION 3. Congress and the several States shall have power to enforce this article by appropriate legislation within their respective jurisdictions.

Senator Helms introduced S.J. Res. 6 in the 94th Congress, providing as follows:

Helms Amendment

SECTION 1. With respect to the right to life guaranteed in this Constitution, every human being, subject to the jurisdiction of the United States, or of any State, shall be deemed, from the moment of fertilization, to be a person and entitled to the right to life.
SECTION 2. Congress and the several States shall have concurrent power to enforce this article by appropriate legislation.

Senator Helms's amendment was introduced in the 97th Congress by Congressman Ashbrook as H.R.J. Res. 13, by Congressman Guyer as H.R.J. Res. 32 and by Congressman Hyde as H.R.J. Res. 50.

The Hogan Amendment would restore to the unborn the protection of "due process of law" and "equal protection of the law" while not explicitly recognizing the unborn as a person. The amendment is intended to "prevent all abortions for reasons less than the preservation of the very life of the mother."[196] In addition, it recognizes the "simple scientific fact, that human life begins at the moment of conception, that is, at the moment of the fertilization of the ovum by the sperm."[197]

The Buckley Amendment has as its "central purpose (with respect to the right to life) . . . to restore a constitutionally compelling identity between the biological category 'human being' and the legal category 'person'."[198] This amendment would therefore make the test of personhood a biological rather than legal one resting on "scientific fact rather than on political, sociological, or other opinion."[199] The fact that the unborn are considered human beings is provided in the phrase "including their unborn offspring at every stage of their biological development." In addition, Section 1 of the Buckley Amendment reaches infanticide and euthanasia by protecting all human beings "irrespective of age, health, function, or condition of dependency." The language of Section 1 of the Buckley Amendment also retains the very language that since at least the 1850s had been utilized by physicians to describe the needed protection for fetal life.[200]

The separation of the traditional concept of *human beings* from the concept of *persons* in *Roe v. Wade,* which would be restored in Section 1 of the Buckley Amendment, destroyed the very work of the framers in the 14th Amendment. Those framers were very cognizant that these two concepts had been separated in the actual administration of the Constitution of the United States by the Supreme Court in *Dred Scott v. Sanford,*[201] and it was their clear, demonstrable purpose to prevent for all time thereafter any separation of these two concepts. The author of the first section of the 14th Amendment, Congressman John A. Bingham of Ohio, stated how it was to operate: "Before that great law the only question to be asked of the creature claiming its protection is this: Is he a man?" And of the due process clause of the 5th Amendment, he stated: "No person, no human being, no member of the family of man shall, by virtue of federal law or under the sanction of the federal authority . . . be deprived of his life, or his liberty, or his property, but by the law of the land."[202] By equating human beings with persons, therefore, the basic error of the Supreme Court in *Roe v. Wade* is thus corrected.

Section 2 of the Buckley Amendment makes an explicit exception for the life of the pregnant woman from its grant of personhood to the unborn in Section 1. Under this section, "there must be an emergency in which reasonable medical certainty exists that continuation of the pregnancy will cause the death of the woman."[203] While "modern obstetrical practice has eliminated almost all medical indications for abortion [,i]n certain limited instances . . . a genuine threat to the woman's life remains, and it is felt that excepting such situations is comparable with long-standing moral custom and legal tradition."[204]

The overriding consideration of the Helms Amendment is "to insure that all human beings enjoy the protection of the right to life."[205] In this intent, the amendment is consistent with the Hogan and Buckley amendments. The Helms Amendment, however, defines the beginning of life as "the moment of fertilization" on the grounds that it is more precise than the word "conception"; that it is the beginning of human development; and that, by using the term "moment," it applies to a given point in time.[206] Additionally, the Helms Amendment does not contain a specific exception clause for the life of the mother since "such a claim is not necessary. As the amendment is presently drafted, the difficult cases can be handled under traditional concepts of due process and equal protection of the laws. . . . [I]t is not intended to invalidate past, present and future laws in the states which permit abortion to save the life of the mother. . . . as a matter of self-defense,". . .[207] or under "the doctrine of legal necessity."[208] Section 2 of the Helms Amendment, just as Section 3 of the Hogan and Buckley amendments, provides for state and federal enforcement of the amendment.

Each of these proposed amendments would declare the unborn to be persons entitled to the right to life as guaranteed in the United States Constitution. The right to life is guaranteed against actions of the federal government by the 5th Amendment, which provides that "[n]o person shall . . . be deprived of life, liberty, or property, without due process of law." Similarly, the 14th Amendment provides that "[n]o state shall . . . deprive any person of life, liberty, or property, without due process of law; nor deny to any person within its jurisdiction the equal protection of the laws." The 5th and 14th amendments, therefore, are the provisions of the Constitution guaranteeing the right to life which are dealt with in these proposed amendments.

As a result of the adoption of any of these amendments, states and the federal government would be prohibited from taking the lives of unborn children "without due process of law." While it is very uncertain what the requirements of "due process of law" would be under future court decisions, this problem does not create much concern since states and the federal government are not taking the lives of unborn children. Except to the extent that some abortions are performed in government facilities or paid at government expense, most abortions are private ones with no state involvement whatsoever. For those abortions performed in government facilities or funded by government, the courts would determine the guidelines of "due process of law." This could only entail committee approval for an abortion or it could result in more extensive protection even to a prohibition against abortion performed in government facilities or funded by government except to prevent the death of the mother.[209]

By application of the equal protection clause of the 14th Amendment, a state would also be required to provide some degree of effective protection to the unborn if the killing of born persons is illegal. The scope of this protection is unclear, however. Under prevailing constitutional standards, equal protection of the laws does not prevent a legislature from recognizing degrees of evil and does not require things which are different in fact or opinion to be treated in the laws as though they were the same. Thus, a state, in the exercise of its police power, need not provide "abstract symmetry."[210] That is, the legislature may recognize "degrees of evil":[211] a class of offenders or a family of offenses may, therefore, receive special treatment.[212]

Still, it is clear that the state must provide some degree of protection to the unborn.[213] A long series of decisions support the general proposition that for government to withdraw protection from one class of the people is for the government to perform an act of discrimination against the group deprived of protection. In one of the classic older cases on this point, Chief Justice Taft stated that

> [i]mmunity granted to a class, however limited, having the effect to deprive another class, however limited, of a personal or property right is just as clearly a denial of the equal protection of the laws to the latter class as if the immunity were in favor of, or the deprivation of right permitted worked against, a larger class.[214]

This fundamental principle has been recently affirmed in a variety of civil rights cases. In *Burton v. Wilmington Parking Authority,*[215] the Supreme Court found it unconstitutional state action for the operator of a restaurant in a building owned by the state to refuse to serve blacks. The state, while taking no affirmative action to discriminate, by its "inaction" made itself a party to the refusal of service. Its failure to prevent the discrimination was itself treated as state action against one class of citizens. In *Rietman v. Mulkey*[216] an amendment to the constitution of California permitting discrimination in private housing was held to be unconstitutional. The state's action in permitting discrimination was itself found to be a form of action against one class of its citizens.

In providing this degree of protection, the state would be free to determine what degree of punishment would be provided for illegal abortions. Thus, all illegal abortions would not be murder in the first degree but could be punished as a felony or even a misdemeanor. Before 1965, when the trend toward permissive abortion laws began, fifty of the fifty-one jurisdictions in the United States made the procurement of nonlifesaving abortions a felony. New Jersey, the lone exception, made it a high misdemeanor.[217] Abortion, in some states, was murder when the woman died as a result of the abortion. In that instance, twenty-two states increased the punishment by characterizing the death as either murder, manslaughter, or assault with intent to murder.[218] Therefore, states would be forced to extend some degree of criminal protection to the unborn against illegal abortions. While the states would have some discretion, the penalty would have to be of sufficient severity to protect the lives of the unborn effectively.[219]

Restoration of personhood would accomplish many of the objectives necessary to restore full legal protection to the unborn. Its adoption would restore to the unborn the constitutional status and protection of persons, with respect to their right to life (Objective 1). It would, therefore, specifically reverse one of the two essential holdings of *Roe v. Wade*—that the unborn are not persons protected by the 14th Amendment. The amendment would also insure that all human beings, regardless of their age, health, or dependency, are protected in the right to life (Objective 2), and, specifically, that the unborn are so protected at all stages of development (Objective 3).

This amendment, however, does not reverse the holding of *Roe v. Wade* that a woman has a constitutional right of privacy to decide whether or not to seek an abortion. The right to life of the unborn under this type of amendment would then be subject to balancing against the woman's right to privacy.[220] Additionally, the unborn's right to life would be subject to devestment by state authorization of health abortions in the exercise of the state's compelling interest in maternal health. The extent of the protection of the unborn under this amendment, therefore, is uncertain.

Proponents of the restoration-of-personhood type of amendment often cite the following quote from *Roe v. Wade* to buttress their position that simple restoration of personhood is sufficient to restore full legal protection to the unborn.

> The appellee [State of Texas] and certain amici argue that the fetus is a "person" within the language and meaning of the Fourteenth Amendment. In support of this, they outline at length and in detail the well-known facts of fetal development. If this suggestion of personhood is established, the appellant's case, of course, collapses, for the fetus' right to life would then be guaranteed specifically by the Amendment.[221]

Clearly, this statement by the Court is a dictum; that is, it does not constitute the holdings of the Court and was not otherwise analyzed by the Court, since they held that the unborn was not a person under the amendment. This is a very slender reed, indeed, upon which to rest the unborn's right to life. Dicta are not binding on the courts[222] and are often ignored in future cases—and even recent *holdings* by the Court are reversed in subsequent cases despite the doctrine of *stare decisis.*[223]

As the analysis above indicates, once the state has a compelling interest in unborn life, the courts will invoke the traditional balancing tests. The Court in *Roe v. Wade* did not do so because the majority found no such compelling interest before the unborn became viable. Ominously, though, the Court did find a compelling state interest in "potential life" after viability but then balanced it against the state interest in maternal health and found the state's interest in maternal health to be greater. Thus, the Court held that the state's compelling interest in "potential life" must give way to maternal health. A state, therefore, could not proscribe health abortions even after viability.[224] There is no assurance that a later Supreme Court, forced to analyze the scope of a state's compelling interest in unborn life, will not strike a similar balance. Restoration of personhood will only invite this balancing without guiding the court to its proper resolution.

The Hogan Amendment refers to the "moment of conception" and the Helms Amendment refers to "the moment of fertilization" as the time at which personhood and the guarantee of the right to life commence. The reference to "moment of conception" in the Hogan Amendment was intended to mean the moment of fertilization.[225] In either case, however, it is now clear that the term is imprecise and ambiguous.

In *Roe v. Wade,* the Supreme Court correctly noted that "new embryological data . . . purport to indicate that conception is a 'process' over time, rather than an event."[226] They were somewhat supported by the American College of Obstetrics and Gynecology which in September 1965 revised the meaning of conception to be implantation of the already fertilized ovum, or zygote, on the mother's uterus—that point at which pregnancy is currently first detectable.

There are in fact several distinguishable events, occurring over a number of hours, culminating in a zygote.[227] As a result, the reference to "moment" of fertilization is inaccurate and vague. Its meaning may be interpreted to be the beginning or the culmination of the process of fertilization. This defect, however, could be cured by using the phrase "inception of fertilization."

The Buckley Amendment has been subject to criticism because of its Section 2, which denies the unborn personhood when "the pregnancy will cause the death of the mother," as "filled with unfortunate phrases that admit ambiguity."[228] Specifically, the terms "emergency," "reasonable," "medical certainty," and "cause" have been criticized as leaving "a great loophole that an unsympathetic court could use to negate the main purpose of the amendment."[229] Additionally, some objected to it for its authorization of abortion where it is necessary to save the life of the mother,[230] in part because the wording would make the saving of the mother's life mandatory.[231]

The personhood type of amendment, however, has been subject to criticism mainly for its failure to "prevent abortions committed by private persons who are not public officials and not otherwise acting under color of state law."[232] Later amendments were proposed to deal with this deficiency.

Prohibition

As a result of the criticism of early constitutional amendments, primarily their failure to deal directly with private killing, two additional types of amendments were proposed: the prohibition type and the life-protective type. In the 93rd Congress, Congressman Roncallo introduced H.R.J. Res. 394[233] which provided as follows:

Roncallo Amendment

SECTION 1. Abortion is hereby prohibited within the United States and all territory subject to the jurisdiction thereof. As used in this article, abortion means the intentional destruction of unborn human life, which life begins at the moment of fertilization.
SECTION 2. Congress and the several States shall have concurrent power to enforce this article by appropriate legislation.

This amendment would cure the primary criticism of the Hogan, Buckley, and Helms amendments, which did not forbid private abortion directly. Additionally, it does not authorize abortions necessary to save the life of the mother or use the criticized term "moment of conception."

The prohibition type of amendment was intended to be a direct prohibition of abortion, comparable to the 13th Amendment's direct prohibition of slavery, whether performed by private parties or state officials.[234] It would forbid all direct abortions even when claimed to be necessary to save the life of the mother but would permit treatment of the cancerous womb and the ectopic pregnancy "where the death of the child is an unintentional result of an independently justified operation."[235] The amendment was not designed to write into the Constitution a sweeping elaboration of the rights of all human beings of all ages but only to stop abortion.[236] This is the only proposed amendment which seeks, as its intended result, to prohibit some abortions—that is, direct ones—which are necessary to save the life of the mother. It would accomplish the result of prohibiting all abortions except indirect ones.

The Roncallo Amendment is subject to criticism on several grounds. First, most congressional supporters of a human life amendment recognize that all medical procedures necessary to preserve the life of the mother should be permitted. The purpose of a constitutional amendment, in their mind, is to restore the right to life of the unborn, not diminish the right to life of the pregnant woman. The Roncallo Amendment, however, employs the Catholic doctrine of double effect to distinguish between direct and indirect abortions[237]—a distinction the law has never recognized. Second, while it attempts to define abortion and thereby avoid the definition problem of the Hatch Federalism Amendment, the Roncallo Amendment includes a definition of abortion which is not widely accepted in either law or medicine. The American College of Obstetrics and Gynecology defines abortion as follows:

Abortion is the expulsion or extraction of all (complete) or any part (incomplete) of the placenta or membranes, without an identifiable fetus or with a liveborn infant or a stillborn infant weighing less than 400 gm.

In the absence of known weight, an estimated length of gestation of less than 20 completed weeks (139 days), calculated from the first day of the last normal menstrual period, may be used. Abortion is a term referring to the birth process culminating before the 20th completed week of gestation.[238]

Most legal authorities define abortion as the expulsion of a non-viable fetus from the womb.[239] The Roncallo Amendment definition, therefore, is more narrow. It is also vague. There appear to be circumstances in which a pregnancy is terminated, with the unborn child extracted from the womb, without the intentional destruction of the child—for instance, by a prostaglandin abortion. Even when there is no intentional destruction of the child, the unborn's right to life may be infringed or deprived. Later amendments have included these circumstances.

Third, the Roncallo Amendment includes the use of the term "moment of fertilization," which is also ambiguous and subject to misconstruction. As a result, this amendment has gained little support and was not reintroduced in the 98th Congress.

Paramount

A fourth type of amendment is referred to as the Paramount Human Life Amendment,[240] introduced in the 98th Congress by Senator Jesse Helms as S.J. Res. 8. It provides as follows:

Paramount Human Life Amendment

The paramount right to life is vested in each human being from the moment of fertilization without regard to age, health, or condition of dependency.

The Paramount Amendment is intended to be a general statement of principle that a court must protect the sanctity of innocent human life.[241] By use of the term "each human being," the amendment restores the right to life of each human being without directly restoring personhood to the unborn under the 14th Amendment. By use of the word "paramount," the amendment insures that the right to life is superior to all other constitutional rights, thereby preventing the courts from eroding the right to life by balancing it against any other constitutional right, including the woman's right to privacy. The amendment refers to "the moment of fertilization" to insure that each human being has legal protection when he or she first comes into existence.[242]

The Paramount Amendment does not contain an explicit exception for maternal lifesaving abortions. The amendment, however, "is not intended to invalidate future laws in the States which permit procedures to save the life of the mother. . . . [n]or is it intended to prevent State legislatures and courts reviewing State laws from continuing to regard abortion to save the life of the mother as a matter of self-defense and therefore legally justifiable according to the general principle of self-defense. . . [,] substantive due process [,and] the doctrine of necessity."[243] The Paramount Amendment, therefore, is intended to permit lifesaving abortions under traditional legal principles. Whether or not they are permitted is a question the sponsor intends "to be determined by state legislatures, courts, and medical communities."[244]

This amendment is written to guarantee to all "human beings" the paramount right to life. Thus, the pregnant woman, as well as the unborn child, is guaranteed this paramount right. This amendment, therefore, would provide an additional basis for a pregnant woman to challenge a restrictive abortion statute which does not provide for maternal lifesaving abortions. The pregnant woman could claim that such a no-exception statute is in violation of her paramount right to life. Her challenge would probably succeed. As a result, the paramount type probably guarantees that maternal lifesaving abortions, of all types, must be permitted under subsequent state and federal legislations.[245]

With reference to the objectives, the paramount type would restore to the unborn the right to life (Objective 1), specifically protect for all persons the right to life (Objective 2), protect all human beings regardless of age, health, or condition of dependency (Objective 3), and establish the right to life as the paramount and most fundamental right (Objective 6). The paramount type, however, does not reverse the second holding of *Roe v. Wade,* which found a right to privacy for a woman to terminate her pregnancy. Additionally, since the unborn are not considered by the amendment as persons, under the 14th Amendment the unborn may not take advantage of the equal protection and due process protection contained therein. The protection of personhood would not be extended under the paramount type. Neither does this amendment prohibit private killing of the unborn, as authorized by *Roe v. Wade* (Objective 5), nor does it create the basis for a private cause of action to protect the unborn (Objective 7). Congress would be precluded, therefore, from passing legislation affecting private killing. The amendment apparently relies upon subsequent state legislation to affect these areas. The amendment is additionally defective in its reference to "moment of fertilization."

The paramount type is subject to additional criticism on the following grounds. First, it has the disadvantage of appearing to be a flat prohibition against any abortions, even lifesaving ones, when in fact it is not. Maternal lifesaving abortions are intended to be permitted by it and probably would be constitutionally required.

Second, while implicitly recognizing that maternal lifesaving abortions are permitted, it is not expressly limited to them. The sponsors of the paramount type would authorize legislatures and courts to carve out an exception for these necessary medical procedures but would intend that the courts and legislatures limit themselves to this exception only. The danger of this approach is demonstrated by the treatment by courts of restrictive abortion statutes which contain no explicit maternal lifesaving provision prior to 1973. Of the four state statutes so drafted before 1965, only two had reported cases interpreting them; both were interpreted to include lifesaving abortions[246] and one was expanded to include health abortions.[247] England's statute, which contains no maternal lifesaving provision, was also interpreted to include health abortions.[248] Further, an explicit maternal lifesaving exception, written in the phrase "necessary to save her life," is not immune from expansion. Of the forty-seven states which had a similar provision, one was interpreted to include health abortions.[249] Other such phrases have been struck down as vague.[250] Unfortunately, the paramount type does not deal with this problem.

Third, the paramount type does not remove from the state its compelling interest in maternal health, which can be used to authorize health abortions. Permitting the legislature and court to authorize health abortions is to authorize abortion on demand.

The paramount type of human life amendment, therefore, contains numerous loopholes whereby legislatures and courts can frustrate the protection intended to be extended to the unborn under its terms. While it does have "the important virtue of simplicity and readability,"[251] its very simplicity prevents it from dealing with the complex legal issues which must be resolved to extend full legal protection to the unborn.

Life Protective

The first life-protective type of amendment was introduced by Congressman Burke in the 94th Congress as H.R.J. Res. 121.[252] It provided that:

Burke Amendment

SECTION 1. With respect to the right of life, the word "person," as used in this article and in the fifth and fourteenth articles of amendment to the Constitution of the United States, applies to all human beings, including their unborn offspring at every stage of their biological development, irrespective of age, health, function, or condition of dependency.

SECTION 2. No abortion shall be performed by any person except under and in conformance with law permitting an abortion to be performed only in an emergency when a reasonable medical certainty exists that continuation of pregnancy will cause the death of the mother and requiring that person to make every reasonable effort, in keeping with good medical practice, to preserve the life of her unborn offspring.
SECTION 3. Congress and the several States shall have power to enforce this article by appropriate legislation within their respective jurisdictions.

It was introduced in the 97th Congress by Congressman Zablocki as H.R.J. Res. 127.

The Burke Amendment combines the Buckley Amendment's restoration of personhood (Section 1) with a specific prohibition against private killing (Section 2). The Burke Amendment was followed by the introduction of the version endorsed by the National Right to Kife Committee and introduced in the 94th Congress as S.J. Res. 11 by Senator Buckley. Senator Jake Garn later became the prime sponsor for that amendment, which reads as follows:

Garn Amendment

SECTION 1. With respect to the right to life, the word "person," as used in this article and in the fifth and fourteenth articles of amendment to the Constitution of the United States, applies to all human beings, irrespective of age, health, function, or condition of dependency, including their unborn offspring at every stage of their biological development.
SECTION 2. No unborn person shall be deprived of life by any person: *Provided, however,* That nothing in this article shall prohibit a law permitting only those medical procedures required to prevent the death of the mother.
SECTION 3. Congress and the several States shall have the power to enforce this article by appropriate legislation within their respective jurisdictions.

This amendment was reintroduced in the 98th Congress by Senator Garn as S.J. Res. 4 (with twenty-five cosponsors) and by Congressman Oberstar as H.R.J. Res. 73 (with thirty-three cosponsors).

On October 4, 1981, the Board of Directors for the National Right to Life Committee unanimously endorsed a revised version of its 1974 Human Life Amendment. The version adopted by NRLC is as follows:

NRLC Amendment

SECTION 1. The right to life is the paramount and most fundamental right of a person.
SECTION 2. With respect to the right to life guaranteed to persons by the fifth and fourteenth articles of amendment to the Constitution, the

word "person" applies to all human beings, irrespective of age, health, function, or condition of dependency, including their unborn offspring at every stage of their biological development including fertilization.
SECTION 3. No unborn person shall be deprived of life by any person: *Provided, however,* That nothing in this article shall prohibit a law allowing justification to be shown for only those medical procedures required to prevent the death of either the pregnant woman or her unborn offspring, as long as such law requires every reasonable effort be made to preserve the life of each.
SECTION 4. Congress and the several States shall have power to enforce this article by appropriate legislation.

The NRLC Amendment was reintroduced in the 98th Congress by Congressman Luken as H.R.J. Res. 114 and by Senator Helms as S.J. Res. 14.

The primary objection to the Burke Amendment has been the use of the term "abortion" in Section 2. As previously discussed, there are substantial definitional problems with the term. As a result, its meaning is not clear and is subject to court construction which might frustrate the intent of the amendment's supporters. In all other respects, the Burke Amendment is quite similar to the Garn, Buckley, and NRLC amendments.

The effect of the Garn Amendment was clearly set forth in the testimony of Professor Joseph Witherspoon in the 1976 House hearings.

One of the principal changes incorporated into the [Garn] amendment, as compared with the Hogan and Buckley Amendments, is its prohibition of private action that would destroy the unborn child's life as well as state or federal action of this type. This change was heavily favored by members of the Legal Advisory Committee due to the fact that the Supreme Court's anti-abortion law decisions had created a constitutional right in private individuals, *viz.* pregnant women and their physicians, to direct the destruction and to destroy, respectively, the lives of the unborn children of the former. The committee felt that an amendment, in order for it to be completely effective, was required to go as far in reversing the Supreme Court decision as the latter had gone in stripping from unborn children their constitutional right to life.

Any lesser protection would leave the lives of unborn children, in varying circumstances, without immediate or adequate constitutional protection. Merely to confer the constitutional status of a person upon unborn children under the Fifth and Fourteenth Amendments, necessary and important as it is to do this, would not provide the full and immediate protection which unborn children require. It was for this reason that the [Garn] amendment proposal adopts the direct protection principle which has been embodied in the Burke Amendment. It was felt that the Hogan and Buckley Amendments needed to be strengthened in this respect.

The proposed [Garn] amendment also adopts the orientation of the Hogan, Buckley and Burke Amendments in protecting unborn children from and after the earliest state of human life, which is fertilization of the female ovum. It does this by language which the committee believed to be better adapted for accomplishing this result than the language of several of the current amendment proposals. The language utilized is very similar to that originally used by the American Medical Association in 1859 and its Committee on Criminal Abortion in describing the period beginning with conception that unborn children exist as human beings and during which they require protection against abortion. The language is "every stage of their biological development". Clearly, "every stage" includes the first stage of biological development, *viz.,* fertilization of the female ovum, and every other subsequent stage of such development.

This language avoids the possibility that the term "conception" would be interpreted as some medical authorities are currently defining it as "implantation" or as the Supreme Court apparently was willing to interpret both that term and the term "fertilization" as constituting some kind of process extending over some indefinite period of time. By firmly grounding protection of the unborn child upon the scientific fact of its existence at the very first stage and all subsequent stages of its biological development, the possibility is clearly avoided that the Supreme Court might cut down the protection of the lives of unborn children by an undue or unwarranted interpretation of the term "conception" or "fertilization" through reference to nonscientific and evaluative factors. Since the science of biology and other related sciences clearly take the position that the first stage of biological development of unborn human offspring occurs with the fertilization of the female ovum by the male sperm, the proposed [Garn] amendment both firmly protects the unborn child throughout its existence and avoids giving the Supreme Court any opportunity of distorting the meaning through interpretation of the words "conception" or "fertilization".

A third important aspect of the proposed [Garn] amendment is its elimination of the possibility that the Supreme Court would take some of the human life amendment proposals, such as the Hogan Amendment, and engage in a so-called balancing process which would engraft numerous exceptions upon the basic anti-abortion policy of the amendment. The [Garn] proposal avoids this result by directly protecting every unborn person from being deprived of its life by any other person.

In this respect, the proposal is modeled upon the Thirteenth Amendment which provides direct protection to a human being from being subject to slavery or involuntary servitude by any other person or by any government. The [Garn] proposal also avoids the possibility of the Court acting to engraft exceptions upon the amendment's anti-abortion policy in a second way: by leaving it up to each state or to Congress whether to create an exception to the policy of this amendment and, in the event a state or Congress does act to create an exception, by limiting that exception to one permitting only those medical procedures required to prevent the death of the mother. This mode of language

> operates most effectively to prevent the Supreme Court from engaging in any general balancing process as between the mother and her unborn child. Moreover, it precludes either a state or Congress from engrafting any exception upon the basic policy of the amendment except one narrowly restricted to preventing the death of the mother. For this reason, the framers of the proposed [Garn] amendment declined to follow the permissive example of the Hogan Amendment which the Supreme Court and legislatures might justifiably read as allowing either to develop broad exceptions to the amendment's anti-abortion policy. It was the committee's opinion that enacting the amendment with the hope that a friendly court would interpret it to allow only a limited number of life-saving exceptions would be to invite the kind of judicial legislation witnessed in the *Wade* and *Bolton* decisions. For this reason, the committee followed the sterner approach of the Buckley and Burke Amendments with respect to the problem of exceptions to the anti-abortion policy of those amendments.[253]
>
> It is to be carefully noted that the [Garn] proposal does not compel recognition by a state or by Congress of any exception to this policy.[254] Moreover, the proposal operates to require reasonable effort to save the life of an unborn child even if an abortion is performed under a state or federal law permitting medical procedures required to prevent the death of the mother. This result necessarily flows from the proposal's provision of direct protection of the life of the unborn child against the action of individuals who would destroy it.[255]

The Garn Amendment, therefore, clearly accomplishes the major objectives of restoring full legal protection to the unborn. The amendment explicitly restores personhood to the unborn through Section 1, thereby reversing the holding of *Roe v. Wade* that the unborn is not a person under the 14th Amendment's guarantee of the right to life. Section 2 would have the effect of prohibiting private taking of the lives of the unborn, thus reversing the second holding of *Roe v. Wade,* creating a constitutional right of privacy for a woman to decide whether or not to terminate her pregnancy. Section 2 also restricts, to only those medical procedures necessary to prevent the death of the mother, the circumstances under which a state may choose to allow abortion. Health abortions would not be permissible under this section.

Further, Section 2 permits Congress to pass laws affecting private conduct and provides the basis for a private cause of action to protect unborn children when state and federal governments refuse to do so. Thus, under the rationale of the existing Supreme Court cases, a person with appropriate standing, such as a parent of an unmarried minor daughter or a spouse, could seek injunctive relief against the performance of an abortion upon their daughter or spouse. Under certain circumstances a guardian *ad litem* for an unborn child could also be appointed who could then seek to civilly enjoin an abortion from taking place. Lastly, appropriate action could be taken to prevent a state from depriving an unborn of life unless it is necessary to prevent the death of the mother.

By use of the phrase "required to prevent the death of the mother" in its maternal lifesaving exception,[256] the Garn Amendment uses a phrase which is more specific and definitive and less subject to court misconstruction. It avoids the word "life," which has been previously expanded to include "health." This section prevents the state from exercising its compelling interest in maternal health by permitting health abortions since the states may "only" authorize, if they wish, abortions "required to prevent the death of the mother."

The Garn Amendment also accomplishes the major objectives of full restoration of legal protection to the unborn. Section 1 would restore personhood to the unborn (Objective 1), protect all persons in their right to life (Objective 2), insure that all human beings are protected as persons (Objective 3), and insure that the unborn are protected from the beginning of life (Objective 4). Section 2 protects the lives of unborn children against both state and private action (Objective 5), provides the basis for a private cause of action to protect unborn lives (Objective 7), and permits maternal lifesaving procedures (Objective 8). Section 3 authorizes both state and federal government enforcement of the amendment (Objective 11).

The NRLC Amendment is the result of more than a year of study to determine if any improvements might be made in the Garn Amendment. In June 1980 Dr. J. C. Willke of Ohio, newly elected president of the National Right to Life Committee, appointed a committee, made up of lawyers and doctors, to reexamine the Garn Amendment.[257] Since 1974, several new versions of amendments had been introduced to Congress and considerable scholarly consideration had been given to the Garn Amendment. Dr. Willke felt that the time had come for NRLC to reexamine that amendment to insure that it was the best vehicle to accomplish the reversal of *Roe v. Wade* and *Doe v. Bolton* and their antecedents and progeny, and to restore fullest legal protection to the right to life of unborn children.

Adding to its concern for insuring maximum protection of the unborn through a constitutional amendment, the new committee sought to form a consensus within the right-to-life movement around one version of a human life amendment. Since this aim was not fully achieved, the committee attempted to narrow the disagreements within the movement and to define those disagreements as clearly as possible. Based upon this work, the committee recommended, on January 23, 1981, certain changes, the most important of which was designed to provide that the right to life is superior to all the rights granted under the Constitution.[258]

The committee was able to agree unanimously on Sections 1, 2, and 4 of the new NRLC Amendment. However, they were not able to agree on the proper formulation of Section 3. This section was intended to provide two essential elements in the formulation of the amendment, the prohibition against private taking of the lives of the unborn and the creation of a basis for a private cause of action to protect unborn children when state and federal governments refuse to do so. Section 3, therefore, would reverse the second essential holding of *Roe v. Wade,* that a woman has the right to take the life of her unborn child. The majority of the committee supported the following:[259]

SECTION 3. No unborn person shall be deprived of life by any person: Provided, however, That nothing in this article shall prohibit a law permitting only those medical procedures required to prevent the death of a pregnant woman; but this law must require every reasonable effort be made to preserve the life and health of the unborn person.

A minority of the committee supported the following language:[260]

SECTION 3. The right to life of an unborn person is protected by the Constitution against infringement by any person.

At the October 1981 meeting of the NRLC Board of Directors, the committee's recommendations were studied by still another group of scholars, some of them prior committee members and some newly appointed as consultants, and the present version of Section 3 was drawn up which was subsequently unanimously adopted by the board.[261]

The intent of the NRLC Amendment is to fully reverse *Roe v. Wade* and meet all of the objectives of full restoration of legal protection to the unborn. Unlike the Garn Amendment, which meets only eight of the eleven objectives, the NRLC Amendment accomplishes them all.

SECTION 1. The right to life is the paramount and most fundamental right of a person.

This section of the NRLC Amendment accomplishes Objective 6 by specifically establishing that the right to life is superior to any other right guaranteed by the Constitution. This section was added to meet this objective not met by the Garn Amendment. This section is inspired by the Paramount Human Life Amendment, which had as its principal thrust the concept that the right to life must be superior to any other right guaranteed by the Constitution, such as the right to privacy, in order to insure that the courts will give priority to the right to life of the unborn when they seek to balance it against the right to privacy of the pregnant woman. By making the right to life superior to any other right, the court, in employing its traditional balancing test, would only balance this constitutional right against the right to life of another person.

SECTION 2. With respect to the right to life guaranteed to persons by the fifth and fourteenth articles of amendment to the Constitution, the word "person" applies to all human beings, irrespective of age, health, function, or condition of dependency, including their unborn offspring at every stage of their biological development including fertilization.

This section restores personhood to the unborn, with respect to the right to life, at every stage of development including fertilization, and protects all human beings in their right to life regardless of age or handicap. This section is similar to the Garn Amendment Section 1 except that it makes explicit that the protection of persons begins at "fertilization."

SECTION 3. No unborn person shall be deprived of life by any person: Provided, however, That nothing in this article shall prohibit a law allowing justification to be shown for only those medical procedures required to prevent the death of either the pregnant woman or her unborn offspring as long as such law requires every reasonable effort be made to preserve the life of each.

This section reverses the second holding of *Roe v. Wade* that a woman has a constitutionally protected right of privacy to decide whether or not to terminate her pregnancy by directly protecting every unborn person from being deprived of its life by another person and is similar to the Garn Amendment's Section 2. It does, however, reformulate the lifesaving exemption by explicitly permitting lifesaving medical procedures necessary to prevent the death of either the mother or her unborn child. Thus, each life involved in a pregnancy, mother and child, is given equal consideration and treatment.

This new formulation accomplishes all of the objectives of the Garn Amendment's Section 2 as well as protecting all human beings equally (Objective 9), and ensuring that, when one life is endangered in a pregnancy, reasonable efforts are used to protect all others (Objective 10).

SECTION 4. Congress and the several States shall have power to enforce this article by appropriate legislation.

This section gives both Congress and the several states the power to enforce this amendment and does not limit this authorization to only "their respective jurisdictions" as provided in the Garn Amendment. A federal minimum applied to all states is thus possible under this amendment. This section is intended to accomplish Objective 11 by giving back to Congress and to the several states the power to enforce the amendment.

The NRLC Amendment, therefore, offers full legal protection to the lives of the unborn.[262] Under its provisions, the holdings of *Roe v. Wade* are fully reversed. The unborn child's right to life, and the state's compelling interest in protecting it, could not be balanced against a woman's right to privacy to decide whether or not to have an abortion since this right to privacy would be abrogated. Additionally, circumstances where abortion would be permitted would be restricted to those necessary to prevent the death of either the mother or her child. A state, therefore, would not permit health abortions which are equivalent to abortion on demand. This amendment alone meets all the objectives of restoration of full legal protection to the lives of the unborn.

Chapter Two

THE EFFECTS OF A HUMAN LIFE AMENDMENT ON FEDERAL AND STATE LAW

Lynn D. Wardle

In *Roe v. Wade*[1] the Supreme Court effectively amended the Constitution of the United States. In "every functional sense," it was as if a new amendment had been proposed and ratified.[2] That is the source of the legal dilemma. For constitutional law—whether created by the laborious amending process outlined in Article Five of the Constitution or by a decision of the United States Supreme Court—is the supreme law of the land. Thus, any examination of a proposed constitutional amendment to correct the abuses of *Roe v. Wade* necessarily must begin with an examination of that decision.

In *Roe v. Wade,* the Supreme Court did the following:

1. *It announced a new constitutional right.* It announced that the 14th Amendment of the Constitution shelters a fundamental right of privacy which encompasses "a woman's decision whether or not to terminate her pregnancy."[3] Under established principles of judicial review, state laws that infringe upon a fundamental constitutional right, such as this right of privacy, may only be sustained if *necessary,* and narrowly drawn, to effectuate a *compelling* state interest.
2. *It held that States have no compelling interest to prohibit abortion generally.* The Court rejected the argument that states have a compelling interest in protecting the lives of unborn persons because it held that the unborn are not persons in a constitutional sense. Likewise, it rejected the argument that states have a compelling interest in maternal health sufficient to justify even minimal medical regulation of abortion until the end of the first trimester, because it found that until then abortion may be safer than childbirth. It also rejected the argument that states have a compelling interest in

---

Lynn D. Wardle, J.D., is professor of law, J. Reuben Clark Law School, Brigham Young University. He is author of THE ABORTION PRIVACY DOCTRINE (1981) and a coauthor of A LAWYER LOOKS AT ABORTION (1982).

The author gratefully acknowledges the research assistance provided by James Bopp, Jr., Robert Dinsmoor, Martin Slater, and Linden Slaugh, and the valuable criticism of Professor C. Douglas Floyd.

preventing the destruction of unborn human life before viability because the Court did not know when life begins.

3. *It concluded that states must permit abortion on demand.* The Court unilaterally enacted a trimester scheme of constitutional abortion regulation. During the first trimester, essentially no regulation of abortion is permitted. During the second trimester, minor regulations of the medical aspects of abortion (such as place and manner) are permitted, but the decision to have an abortion may not be restricted. After viability, abortion may be prohibited except when necessary to save the life of the mother (and that exception has been interpreted by some judges so broadly as to swallow the rule).[4]
4. *It declared existing abortion laws invalid.* In *Roe,* a traditional nineteenth-century abortion statute was declared unconstitutional. In the companion case, *Doe v. Bolton,*[5] the carefully drafted and very progressive Model Penal Code was likewise declared unconstitutional. In effect, the abortion laws in all fifty states, totally or in part, were invalidated by the Supreme Court decisions in *Roe v. Wade* and *Doe v. Bolton.*

Roe v. Wade has had four major consequences. First, the decision substantially modified the structure of our constitutional form of government. *Roe v. Wade* took from the states the authority to restrict abortion just as if the 10th Amendment had been partially repealed. The authority to prohibit or restrict abortion, by common law or by statute, has been exercised by the states as long as there have been states.[6] This right to regulate abortion, which was reserved to the states by the 10th Amendment, was substantially curtailed by *Roe v. Wade.* Moreover, by declaring that the right to choose to have an abortion is a fundamental right, the Court brought abortion regulations under the direct supervision of the federal judiciary, just as if Article Three, section 2 had been expanded. These two shifts in governmental authority effected a severe curtailment of state legislative power and a substantial expansion of federal judicial jurisdiction. Abortion, constitutionally, became a matter for special federal judicial supervision rather than ordinary state legislative direction.

Second, the decision in *Roe v. Wade* has had a significant, and severely detrimental, impact on the federal judiciary. No decision in the last quarter of a century has brought upon the courts such widespread, and such justly deserved, condemnation. Never in the twentieth century has the legitimacy of a Supreme Court decision rested on so tenuous a basis. The opinion in *Roe*—the official justification for the aforementioned restructuring of our federal government—is ineptly written. It is, in fact, an embarrassment to the legal profession. Richard Epstein put it well when he wrote that the decision was so poorly reasoned that "[w]hat seemed to make a lot of sense as a matter of principle to a lot of people and a lot of lawyers [became] all of a sudden suspect."[7]

Thus, *Roe* is a negative example for judges in the federal judicial system. Judicial craftsmanship and credible legal analysis are generally absent in post-*Roe* abortion decisions. Instead of legal analysis, courts have often been satisfied to employ mere rhetorical slogans to justify their results in abortion cases. Since *Roe* there has also been a startling absence of *vertical* dissent or criticism in federal court abortion decisions. That is an unhealthy development. When criticism ceases and legal doctrines are "sheltered" from the historical process of reexamination and refinement, the law stagnates. Evidence of stagnation has already appeared in the form of the excessive resort to *stare decisis* to resolve new abortion issues without analysis. This is reminiscent of the days of "high formalism" of the last part of the nineteenth century. Finally, the unconcealed hostility of some federal judges—including some of the Justices of the Supreme Court—against almost any type of abortion restriction is apparent.[8] The deterioration of the quality and integrity of the federal judicial system in the wake of *Roe* is therefore a serious concern.[9]

Third, *Roe v. Wade* has had an enormous effect on the substantive law of abortion. For one thing, the Supreme Court decision nationalized and standardized the abortion law. The Court put the law in a constitutional straitjacket; that is, it left no more room for difference of opinion, no more room to account for local feelings and morality. The Supreme Court rulings had the further effect of drastically liberalizing the substance of abortion law. Indeed, the "trimester doctrine" created by the Court went further to decriminalize abortion than any state had previously gone, even further than those states in which the abortion law reformers of the 1960s had achieved their most spectacular successes. In no other modern cases, not even in the Japanese concentration camp cases,[10] has the Court so completely turned its back on so large a class of the defenseless, the unwanted, or the unprotected.

Finally, the impact of *Roe v. Wade* on life in the United States has been devastating. Since 1973 more than eleven million abortions have been performed in this country.[11] Abortion is now the most common surgical procedure performed in America.[12] One-third of all abortions obtained every year are obtained by teenagers.[13] Thirty percent of all known pregnancies in the United States are now terminated by abortion, and in some areas of the country the abortion rate exceeds the birth rate.[14] Thirty percent of all abortions are being obtained by abortion repeaters; that is, women who have previously had one or more abortions.[15] The destruction of life that has resulted under the legal regime of abortion on demand is overwhelming. The effect on the values and composition of the growing generation of Americans is frightening. It is therefore imperative, in my opinion, that *Roe v. Wade* be repudiated. However, since the Supreme Court was acting under its authority to interpret the Constitution when it decided *Roe v. Wade* as it did, its declaration of constitutional law can only be repudiated in one of two ways—by judicial rejection (the Supreme Court overturning the decision itself in a subsequent case) or by a constitutional repeal (the adoption of a formal amendment to the Constitution repealing the judicial amendment effected by *Roe v. Wade*). Subsequent decisions of the Court, particularly those of June 1983,[16] clearly indicate that the Court as presently constituted will staunchly continue to support *Roe v. Wade.* Constitutional repeal is therefore the only practicable avenue of repeal that is presently open.

Moreover, this single open option will be most difficult to accomplish successfully. Two problems are paramount. First, strong political support must be mustered to enact an amendment; and second, even if the amendment is passed by Congress and ratified by the states, there is no guarantee by enactment alone that the desired objectives of the amendment will be fully achieved or that such achievement will not cause unacceptable side effects.

It is important to note that the process of amending the Constitution is an intentionally difficult process. The drafters of the Constitution were not sympathetic to the notion that the document should be freely amended. For example, James Madison, writing in *The Federalist,* expressed his "serious objection against a frequent" use of the amending process.[17]

The difficulty of amending the Constitution is borne out by the few times the task has been successfully accomplished, particularly in comparison to the number of amendments that have been attempted. Excluding the first ten amendments, the Bill of Rights, because their adoption in 1791 represented the fulfillment of a commitment made during the campaign to secure ratification of the Constitution,[18] there have been only sixteen formal amendments to the Constitution adopted. That works out to an average of less than one amendment every decade. By contrast, from 1789 to the present nearly ten thousand proposals to amend the Constitution have been introduced in Congress.

Amending the Constitution is a two-step process: proposal by Congress (or by convention), and ratification by the states. Historically, the major hurdle for constitutional amendments has been the first step—obtaining approval by two-thirds of the House and Senate. (Amendment by convention has never been attempted.)

Only thirty-four proposals to amend the Constitution have been passed by Congress. That means that only one out of about every three hundred proposals to amend the Constitution presented to Congress is approved by Congress. On the other hand, twenty-six of the thirty-four amendments that have been proposed by Congress have ultimately been ratified by the necessary three-fourths of the states.[19] Thus, in discussing any proposed amendment to the Constitution which has not passed Congress, it is apparent that the "odds" are clearly in favor of the opponents. However, if a proposed amendment does get through Congress, the chance of success dramatically changes. Then the odds are three to one that the proposed amendment will be ratified.

In examining the effects of any antiabortion amendment on state law and prosecutions we must be aware of four important qualifications. First, a constitutional amendment will not be a panacea. This is particularly true in the context of the objectives of the right-to-life movement. Some objectives—the ultimate objectives—are really not legal but are behavioral and attitudinal. These are affected by many influences, of which law is only one. No law, either constitutional or statutory, will stop all abortions, and anyone who thinks that passage of any proposed amendment will achieve that result, or even come close to achieving it, has lost touch with reality.

By the same token, adoption of an amendment to the Constitution will not automatically accomplish all of the legal objectives either. As Professor David Louisell put it, "[a] Constitutional Amendment fixes the path, but cannot alone achieve the desired goal."[20] State or federal legislation will be necessary under *any* version of a human life amendment.

Second, a constitutional amendment, when ratified, becomes the supreme law of the land. Article Six of the Constitution, the supremacy clause, explicitly so provides. John Marshall wrote, in 1803, that it was the intent of the framers that the Constitution be "the fundamental and paramount law of the nation, and . . . that an act of the legislature, repugnant to the Constitution, [be] void."[21] Ever since that statement it has been the cardinal principle of constitutional law that provisions of the Constitution, including the articles of amendment, supersede all conflicting statutes, rules, or regulations—whether federal or state; whether executive, legislative, or judicial.[22] It is also clear that an amendment to the Constitution takes priority over a previously adopted provision of the Constitution when there is a conflict between them.[23]

Third, the federal judiciary, particularly the Supreme Court, has a special responsibility for interpreting the provisions of the

Constitution, including the amendments. Since the Constitution was first ratified it has been recognized that "[i]t is emphatically the province and duty of the judicial department to say what the law is. [Judges] must of necessity expound and interpret [the Constitution and laws]. . . . This is the very essence of judicial duty."[24]

Just how the Court will interpret documentary law is not entirely predictable. The tradition of adherence to the original intent is well established, but so also is a history of numerous exceptions. And in dealing with a constitutional amendment there is the further complication of the absence of "a" legislative intent—because an amendment to the Constitution must be passed by at least thirty-nine separate and independent state legislatures to become effective.

Furthermore, legal analysis seldom provides one specific answer to an issue. Rather, legal analysis narrows the range of technically justifiable solutions. This poses a real problem for a human life amendment. For the federal judges who will be deciding which of the technically plausible interpretions of a human life amendment is to be given operative effect are the same judges who have been responsible for creating and expanding the doctrine of abortion privacy. Thus, writing a substantive rule of law concerning abortion directly into the Constitution may invite the frustration of right-to-life objectives by the same hostile judiciary which since 1973 has successfully thwarted efforts to extend even minimal protection to the unborn. To use Professor Louisell's words again, that "would but embrace the trap, by popular action, which *Roe* and *Doe* set by judicial fiat."[25]

Fourth, it must be recognized that interpretations of the Constitution change. Judicial interpretation of the 13th, 14th, and 15th amendments (the Civil Rights Amendments) provides the classic example. Anyone who judges the past effectiveness of those amendments on the basis of their present effectiveness will get a distorted picture of what has actually occurred. For three-quarters of a century, the Civil Rights Amendments were interpreted so narrowly as to constitute an obstacle to the achievement of the objectives of those amendments.[26] Only in the last three decades have they been given meaningful, effective interpretation.

Thus, it is possible that even a substantively "tough" human life amendment—one that by its terms provided total protection for the unborn—could receive such a narrow construction by the courts that effective achievement of the real objectives could be thwarted for decades. By the same token, even if such an amendment were immediately given a proper reading by the judiciary, that does not insure that it would be interpreted the same way in the future.

Since *Roe v. Wade* was decided, dozens of human life amendments have been proposed.[27] Some of these differ only in choice of specific language; others differ significantly in both language and intent. All of them, however, contain one or more of just three distinct provisions: (1) those establishing the legal personhood of the unborn, (2) those specifically prohibiting abortions to some extent, and (3) those empowering federal and/or state legislatures to enforce the prohibition or otherwise regulation of abortion. A number of proposed amendments include all three of the above-stated provisions. In my opinion, one of these, the Garn Amendment,[28] has the most promise both as regards its chances of receiving sufficient political support for enactment and as regards its achieving the objectives of the right-to-life movement with minimum risk of unacceptable side effects. The following examination therefore has as its central focus the Garn Amendment, with its personhood, prohibiting, and enforcement (empowerment) provisions.

The Garn Amendment

Nonlegal Aspects

The Garn Amendment is the most widely known of the several human life amendments and has served both as a rallying point and as a lightning rod for the right-to-life movement. Sponsored by the National Right to Life Committee, it was introduced in Congress in 1974 and has been reintroduced every year since.[29] The Garn Amendment is appealing to the right-to-life movement for several good, nonlegal reasons. First, it seems right. As a statement of fundamental value or belief it is very good; it sounds very attractive. Second, it is the most familiar amendment; it has been the banner of the right-to-life movement since 1974. Third, the philosophical parallelism and historical symmetry embodied in the language are intellectually satisfying. Still, all such attractiveness aside, the Garn Amendment—or any of the proposed human life amendments, for that matter—must be critically examined, and must pass or fail, against the standard of cold legal analysis.[30] Measurement by any other standard risks passage of a constitutional amendment that would be ineffective in operation or produce wholly unnecessary and undesirable unplanned consequences. Such a legal analysis, which must ultimately predict actual legal consequences, is risky. But the risks can be minimized by examining carefully and systematically each provision.

Personhood

Section 1 of the Garn Amendment makes the unborn "persons" for purposes of the 5th and 14th amendments. Those amendments, generally, only restrict actions of the federal and state governments, not private acts of private individuals.[31] As most abortions are performed by private individuals, a restrictive reading of a pure personhood provision, like Section 1, would have virtually no direct effect on the current practice of abortion. Only government acts—probably including government funding of private abortion, but little more—would be prohibited under a personhood provision.

However, there are also several arguments whereby privately performed abortions could be held subject to the provisions of the 5th and 14th amendments under a personhood amendment. Legalized abortions could be deemed to be a state action by invoking an argument that the Supreme Court relied on in *Planned Parenthood v. Danforth*[32] to invalidate parental and spousal consent requirements. In *Danforth* the Court characterized Missouri's formal recognition and enforcement of the constitutionally protected rights of parents and husbands to participate in making the abortion decision of minor children and wives as an impermissible "delegation" by the state of a power (to prohibit abortion) which the state itself did not possess. By similar logic, one could argue that under Section 1 a state could not "delegate" to private doctors and others a power (to deprive unborn persons of their lives) which the state does not possess. This argument is a very shallow one, for it completely reverses what has been the historical perception of the constitutional source and flow of personal rights and governmental powers (i.e., from the people to their government, not vice versa). But it is a plausible technical argument.

A second argument under which private abortions might be reached by a pure personhood provision is that the failure of a state to prohibit abortion (state inaction) is a form of state action. The U.S. Supreme Court rejected an analogous argument in a recent case. The survivors of a fifteen-year-old girl murdered by a parolee in California brought an action for damages under 42 U.S.C. § 1983 and state law claiming that the action of the parole board in releasing the criminal, together with a California statute immunizing parole authorities from liability, constituted state action depriving the victim of her life without due process of law. In *Martinez v. State,* the U.S. Supreme Court sustained the dismissal of the action, reasoning among other things that a "legislative decision that has an incremental impact on the probability that death will result in a given situation . . . cannot be characterized as state action depriving a person of life just because it may set in motion a chain of events that ultimately leads to the random death of an innocent bystander."[33] But a state legislative policy of abortion on demand has more than "an *incremental* impact on the probability that death will result in a given situation." The

Court's rejection of the state action claim in *Martinez* does not foreclose the possibility that it might find state action in a failure to legislate which directly led to the foreseeable death of deliberately selected victims at the hands of private persons.

Thus, there are several plausible grounds for concluding that the 5th and 14th amendments could be read so as to cover private abortions. At least one commentator believes that Justice Blackmun implied as much in one of the many tangential and ambiguous passages in the *Roe v. Wade* opinion.[34] On the other hand, there is a good argument in support of the position that a pure personhood amendment would have no effect on private abortions. Technically, both conclusions would be supportable.

The effective reach of the personhood section is not its only questionable aspect. A pure personhood provision would make the unborn "persons" for the purposes of the 5th and 14th amendments only. Those amendments contain the due process and equal protection guarantees of the Constitution.

Under the due process clause, it is possible to argue that a personhood amendment would prohibit abortion, but it is also possible to argue that it would have absolutely no effect on the result of *Roe v. Wade.* The argument that a personhood section would prohibit abortion is based upon a dictum in *Roe v. Wade* wherein Justice Blackmun suggested that, if the unborn were persons, the argument that states cannot regulate abortion would fall to pieces because the states' interest in protecting the right to life of such unborn persons would provide sufficient justification for adopting a law which infringed upon a woman's right to choose to have an abortion.[35] Justice Blackmun's dictum suggests more than it explains—yet it is not an implausible analysis.

But there is another possible interpretation. The 5th and 14th amendments do not guarantee any person—including the unborn, if they are persons—an *absolute* right to life. It only guarantees that persons will not be deprived of life without due process of law. Calling a fetus a "person" might only mean that the Court would have to explain that an abortion clinic "consultation" constituted all the "process" that was "due" the unborn person. Thus, it is possible that all that "would be established by [a personhood amendment] is that one right granted specific protection by the Fourteenth Amendment [would be] in conflict with what the Court felt was another; it would not tell us which must prevail."[36] Thus, it is possible (although unlikely, in my opinion) that a pure personhood amendment would not change the *Roe v. Wade* holding that states are constitutionally required to allow abortion on demand. It is also possible (and equally unlikely) that it could be read as requiring states to prohibit abortion. Most likely, a personhood amendment alone would be read as providing states with a justification for abortion laws if they chose to pass such laws—a states' rights effect.[37]

A personhood provision, such as Section 1 of the Garn Amendment, arguably could prohibit abortion under the equal protection clause of the 14th Amendment. The argument for this result is as follows: State homicide laws prohibit the taking of life of born persons. The equal protection clause provides that all persons shall reserve the equal protection of the law. The unborn are persons. Therefore, the unborn are entitled to protection of their lives equivalent to that which is provided for born persons. This is a logical, very plausible analysis. But it is not the only possible analysis.

An alternative argument is that, like the due process clause, the equal protection clause is not absolute. It does not prohibit all class distinctions; it only requires that distinctions in the law be justified. How much justification is required depends upon the nature of the classification. Even detrimental discrimination against the classes entitled to the greatest constitutional protection will be permitted if justified by a compelling reason. Thus, one could call the fetus a person and still conclude, as does Professor Laurence H. Tribe, "that to deny such a person protection from the woman's choice until the point of viability is a reasonable policy, entirely consistent with due process and equal protection."[38]

How would the Court actually interpret a personhood provision? No one really knows for sure. Hopefully, the Court would read it in light of the obvious intent to repeal *Roe v. Wade.* But that is not certain. And it is analytically possible—in fact, it would be quite easy—for a Court to perpetuate the legal doctrine of abortion on demand even under a pure personhood provision.

Before leaving the personhood section, we must note that it clearly *does* achieve another major objective—one of particular significance for reasons of philosophical parallelism and historical integrity. That is, it expressly establishes the legal personhood of the unborn and all other living human beings. This objective is not primarily a legal objective in an operational sense. As explained above, the "personhood" of the unborn is only of debatable significance so far as the legality of abortion is concerned. But it is of enormous philosophical and political significance to many people. And the argument that it is not inappropriate to add to the Constitution clear declarations of fundamental beliefs that are of only minor functional significance has merit. The counterpoint is that to do so invites all sorts of unintended consequences—the parade of horribles. Whether constitutionalizing the personhood of the unborn is a good objective to be achieved by constitutional amendment is beyond the scope of this chapter. Suffice to state that this is an apparent objective of those who drafted the personhood section of the Garn Amendment, and other human life amendments as well, and that it clearly will be achieved if language like that in Section 1 of the Garn Amendment is adopted.

Prohibition

It is obvious that prohibition provisions (like Section 2 of the Garn Amendment) have been designed to outlaw abortion. Undoubtedly, Section 2 of the Garn Amendment would do that, providing one narrow exception for death-preventing abortions.

Prohibition provisions do not suffer from the same "private action" controversy as personhood provisions. Clearly, by express language, private actions are covered. State action is also reached, to the extent that states are persons. It also seems that provisions such as Section 2 would not be subject to the balancing tests that apply under the due process and equal protection clauses. The prohibition section is an express prohibition of specific conduct. Only two other amendments have directly prohibited all activity of a specific nature: the 13th Amendment,[39] which abolished slavery, and the 18th Amendment,[40] which prohibited production or sale of alcoholic beverages. Examining each of these amendments to see what effect these direct constitutional prohibitions had on state law will shed some light on what effect the prohibition section of the Garn Amendment could be expected to have.

Like the Garn Amendment, the 13th Amendment contains both a direct prohibition clause and an enforcement clause. Slavery is directly abolished, and the enforcement clause confers power on Congress to enforce the abolition provision.

In 1883 the United States Supreme Court interpreted the prohibition clause of the 13th Amendment. In the *Civil Rights Cases* it declared: "This Amendment . . . is undoubtedly self-executing without any ancillary legislation, so far as its terms are applicable to any existing state of circumstances. By its own unaided force and effect it abolished slavery, and established universal freedom."[41]

For nearly a century this statement has been accepted and noncontroversial but of little real effect. "The force and effect of the Amendment itself has been invoked only a few times by the Court to strike down state legislation which it considered to have reintroduced servitude of persons and it has not used Section One of the Amendment against private parties."[42] Recently the Second Circuit summarized the status of the prohibitory clause of the 13th Amendment as follows: "[T]he [Supreme] Court has directly invoked the Amendment only to strike down state laws imposing the condition of peonage. . . . Moreover, the Court has indicated that for purposes of judicial enforcement under the express prohibition of the Amendment itself . . . the Court will define slavery narrowly."[43]

Think of the significance of that. If the Supreme Court will give a deliberately narrow interpretation to an amendment dealing with a subject it finds odious is it realistic to expect a more generous treatment of the prohibition section of an amendment outlawing behavior it favors? Even if the Garn Amendment were given the same judicial construction as the 13th Amendment, that would only mean that the federal courts would invoke the prohibition section cautiously and probably would give a very narrow definition to the proscribed activity.

Additionally, historians now write that, within a decade after its passage, the 13th Amendment was functionally obsolete and that, because of the failure of the 13th Amendment to achieve its desired ends, Congress later felt it necessary to pass the 14th and 15th Amendments—and the Civil Rights Acts of 1870–75.[44] That may suggest that even if we had a cooperative Congress and a docile Supreme Court it would necessitate substantial subsequent action—both constitutional and statutory—to achieve right-to-life goals even after the Garn Amendment were passed.

The 18th Amendment to the Constitution likewise contained two operative provisions. The first directly prohibited the manufacture, sale, and transportation of beverage liquor, and the second gave the states and Congress "concurrent power to enforce" prohibition.

Soon after its enactment, the Supreme Court reviewed the constitutionality of the 18th Amendment. In the *National Prohibition Cases,* it held that

> [T]he first section of the Amendment—the one embodying the prohibition—is operative throughout the entire territorial limits of the United States, binds all legislative bodies, courts, public officers, and individuals within those limits, and of its own force invalidates every legislative act—whether by Congress, by a state legislature, or by a territorial assembly—which authorizes or sanctions what the section prohibits.[45]

As was the case with the 13th Amendment, the language used by the Court to describe the effect of the amendment was broad but, again, the Court did not follow up with action to match its words.

The operative impotence of the direct-prohibition provision of the 18th Amendment is best illustrated by the case of *Vigliotti v. Commonwealth.*[46] Pennsylvania's "Brook's Law," enacted thirty years before the 18th Amendment, prohibited the sale of liquor without a license. Vigliotti was convicted of violating this law after the 18th Amendment was enacted. He appealed his conviction arguing that Brook's Law was inconsistent with, and therefore unconstitutional under, the 18th Amendment. The amendment, he correctly argued, was intended to prevent completely all traffic in liquor, while the purpose of Brook's Law was only to minimize the evils of unregulated liquor sales. The United States Supreme Court rejected this argument and affirmed his conviction, stating that Brook's Law "merely grants to the appropriate officials . . . discretion to give or to withhold the license [to sell liquor] under the conditions prescribed. . . . It is thus primarily a prohibitory law."[47] The Court reasoned that this licensing scheme was not unconstitutional under the amendment.

> The Brooks law as thus construed does not purport to authorize or sanction anything which the Eighteenth Amendment or the Volstead Act prohibits. And there is nothing in it which conflicts with any provision of either. It is merely an additional instrument which the State supplies in an effort to make prohibition effective.[48]

Similarly, the fact that Brook's Law was enacted decades before the 18th Amendment was irrelevant to its constitutionality.

If the prohibition section of the Garn Amendment were interpreted similarly, it would mean—despite the very tough language and the narrow exception contained therein, and despite the obvious intent to proscribe all abortions completely, save only those few necessary to prevent the death of the mother—that an abortion-on-demand statute could be passed by a state, or a previously enacted abortion-on-demand statute could continue to be the law in a state, and the argument might be made (unsuccessfully, I believe, but it could be argued) that it is not inconsistent with the prohibition section of the Garn Amendment because it merely gives to appropriate officials (doctors) discretion to grant or deny an abortion under prescribed conditions.

Enforcement

The third major intended objective of the Garn Amendment is to permit both federal and state regulation of abortion. A general police power was not among the powers given to Congress but was reserved to the states.[49] Congress's limited power to enact criminal laws derives from its constitutional authority to exercise control over specific subjects such as federal lands (e.g., federal territories, national parks, etc.), the armed services (military law), and interstate commerce (interstate transportation crimes, etc.). Thus, without an amendment specifically providing that Congress has the authority to prohibit or restrict abortion, Congress would not, generally, be able to do so. The states, however, could.

The enforcement provision of the Garn Amendment (Section 3) not only restores to the states their historic authority to prohibit or otherwise restrict and/or regulate abortion, but confers new power on Congress. The apparent intent is to let Congress create a "floor," or minimum level of nationwide protection for the unborn, and let the states individually provide greater protection if they so choose. Under the enforcement section it is likely that a "federalization" of abortion law would occur, at least to some extent. States would not recover the same police power they had before *Roe v. Wade.* That power was an exclusive power within their respective territorial jurisdiction. Under the enforcement section the states would give up that exclusiveness by giving to Congress the authority to regulate in this area also.

There is only one technical point of possible concern resulting from this "dual jurisdiction" approach. The exact nature of jurisdictional overlap or division of power between Congress and the states is not certain. It would probably be similar to that established by the 18th Amendment, however. The enforcement section of the 18th Amendment provided that Congress and the states had "concurrent power" to enforce prohibition. There is a good body of case law interpreting that section.[50] However, the word "concurrent" is not used in the Garn Amendment. It is possible, therefore, that the method of sharing power under the Garn Amendment could be different than it was under the 18th Amendment.

To date, only two proposed human life amendments have emerged out of committee in Congress, and both have contained only enforcement (or empowering) provisions. The first was S.J. Res. 110, introduced by Senator Hatch in the 97th Congress in the fall of 1981.[51] The Subcommittee on the Constitution of the Senate Judiciary Committee held nine days of hearings on the subject of proposed constitutional amendments, particularly focusing on the proposed Hatch Federalism Amendment, from October through December 1981.[52] On December 16, 1981, the Subcommittee on the Constitution voted four to one in favor of reporting out the proposed amendment, modified to read:

> A right to abortion is not secured by this Constitution. The Congress and several States shall have concurrent power to restrict and prohibit abortion: *Provided* That a provision of a law of a State which is more restrictive than a conflicting provision of a law of Congress shall govern.[53]

On March 10, 1982, the Senate Committee on the Judiciary voted to favorably report out the proposed amendment (as above modified) by a vote of ten to seven.[54] On September 15, 1982, with the Congress approaching the end of its work year and with a filibuster underway regarding another right-to-life proposal, Senator Hatch announced his intention to withdraw his proposed amendment from further consideration because he did not have the votes to support the measure.[55]

The full operative legal effect of the Hatch Federalism Amendment has been explained in a senate report. The second sentence of that amendment embodies the concept of "federalism" discussed earlier.[56] "By the phrase 'concurrent power to restrict and prohibit abortion,' it is intended that Congress and the States have the power to enact and enforce any laws rationally related to restricting abortion which they may deem appropriate."[57] The proviso clause was included so that if there should arise a conflict between a law on the subject of abortion passed by Congress and a law on the same subject passed by a state, the supremacy clause of the Constitution would not result in the preemption of a more restrictive state law by a more liberal congressional abortion enactment.[58]

The first ten words of the Hatch Federalism Amendment would repeal the doctrine of abortion privacy developed by the federal courts. "[T]he first sentence is intended to reverse *Roe v. Wade* and its companion *Doe v. Bolton* insofar as these cases hold that the constitution protects an abortion liberty."[59]

In 1983 Senator Hatch reintroduced the amendment,[60] this time modified, in collaboration with Senator Eagleton, to include only the essential language necessary to reverse *Roe v. Wade.* This, the Hatch-Eagleton Amendment, contains just the ten-word opening statement of the Hatch Federalism Amendment, that is, "[a] right to abortion is not secured by this Constitution." The new proposal was "designed to establish a new locus for decision-making authority; i.e., legislatures. S.J. Res. 3 merely reaffirms the power of legislatures to legislate with respect to 'abortion' and denies the existence of any constitutional protection for abortion."[61] The proposal passed the subcommittee, and the Senate Judiciary Committee sent it on to the floor of the Senate.[62] On June 28, 1983, after several days of debate, the Senate voted and the proposal was defeated fifty against to forty-nine for, with one abstention.[63]

It is crucial to note that neither the original Hatch Federalism Amendment nor the Hatch-Eagleton Amendment would establish any substantive constitutional position regarding abortion. Rather, they would *disestablish* a substantive rule of law—that created in *Roe.* The proposed amendments provide "only that the doctrine of abortion on demand is *not* a constitutional doctrine of law; [they do] not purport to declare what balance, if any, the

Constitution strikes between the rights of a pregnant woman who desires to terminate pregnancy and the rights of the unborn child [or of the state to prohibit abortion]."[64] Thus, either of the Hatch-sponsored proposals would largely deconstitutionalize the abortion controversy. State and federal legislators would have the responsibility to resolve the question. However, courts would not be precluded from finding that other provisions of the Constitution protect a right to life or impact on the resolution of the controversy, except that judicial interpretation could not, directly or indirectly, reestablish a right to abortion.

Before refocusing on the Garn Amendment, it is appropriate to address one particular new modification proposal, one that would declare an additional, fourth provision. Just one month after the conference at which this paper was presented, the Board of Directors of the National Right to Life Committee endorsed a modified version of the Garn Amendment. Soon thereafter, that revised proposal—to be called the NRLC Amendment—was introduced in Congress by Senator Jesse Helms[65] and Representative Thomas Luken.[66] In addition to personhood, prohibition, and empowering provisions, this proposal contains a "paramount" provision which reads, "[t]he right to life is the paramount and most fundamental right of a person."[67]

The personhood, prohibition, and enforcement provisions of the NRLC Amendment do not vary significantly from those contained in the Garn Amendment. The exception clauses of the prohibition sections (Section 2 of Garn, Section 3 of NRLC) are defined in different language, but the technical distinctions have more symbolic significance (at least to some right-to-life thinkers) than practical legal significance. Essentially, the NRLC proposal defines more narrowly the life-threatening (death-threatening) circumstances which would justify abortion than does the language of the Garn proposal.

But the paramount provision creates a difference between the NRLC and Garn amendments that is of potentially greater constitutional significance. Section 1 of NRLC declares that the right to life is "the paramount and most fundamental right of a person." This is apparently intended to reverse the hierarchy of values established by the Supreme Court in *Roe v. Wade,* wherein a woman's right to abortion was given priority over the interest in life of the unborn. Thus, the language is an attempt to establish the superiority of the value of "actual life" over "quality of life" values. But both symbolically and as operational law this language could be very problematic.

Symbolically, it is questionable whether all Americans, now or at any time in our history, would agree that life is truly the paramount, or ultimate, value. Our liberties were won, and have been preserved, by many men and women who believed that it was better to die for freedom than to submit to intolerable political or religious oppression.

As operative law, the declaration that the right to life is paramount might conceivably raise questions about the constitutionality of laws, regulations, and programs pertaining to military service and capital punishment. The possible impact on state law and prosecution could be substantial, depending on whether or not the "paramount" right to life were deemed absolute and, if not, just how "fundamental" and "paramount" it is.

The scope of the right to life (exactly what activities that right protects) and the standard of judicial review (the test for judicial scrutiny applicable whenever laws infringing on the right to life were challenged) would be critical under a paramount provision. Clearly, they would be matters for the Court to decide. The language of Section 1 of the proposed NRLC Amendment gives very little guidance. Standing alone, it is as broad and as vague as any provision of the 14th Amendment or of the recently defeated (in part because of its vagueness) Equal Rights Amendment. Fortunately, Section 1 of the NRLC Amendment does not stand alone. The personhood, prohibition, and enforcing sections provide a context for interpretation and would be reference points for judges given the task of interpreting Section 1. Thus, a narrow interpretation of the scope of the right to life (limited to protection against abortion and its equivalents) is probably the intended meaning and a likely interpretation. But it is certainly not the only plausible interpretation of the scope of the right to life. And while the use of the terms "paramount" and "fundamental" suggest that the standard of judicial review should be at least strict scrutiny, it could be an even more demanding standard of review. In short, because of its generality and breadth, a paramount provision could provide the judiciary with enormous interpretative potential. And that is probably just the opposite of what those who drafted the NRLC Amendment intend.

* * *

Writing in a 1974 issue of *Family Planning Perspectives,* Harriett F. Pilpel, counsel to Planned Parenthood/World Population, declared that "legal chaos" would result if a human life amendment were ratified.[68] In two pages she presented twenty-five questions postulating such drastic consequences as criminal liability for pregnant women who smoke, drink, or get inadequate rest; mandatory monthly pregnancy tests for all fertile women; and the enumeration of every fertilized ovum in census reports. Two years later she testified before Congress that adoption of a human life amendment could lead to imposition of a prosecutorial duty to investigate every miscarriage,[69] and to the creation of a powerful federal bureaucracy to enforce antiabortion laws.[70] In February 1981 Ms. Pilpel repeated similar claims. Ratification of a human life amendment "might call into being a doctrine of federal entitlement. . . . This could mean an entitlement to food, shelter, education and health care (for all persons)."[71]

Writing in the February issues of *Ms.,* another proabortion attorney predicted that enactment into law of a human life amendment could, among other things, "permit attacking and even killing anyone about to perform an abortion,"[72] lead to "fetuses be[ing] involuntarily removed from endangered or unwilling women and transferred to willing surrogates,"[73] and ordain "the state [to] prescribe dangerous experimental drugs, not withstanding their impact on a woman's health or their likelihood of producing diseased, deformed, or doomed children."[74]

The ACLU Foundation recently published a pamphlet predicting that the passage of a human life amendment would mean that "women would become machines bearing 'human life,' and the machines would be expendable, while fertilized eggs would acquire unprecedented legal protection."[75] "Monthly pregnancy tests for all women from puberty to menopause may be required, or registration of every pregnancy or suspected pregnancy could be mandated. . . . The government could conceivably set up a Federal Bureau of Pregnancy Investigation."[76]

The notorious 1975 report of the United States Commission on Civil Rights dealing with this subject devoted the better part of one hundred pages to describing the horrors that might ensue if a human life amendment were enacted into law. It speculated that the rules of inheritance in each state would change,[77] that a human life amendment would "create chaos" in the law of torts,[78] and that it would undermine the 1st, 9th, and 14th amendments.[79] The chairman of that commission, Arthur S. Flemming, reiterated these sensational claims when he testified before Congress in 1976.[80]

Most of these allegations are exaggerated, deceptive, or spurious. They are not offered in honest intellectual inquiry, and to respond to them would be to endow them with unmerited dignity. For example, Ms. Pilpel suggests that there is a serious possibility that a constitutional amendment defining "person" to include the unborn would confer citizenship on the unborn.[81] But the 14th Amendment expressly defines "citizens" not simply as persons but as "persons *born* or naturalized in the United States." In fact, there is no controversy about the effect of a personhood amendment on citizenship. In the words of one Planned Parenthood worker, such allegations are simply being used "as a scare tactic."[82] A few other "horribles" deserve comment, however.

What effect would adoption of the Garn Amendment have on property, tort, and criminal laws in the states? Under both the 13th and 18th amendments, the direct effect of the prohibitory sections was restricted. Congress and the states were given sweeping power to regulate the collateral matters—to reach "the badges and incidents" of the proscribed activity. The Court recognized broad legislative prerogative and indicated that regulation of collateral activities (e.g., property, tort, and criminal law, etc.) would be upheld *if* the state or federal legislature chose to enact such legislation. But if the legislature did not attempt to reach those collateral matters, the courts themselves were unwilling to do so. The enforcement sections of those amendments were construed as taking the initiative—the power to proceed in the first instance—away from the judiciary and vesting it in the legislative branch of government.

Likewise, the enforcement section of the Garn Amendment might be read as implicitly depriving the courts of the initiative to regulate collateral matters. In any event, it is unlikely that the courts would, upon the bare authority of the substantive sections of the Garn Amendment, impose a change in a collateral area of law such as property, tort, or other criminal regulations.

If the Garn Amendment were to have collateral effects upon property, tort, and criminal law, it would probably be as a result of the equal protection clause being extended to the unborn. The argument for such consequences is as follows: The 14th Amendment guarantees equal protection to all persons. The unborn are persons. Therefore, they are entitled to the same protections and rights in the law as are other (born) persons. This argument might even be enhanced by the assertion that the constitutional rights of the unborn are fundamental, or that laws discriminatory against the unborn are constitutionally "suspect." If this argument were accepted, laws discriminating between unborn and born persons would be subjected to strict judicial scrutiny and upheld only if necessary to effectuate a compelling state interest.

This position is plausible but not probable. In the first place, the only "fundamental" right extended to the unborn by the Garn Amendment is the right to life. Other rights which the unborn may have do not rise to the level or dignity of being "fundamental." Thus, it is virtually inconceivable that a court would examine distinctions between born and unborn persons in tort or property laws under the standard of strict scrutiny. Furthermore, as explained earlier, the equal protection clause does not guarantee absolute equality. It just requires that inequality be justifiable on the basis of some legitimate state interest. And it is more than likely that most historic distinctions between the property, tort, and criminal law rights of born and unborn persons would be found to be well justified. After all, the law has been wrestling with these problems—the personal and property rights of the unborn—for centuries, not just since *Roe v. Wade.* The doctrines that have developed were examined by courts (even under equal protection analysis) for many years before *Roe v. Wade* was decided.

Moreover, it is very unlikely that adoption of the Garn Amendment would have any significant impact on the law in these collateral areas because even *Roe v. Wade* has had virtually no effect on the development of these doctrines. The trend of the law in property and tort, for the last forty years, has been uniformly in the direction of greater recognition of the rights of the unborn, and *Roe v. Wade* has not produced even as much as a hesitation in that trend.

Property law illustrates this most clearly. While the Constitution refers to "life, liberty and property," the Garn Amendment addresses only the "right to life." Applying the ancient and elementary legal maxim *inclusio unius est exclusio alterius* [the inclusion of one is the exclusion of another],[83] it is clear that the exclusivity of the reference to "life" precludes the possibility of finding that "property rights" are within the direct purview of that amendment. As Professor Robert Byrn has succinctly stated: "The Fifth and Fourteenth Amendments speak of life, liberty and property. The Human Life Amendment speaks only of life. The Amendment will not mandate a change in *property law.*"[84]

However, even given that the Garn Amendment might raise the property rights issue, such a likelihood would not create a precedent. The law of property has traditionally accorded broad recognition to the rights of unborn children. Existence of a being *in utero* is all that has been necessary to have a legal right to inherit. Birth is only significant as marking the point at which the right can be asserted. Laws of descent and inheritance have historically recognized the unborn child from the moment of conception for most purposes concerned with property rights.[85] The unborn child may be an actual-income recipient prior to the time of birth, as well as a tenant in common with his or her mother.[86] Likewise, the unborn have been recognized as living heirs for purposes of taking an estate, whether by devise or intestate succession.[87] Moreover, relatives of the deceased conceived before his death but born thereafter inherit under the UNIFORM PROBATE CODE as if they had been born in the lifetime of the decedent.[88] And in some circumstances the law also recognizes an equitable interest in possible future children who at the time of the creation of the right have not yet been conceived and thus have no physical existence whatever.[89] Thus, even if the Garn Amendment were given such a broad interpretation as to impact upon the collateral matters of property law, it would have very little substantive impact on this area.

Regarding the law of tort, the aim of the Garn Amendment is only to protect the right to life of the unborn child and other human beings, not to guarantee the unborn's "liberty"—even if that term could be construed to mean that there is a constitutional right to be free from tort. At the common law the unborn child was deemed to have no cause of action for tortious injury sustained prior to birth. This was the law followed in the American states until after World War II, when, as Professor William L. Prosser has described it, "the most spectacular abrupt reversal of a well settled rule in the whole history of the law of torts" occurred.[90] It is now well established that there is a cause of action for injuries suffered by a child, even though the child be in the womb, if the child was viable at the time of injury.[91] The trend of modern courts is even to reject the viability requirement and to allow actions for all postconception injuries. It is noteworthy that nearly half of the jurisdictions that have extended their right to recover for prenatal injuries to include injuries received before viability have donc so by judicial actions since *Roe v. Wade* was decided.[92] Even the present RESTATEMENT, SECOND, OF THE LAW OF TORTS, published six years after *Roe,* rejects the viability requirement and recognizes a cause of action for injuries to unborn children whether they occur before or after viability.[93]

Wrongful death actions, generally, are not so uniform. This is due, in large part, to the fact that wrongful death actions are statutory, and the courts have had to apply the specific language of various wrongful death statutes. While the majority rule requires a fetus to have been viable at the time of the wrongful death, some states allow recovery irrespective of viability for the wrongful death of the fetus.[94]

It is most unlikely that the adoption of the Garn Amendment would have any substantial effect on the ongoing development of the law of tort. To state that a fetus is a "person" for 14th Amendment purposes does not mean that the rights of that unborn person must be the same as the rights of all other persons irrespective of the differences in their circumstances and conditions. The equal protection clause only requires a balancing of rights and a justification for discrimination between classes. It would not mean that courts must ignore traditional concerns regarding proof, foreseeability, proximate cause, or important policy considerations relevant to differences between the unborn and other persons.

The issue has been raised that the unborn would be deemed to be foreseeable victims to whom duty of care is owed. Thus, it is argued, the unborn child or its representative could sue third parties for injuries to the mother which also caused injuries to the child (raising the spectre of "double recovery").[95] And it is further alleged that the unborn child or its representative could sue the mother for engaging in negligently harmful activity while pregnant—for example, not getting enough rest, drinking alcohol, or using other fetal-injury-producing drugs.[96] These arguments, however, prove both too little and too much.

These arguments prove too little in that what they claim may result from the adoption of a human life amendment is already the law. As just noted, the unborn child is deemed a foreseeable victim and is entitled to due care in the law of tort. That is exactly what the post-World War II "abrupt reversal" in the law of torts was all about. As Professor Prosser noted in his classic treatise on torts, all of the major writers in recent years have joined "in maintaining that the unborn child in the path of an automobile is as much a person in the street as the mother and in urging that recovery should be allowed upon proper proof."[97] Moreover, state laws uniformly protect children from intentional or seriously negligent injury by the parent. Courts in every state are authorized, and are not reluctant, to order parents to perform acts, or to require that parents refrain from certain conduct, when necessary to protect the lives or well-being of children. And under the *parens patriae* power, state courts, even since *Roe v. Wade,* have enjoined pregnant women from engaging in activities which are sure to have seriously detrimental impact on viable unborn children.[98]

The argument is also overdone. The spectre that the mother would be restrained from smoking, drinking, or would be suable in damages for injuries to the unborn child caused by the mother's simple negligence ignores the fact that even if the equal protection clause did require the unborn child to be treated the same as born children for purposes of tort doctrine, it would not require that they be treated any better than other children. So one must ask whether born children can sue their mothers to stop them from smoking, drinking, and other conduct similarly "dangerous" for the child. And the answer, obviously, is no. Furthermore, parents have historically been protected by the doctrine of parental immunity. And although that doctrine has been modified in special circumstances in recent years, it still is widely followed and the policies behind the rule are still strong.[99] Not only do the states have a profound conceptual interest in encouraging family integrity and supporting good-faith childrearing efforts by parents, but such practical concerns as proof, proximate cause, and potential fraud support the existence of such a doctrine. Those concerns, and that doctrine, would be just as valid with respect to treatment in law of unborn children as they are with respect to born children.

Finally, it is unlikely that a human life amendment would be read as compelling the states or Congress to accord unborn persons the same protection under criminal laws that born persons receive. Again, reviewing principles of equal protection, we must remember that not all distinctions between persons similarly situated are prohibited. Rather, only unjustifiable or arbitrary distinctions are forbidden. And in the area of criminal law, it should be abundantly clear that all "killings" of "persons" are not subject to the same penal restrictions. There have always been definite "degrees" of homicide and manslaughter. So, also, different degrees of punishment or different schemes of prohibition for the killing of born and unborn persons could be justified. Such factors as degree of malice, degree of public sympathy, difficulties of proof, strength of public policy to be served, and countervailing public policies would all have to be considered by any court examining an equal protection challenge to a law that treated abortion differently from homicide.[100] It is, of course, rhetorically possible to say that a court could conclude that any distinction between the protection of the criminal laws afforded the unborn and the protection of the criminal laws afforded born persons is unconstitutional. But the analysis necessary to support such a conclusion is as unlikely as it is strained. It is far more likely that reasonable distinctions would be upheld. Abortion would not have to be treated the same as murder. Before *Roe v. Wade* the two crimes were not equal. Punishment for the crime of abortion could vary significantly from punishment for the crime of homicide or manslaughter. Even distinctions in the criminality of different types of abortions would very likely be upheld on the basis of difficulty of proof, countervailing public policies, or differences in the degree of malice.[101]

Purveyors of the "horrible hypotheticals" frequently argue that the prohibition section of the Garn Amendment would give to the unborn greater protection against the destruction of life than is afforded under the Constitution to the mother or any other born person inasmuch as no due process or equal protection qualifications apply. The prohibition against destruction is absolute save in the case of a death-preventing abortion. The exception, however, negates the "greater protection" notion, for the exception indicates that the life of a living person (the mother) is of greater value than the life of the unborn.

At the common law, generally the woman was deemed to be immune from prosecution inasmuch as the law viewed her as a victim of the crime of abortion, rather than the criminal.[102] In a few states, however, exceptions to this rule were recognized. Whether the traditional position of immunity from prosecution would continue after the adoption of a human life amendment is uncertain. The argument against its continuation refers to the strict language of a prohibition section that would seem to give the unborn greater rights than their mothers. The argument against such a result focuses on whatever exception might be written into the section. And to the extent that such an amendment were read as restoring the *status quo ante,* it would leave the matter entirely to the discretion of the states. Inasmuch as good reasons for immunity from prosecution could be articulated (e.g., difficulty of proof and conviction if the woman who had the abortion is unwilling to cooperate, etc.), it is likely (barring a significant change in abortion technology) that an immunity doctrine would not be found unconstitutional under a human life amendment.

* * *

If this discussion has illustrated anything, it is the substantial problems that exist if the substantive legal issue of abortion remains in the special domain of the judiciary. As a matter of simple constitutional structure, the issue does not belong in the judicial arena. By trying to carry on the battle to restore protection for the unborn in the judicial arena, right-to-life advocates may well have "embraced the trap" that will ensure frustration of an effective rule of law—even the frustration of an amendment that expressly provides absolute protection for the unborn.

The first step that should be taken to ensure effective legal protection for the life of the unborn is to take this issue away from the courts and return it to the legislatures of the states, or to the legislatures of the states and to Congress. A simple enforcement, or empowering, provision (e.g., the Hatch Federalism or Hatch-Eagleton Amendment) would do this. That is, an empowering provision (or amendment) would return to the states, and expressly give to Congress, the authority to prohibit or restrict abortion.

The operative effect of an empowering provision would be similar to the operational effect of the 21st Amendment. The 18th Amendment did two things. Procedurally, it severely restricted the authority of the states to decide a very controversial issue (concerning the use of liquor). Substantively, it adopted about the most extreme position possible on the issue (total prohibition). The 21st Amendment restored to the states their plenary authority to deal with the issue, and it substantively repealed the prohibition rule. The 21st Amendment was intended to allow states to authorize the use and manufacture of beverage liquor. The effect is that alcoholic beverages were again made freely available.

By analogy, the effect of *Roe v. Wade* on constitutional law was the same as the 18th Amendment. Procedurally, it severely restricted the authority of the states to decide and regulate this controversial issue (the legality of abortion). Substantively, it adopted one of the most extreme positions on the issue (abortion on demand). An empowering provision would restore to the states their plenary authority to deal with the issue. Also, it might—like the Hatch Federalism Amendment—give to Congress the authority to deal with the issue by passing a "floor" or nationwide minimum protection for unborn human life. The effect would be a giant step toward restoration of legal protection for unborn children. While this approach would not directly accomplish all of the objectives of the right-to-life movement, it would constitute a major step in that direction.

2

PHILOSOPHICAL ASPECTS OF ABORTION

Chapter Three

THE UNBORN AS PERSON

John P. Doyle

If most of us were asked what it is that makes a person, without hesitation we would answer that it is the possession of understanding or intelligence. In possession of intelligence, human persons not only can know but they can also know that they are knowing—which is to say, they can be fully self-conscious. Because they have intelligence, human persons are able to range universally over eligible goods or goals and know that none of them is so perfect or attractive that it must be chosen without fail. For this reason, human persons are not necessitated to act by any good outside themselves. They are in fact what each of us experiences himself to be—namely, self-determined. They can and do intelligently set goals for their own activity. And in this they demonstrate that they are so dominating the order of means and ends as to be ends in themselves and never simply means.[1]

Yet, even rather benighted people will allow that persons exist and that they should be accorded rights, whether they are *actually* thinking or not. They can, in truth, be asleep, they can be unconscious, they can even be in a prolonged coma. They can be newborn or senile. They can be retarded or insane, and still their personhood is accepted and respected. Personhood is thus implicitly acknowledged to run deeper than the actual exercise of intelligence. While exercise comes and goes, personhood remains. Personhood, in fact, is the abiding substrate of intellectual activity. For that reason, we all will attribute a succession of different actions to our continuing person.

An abiding substrate can exist on at least two levels. Penultimately, on a level a philosopher might call "accidental," there is, continuing through different acts, the power to cause those acts—in this instance, especially, the power of understanding. And then there is what from the time of Aristotle has been called "nature"—the ultimate source of each being's powers and activity.

"Properly speaking," Aristotle tells us, "nature is the essence of things which have in themselves, as such, a principle of activity."[2] In the ensuing tradition of western philosophy, essence and nature

John P. Doyle, Ph.D., is professor of philosophy, St. Louis University. He is former chairman, Missouri Governor's Committee on Employment of the Handicapped (1977-1981).

have been differentiated inasmuch as essence has signified the underlying reality of a thing as somehow static, while nature has signified it as dynamic, that is in relation to its operation.[3] To this, I shall return. But first let me say a person is one with a concrete nature of which we take cognizance under the concept of "self." It is the enduring and unitary subject and source of all the states and acts which manifest a human life.

It is true that certain philosophers, especially of the Humean persuasion, deny the existence of an enduring self.[4] But ordinary people, as well as most philosophers possessing common sense, realize that Hume and his followers, while intending to account for the phenomena of self-consciousness, have strangely ignored its most important witness—that is, a self who owns these phenomena and who is directly experienced in them. This is to say that the basic continuing self is an experienced fact that can be explained only if there is something more to our reality than what is merely peripheral or phenomenal. Deeper than phenomena, everyman in fact intuits the level of his own substantial reality,[5] of his own nature as the unitary source of various powers from which in turn proceed various activities. Each of us knows and also remembers himself as the one substrate-source of different powers such as seeing and hearing, as well as understanding, and through them as the source of different activities.

Precisely, then, personhood is either to be identified with or to be rooted in what may, from its highest and most distinctive manifestation, be specified as *intellectual* nature. This, indeed, is the burden of that definition of person which is of longest standing in the history of philosophy. "Person," Boethius defined in the sixth century, "is an individual substance of rational nature."[6] St. Thomas would later modify this to allow for the nondiscursive, purely intellectual operation of angels and God, in whose cases personhood would be separate from bodily existence.[7] But in the case of human beings no such separation is possible.

Evidently, there is a distinction between intellectual and bodily functions. We do not understand with our ears. Otherwise, as someone said, we would have only to hear Chinese in order to comprehend it. Still, there is no sharp separation of our intellectual and bodily functions. It is an axiom whose truth I believe a majority would accept that "there is nothing in the intellect which was not first in the senses." That axiom attests to the fact that for ideogenesis a continuity is required between understanding and sensation. One hundred and eighty degrees away from ideogenesis, the same continuity appears equally requisite across the spectrum from scientific verification to the use of evidence in a courtroom. For Einstein's most abstract theories, as well as for the concrete "smoking gun" argument of the local district attorney, proof is in a return to sensation, a return which would not be possible without continuity between human reasoning and sensation.

That such a continuity requires in man a single unitary nature seems clear. Rather obviously, a yawning chasm between bodily existence and intellectual existence will preclude any continuity between sensation and intelligence. Just as obviously, two things of fundamentally different natures, the one purely bodily and the other purely intellectual, cannot by any stretch of imagination be contiguous with one another. By process of elimination, some single nature that would unify both bodily and intellectual functions seems necessary as the foundation of the continuity that exists between human sensation and understanding.

Once more, Hume notwithstanding, we experience ourselves as basically unified. We are conscious of ourselves as complex, but equally conscious that we are fundamentally one in our being. And, remarkably enough, that being is corporeal; we do not experience ourselves as disembodied spirits. Neither are we spirits who are only extrinsically linked or forcibly yoked to a body. Even though great names—for example, Plato and Descartes—may be attached to it, a radical psychosomatic dualism runs squarely against everyman's awareness that he is one thing and not two.

In line with this, dualism involves problems respecting personal integrity and/or identity. For example, who or what am I? a body? a soul? or a team of both together? It also raises epistemological problems of a kind toward which I have just nodded. If there is in man a separation between two very different things—call them body and soul, body and mind, or body and intelligence—how can the one, that is, the body, provide information to the other? Would not soul or mind knowledge be of an altogether different sort from sense knowledge? Would there not in fact be an opposition between the two? If there is, where would that leave the whole enterprise of knowledge? Empirical science, especially, would be, as I have implied, impossible not only in its advent but also in its verification.

Further problems involved by psychosomatic dualism run into the area of ethics. If body and soul, body and mind, or body and *person* are two separate things of radically diverse nature, how can one explain the experience we all have of willing our own bodily activity? How could a person control his body? Or why should he even try? Why not simply ignore the body as something outside oneself and just cultivate "the right intention" about everything? Why not indeed, as long as one chooses also to ignore the antinomian and Manichean corpses strewn along the highways of history?

As a kind of addendum here, one medieval argument makes, I think, a point worth repeating. A mind or an intelligence merely yoked to a body would be like an angel—that is, in itself a pure spirit. There would then logically be more of a gap between it and the human body, with which it would be yoked, than there would be between that human body and the body of a donkey. In other words, one of the parts of such a split man would be closer in kind to an ass than it would be to its companion part.

Still in a vein of medievalism, let me recall the antique question of the "plurality of forms." First explicitly taught by the eleventh-century Jewish philosopher Ibn Gabirol[8] but already adumbrated in the three-souls doctrine of Plato's *Republic,*[9] the plurality-of-forms theory maintained that in any complex reality such as man there were in fact a number of complete entities, each structured or coded by its own proper "substantial form." Thus, a man would have, in common with inorganic things, a corporeal existence and on that level would be structured by a form which conferred tridimensionality, the so-called form of corporeity. In common with plants, a man would have a simple biological existence and on that level would be structured by the "vegetative form." Again, commonly with worms, dogs, and great apes, a man would have sensitive life and for that he would be structured by a "sensitive form." At last, over it all, would be the level of existence proper to a man as such, and for that he would be structured by the "intellective form."

In the thirteenth century, St. Thomas Aquinas opposed both the dualism of Plato and the plurality of forms doctrine. His basic argument was that they contradicted man's manifest unity.[10] Far from being one thing, man in the view especially of Ibn Gabirol would be like a gang of things. Yet even as he opposed it, St. Thomas was constrained by bad biology to give the plurality doctrine some credence. Obviously, a human being as it exists at the present time cannot be more than one thing. But what about its past existence? Might it not, during the period of its generation, have undergone a succession of formal structures such that it first existed as infrahuman and then in the course of its development crossed the threshold of humanity? St. Thomas thought yes.[11] Aristotle, easily the greatest biologist up to that time, was of the opinion that in human embryonic development such threshold was not crossed until the fortieth day in the case of a male and the eightieth day in the case of a female.[12]

I will come back to this. But now I take it as certain that human intelligence cannot in the normal order of things be separated from bodily existence. I further take it to be shown that the continuity which this requires in its turn again requires a unitary nature in a man possessed of intelligence. The harder question is in the opposite direction; that is, whether *human* bodily existence can ever be separated from intelligence. To be sure, such bodily existence is separable from the actual exercise of intelligence. Moreover, human bodily existence may be separated from the power of intelligence, for the only way one could be sure of the presence of the power would appear to be from acts of understanding as its effects. Whatever, it does not seem possible that a whole human bodily existence could ever be separable from intellectual nature. (I have put in the word "whole" here in order to limit the question to a human organism as such and to avoid side questions about the status of transplanted parts or of transfused blood.) Again, there is in man only one nature that, as is well known, has a biological identity from beginning to end of its existence[13] and that is properly specified as "intellectual" from its most distinctive feature.

Of course, if we have no experience of ourselves as split into two discrete parts, body and spirit, still less do we have any experience of ourselves as living with a "merely biological" life. In a related vein, in principle a complete materialism ought to reduce all life to the merely biological or perhaps even to the merely mechanical. That should entail an equally high or low valuation of all life, human or otherwise, at every stage of its development. At the least, it should lead to valuations that would differ only by degrees, but never in kind. A materialist might, of course, like one of Wambaugh's "Blue Knights," think that all human beings, born or unborn, are "garbage." But if he instead puts value on any human beings, he ought to put equal value on all. He ought to, that is, if he is consistent. Perhaps, however, the mind of the materialist is not daunted by the hobgoblin of consistency.

Anyone, materialist or not, who cares about consistency, and who experiences his own nature as unitary—intellectual and corporeal facets together making one thing—should reason that from its earliest onset he has been equally unitary, even without intellectual operations. This he should do in face of undeniable evidence attesting to the presence of a whole human corporeal nature in the earliest zygote.[14] This he should do in face of cogent evidence for the continued existence of that same, individual, human corporeal nature from his existence as a zygote right on through to his present stage of development.[15] This he should do in the absence of any evidence—biological, psychological, or ontological—of another nature, different in kind, either existing side by side with his corporeal nature or succeeding it in some mysterious way. That is to say, in the absence of any evidence for the coming of a new intellectual nature, so different that it would either make the developing human being "two things" or change it totally into another thing, we should all reason that from our earliest biological beginning we were personal in the sense of being what each of us is right now: an individual intellectual nature.

At this point, let me note some similarity between the medieval plurality-of-forms doctrine and any contemporary doctrine maintaining that personhood is added at some stage in gestation, or that it comes to a fully formed human being at some stage after birth.[16] I believe that any such doctrine clearly implies the same objectionable denial of human integrity and/or identity found in the doctrine of Ibn Gabirol. As much as other psychosomatic dualist doctrines, it also contradicts experience and entails problems in areas of epistemology and ethics.

But let me note further the unacceptable character of any doctrine today that maintains the unity of man by the strategem of different natures succeeding one another. Such, for example, is the apparent doctrine of H. Tristram Engelhardt, Jr., for whom two stages in man's development must be distinguished, the one merely "human" and the other "personal."[17] Or Joseph Donceel[18] and James Diamond,[19] who perceived that humanization itself comes in human development only at a stage after the vegetative and sensitive stages. Even in the era of Queen Victoria and of Ernst Haeckel it was respectable to believe that "ontogeny recapitulates phylogeny," or that in its development "each individual climbs up its own family tree."[20] But the only doctrine of reputable biologists now is that, in developing from zygote to adult, each individual, even though he has apparently passed through various stages, has always been human and nothing but human.[21]

Further, if there was in fact some succession of totally different natures in the generation of a person, it would seem that some causal account of that succession could be given. Whence the new nature? By what agency? Rather obviously, not from the previous nature, for, as Engelhardt admits,[22] there would be a radical discontinuity between it and its successor. But even putting that aside, the previous nature would not have the principal feature—that is, intellection—characteristic of the new nature and, as everyone knows, *nemo dat quod non habet* (no one can give what he does not have). Again, it could not come from the air or from the environment. That would be carrying epigenesis too far. But surely not from God directly? While I for one would not deny God's power to intervene in His creation, I think it uneconomical to multiply such interventions without necessity.

In this regard, anyone resorting to divine intervention, in the absence of clear evidence accessible to all, would be introducing a private religious element into the discussion. This criticism can cut both ways. For example, the dualism espoused by some proponents of abortion has such a religious—or at least a quasi-religious—ring to it that it is surprising that it goes unchallenged while those of opposite persuasion are accused of trying to impose their religion. And, finally, in the same connection the ontological (as opposed especially to legal) distinction between a merely human life and a further personal life has always been for me redolent of religion. In fact, the concept has been acknowledged as having its origins in the Christian dogmas of the Trinity and the Incarnation. It has also been generally acknowledged that, since there was no natural evidence for this distinction, without a divine revelation we would never have suspected its existence. There is no natural evidence still, arguments of proabortionists and the Supreme Court notwithstanding; but now what was formerly supernatural has apparently become commonplace.

Another thought here concerns the practice of abortion and the "right intention" morality which has accepted the dogma of psychosomatic dualism. It is logical enough that such a morality should be "agent centered." If one's own body is outside one's control and therefore beyond concern, so also would be one's external act, and even more so would be the body of the patient on whom this act falls. Against such a backdrop, when "right intention" moralists ignore the character of the fetus on whom the act of abortion falls and concentrate exclusively on their own and others' attitudes toward that act, some people display nothing so much as their own dualist conception, not just of the fetus but also of themselves.

My final thoughts are to return to the idea of nature as dynamic. From the moment of conception, the zygote is present and growing. From out of it, in a process primarily caused by *it* and not just by its environment, comes the rest of the human individual.[23] That is to say, from the beginning a living organism of intellectual nature builds itself up in a myriad of ways. From the beginning an incipient embodied human person, in contrast to a pure spirit, is embarked upon a historical career in space and time. By convention of language, itself based upon a recognition of the ontological root of personality, we associate personal growth in a special way with intellectual and affective development. It is especially along the line of the latter, I believe, that we should look for the role of society in the making of a person. This, I believe, is the core of the truth so well stressed by such thinkers as Buber,[24] Marcel,[25] and Macmurray.[26] But I would like to stress three other truths.

First, as important as society is, unless there is presupposed in the developing human being an intellectual nature, socialization will produce nothing more than the kind of domestication we associate with animals.[27] Second, speaking of a certain sort of "gradualist approach" in which personhood would come at a later stage of development, Robert Joyce has rightly noted its confusion of the growth of a living organism with a mechanistic model of development. In his words: "It fails to distinguish between natural process and artifactual process. Only artifacts, such as clocks and spaceships, come into existence part by part. Living beings come into existence all at once and then gradually unfold to themselves and to the world what they already, but only incipiently, *are.*"[28] Third, bodily growth itself, inasmuch as it is the growth from within of a unitary human nature, is also at every stage from the zygote on very definitely personal growth.[29]

Chapter Four

MORALITY AND VIRTUE IN A PLURALISTIC SOCIETY

Robert J. Henle

The pluralism discussed in this paper is not simply diversity or multiplicity; it is diversity within a unity. That unity is the unity of society and the political state, a unity which can be maintained either by force—as in a dictatorship—or by some consensus.

Modern political states have developed under the perception that unity and consensus in most matters were necessary. Thus, in the matter of language, not only have official languages been established, but all citizens have been required to use it as their first language. Thus, Welsh children were punished at the end of the school day by one stroke of the cane for every Welsh word they had used during the day. The question of language has continually created bitterness in Belgium and Canada. Yet, Switzerland showed that a country could have a stable and peaceful political life even with four official and living languages. We also, here in the United States, have problems with languages. When, in some Hispanic areas, ballots or other public documents are printed in Spanish and English, many Americans are resentful. I make these opening remarks only to stimulate reflection on the wide range and seriousness of the problems of pluralism. But the pluralism we are concerned with here is in the area of religion, morality, politics, and law.

Perhaps the best example of a completely homogeneous and unified society is that of an isolated, unsophisticated, primitive tribe such as were the Igorots of the Philippines or the pygmies of the African rain forests. Holistic anthropologists such as Robert Redfield have given us splendid interpretations of such societies.

Everybody accepts the total way of life of the tribe. There is a minimum of dissension, and cultural change is slow.[1] Such a culture is made up of all sorts of rules, ways of doing things, insights into intrinsic values, and historical traditions. Those living within such societies do not reflect upon the various levels or types of rules and procedures. They see it from the inside as one complex

Robert J. Henle, S.J., is professor emeritus of philosophy and jurisprudence, St. Louis University. He is former president of Georgetown University. He is author of numerous books and articles in the fields of the classics, philosophy, and education.

way of life. They often give an almost absolute rightness to their ways of doing things. A simple and humorous modern example is the feeling of Europeans that the American habit of moving a fork back and forth between the hands while eating is a silly piece of etiquette. As a fictional example, recall in *Gulliver's Travels* the Lilliputians' deeply held conviction about which end of a boiled egg was the proper end to open.

Looking at these societies from the outside we can discern different elements within their culture. It is easy to distinguish matters of convention. In all societies, showing respect to people—at least to some people—is universal, but the ways of doing so vary: a warm handshake, a curtsy, a bow, a kneeling posture, a kiss on the cheek.

But we can discern in such cultures overriding principles of conduct that rest not on convention but on a conviction of their intrinsic rightness. These principles appear—in modified forms, to be sure—in all human cultures.

Thus, the anthropologist Robert Redfield wrote:

> Everywhere there are recognized obligations, commitments, sentiments and judgments of what is good and what is bad . . . if we let "morality" stand for all such judgments and commitments as to what is felt to be right or wrong to do, not because it is merely prudential or expedient but because it is in itself right and obligatory, then morality is universal.[2]

Thus, despite the diversity of cultures, there is in the rules of conduct of every society and of every culture, implicitly or explicitly, rules and modes of behavior which are seen to be obligatory in themselves and are therefore to be overriding in the direction of human conduct. The empirical note of "morality" as distinguished from positive customs or matters of etiquette and so forth is that some actions are regarded as simply wrong or as simply good and as overriding all other partial or subordinate considerations. Thus, there is no society in which the killing of human beings needs no justification at all. It may be thought, in a given culture, that perennial enemies might be killed without any further reasoning, or that captives of war may be killed and even eaten; but there is always a justification of some sort, so that the universal conception of an intrinsic right to life can be found in all cultures, and in fact to some degree in all human beings.

I accept those elements that can be abstracted from the concrete totality of a culture and are found with more or less definiteness in all cultures as being the primitive and partial discovery of the natural law.[3] St. Thomas Aquinas argued that knowledge of the natural law varies greatly among men but that all men have some knowledge of the natural law. Philosopher/anthropologist David Bidney implies the same:

> I suspect that on the whole, there are more concrete similarities and identities in the cultural values of different societies than the cultural relativists have so far explicitly recognized. Otherwise, even the degree of cooperation in world affairs which mankind has so far attained would not have been possible.[4]

I am not arguing that the morality imbedded in a primitive culture is simply a reflection of natural law. The amount of natural law perceived by such peoples is often very minimal and in the concrete appears limited, crudely interpreted, even distorted by custom, convention, or positive action of chiefs or councils.

From the standpoint of normative ethics (of which I will speak later) we can also discern within the concrete "morality" of any society certain rules that are apparently contrary to natural (or moral) law. St. Thomas cites from Julius Caesar's report that among the ancient Germanic tribes theft was not regarded as reprehensible. One also thinks of human sacrifice among the Mayans, infanticide in the Roman Empire, and suttee among the Hindus.

We can therefore see in the concrete morality of any particular culture or society, three elements: natural law insights; customs and conventions applying, determining, or extending the moral rules in accord with natural law; and customs and convention contrary to natural law. The complex in its concrete totality I call the "accepted morality of a society."[5] There has never been a society in which the accepted morality was in full accord with the natural law or with Christian morality. We must distinguish, then, in a general way, the accepted morality of a society from other sorts of rules—rules of etiquette, grammatical rules, liturgical rules, and others.

In a simple, unsophisticated society, there is generally little reflective understanding of the various rules and ideals of the community and little effort to distinguish the different levels within those rules. As societies become complex and cosmopolitan, however, the very intercultural differences that are noticed give rise to a reflexive examination of the accepted morality and ultimately to the isolation of moral questions and their investigation. This is what happened in Greek culture just before Socrates and Plato. Plato then undertook a very elaborate investigation of human morality. From this investigation has grown up what we have traditionally called ethics or moral philosophy. This is an intellectual, philosophical discipline that attempts to lay out general norms that should guide the overreaching, totally human evaluation of human conduct. For this reason we can refer to this intellectual discipline as normative ethics. Once ethics has become an independent discipline, it can then be used as a basis for criticizing—that is, for affirming or rejecting various principles and rules which constitute the accepted morality of any society (and of its legal system as well).

Now, we must face the question of the religious guidance of human conduct. In primitive society it is difficult to distinguish the religious rules of conduct from moral rules of conduct. In fact, the rules are often identical, without any reflective awareness of their source. Religion is imbedded in the total culture; it is indigenous to the tribe and is thus at all times thoroughly inculturated.

The situation is quite different when a religion claiming a supracultural authority and origin is introduced from without into an existing culture. There then ensues a period of inculturation during which the accepted morality of the society is modified by the moral directives of the new religion—and the new religion is at the same time modified, and perhaps limited and reinterpreted, by the culture. For example, Christianity put an end to polygamy in many parts of the world. Likewise, it was not Platonism, Aristotelianism, or stoic philosophy that stopped infanticide in the Roman Empire. The spread of the Christian religion effected that.[6] Yet, Christianity has taken on a distinctly indigenous character in the process of being inculturated in India, China, and black Africa. Whatever the modifications, however, religions, where vital, have clearly influenced the accepted morality of societies worldwide. If there has been a common religious consensus, the religious rules have become a part of the accepted morality of the society and religious motives have strengthened natural law insights.

One of the political innovations in modern times has been the development of states that are neutral with regard to profound differences of belief, ideology, and morality among the citizenry. Correlative to such states, each citizen—regardless of any personal belief or position—is considered to be a full citizen, with rights before the state and the law equal to those of any other citizen.

In the thirteenth century in Europe, nobody conceived of a state that would not be at the same time a religious unity. This can be seen clearly in the fact that medieval society had within it really two different communities: the Christian community and the Jewish community. While the Christian state had to deal with the Jewish community residing within its borders, to a very large extent the Jewish community was self-contained. It took care of its own internal affairs, could maintain its religion and its religious practice and its own system of organization and laws. Obviously, problems arose when there was a question of a dispute between a Jew and a Christian. This, however, does not modify the basic fact that a medieval Jew living in Christian Europe was not a citizen of any of the Christian states. It was therefore possible for medieval people to think of coexistence of different religious groups within the same territory and, ultimately, some shared relationship to the common authority—but not of shared citizenship.

Among citizens, however, heresy was regarded as a disaster for the state and the community, as well as an attack on the dominant religion. St. Thomas Aquinas justified state action against heresy by comparing heresy to falsification of the coinage—counterfeiting. Just as the counterfeiting of money struck at the very basis of the society's economic life, so heresy struck at the very basis of the consensus on which the unity and existence of civil society rested.

In the sixteenth century, when Christianity was broken up into various sects and national states were emerging, there was a realization that some rethinking had to be done. There was considerable discussion on the matter of tolerance in the first part of the sixteenth century, particularly in France, but it seems to have been put into political practice first of all in Poland. So the first modification of the notion of the unified state maintaining and being maintained by a unified religion was for a state officially professing a certain religion to *tolerate* citizens who professed and practiced a different religion.

It is important to note that "tolerance" was not full acceptance. When a state with an established religion allowed other religions to exist, in most cases civil disabilities attached to such toleration. For example, when Catholics were tolerated in England, they were still unable to be elected to the House of Commons; and, during English rule of Ireland, Catholics were often denied access to education and ownership of property.

The only way to move from tolerance to universal equal citizenship was to divorce the state from an established religion, either entirely, as was constitutionally decreed in the United States, or *virtually,* as has been the case in England—though even today one last disability for Catholics in England exists: the king or queen must be a Protestant. It should be noted that, in the world today, communist nations, which have no established religion (in the traditional sense), are the equivalents of the sectarian state inasmuch as the ideology which governs such states is a surrogate religion competing with traditional forms of religion. Christians are tolerated in Russia, but there are many restrictions placed upon their practice of religion and their participation in the life of the country. An innovation suggested in Poland has been for practicing Catholics to be admitted to the Communist party!

In the United States, we have attempted to establish a political state in which everyone—regardless of race, creed, ethnic origin, or ideology—can participate at least according to a proper and proportionate justice. Under the 1st Amendment the state is not supposed to be the enemy of any religion, nor is it supposed to foster any specific religion or (within restrictions) to directly support religion in general. The American state is not neutral in the sense that it is positively secularist. If the United States government ignored religion and made no accommodations to the religious conscience of the citizenry (as vociferously espoused by some Americans), it would, in fact, become a positively secular state,[7] promoting secularism as an alternative to religious belief. Obviously, this raises difficult questions. It is easy enough for an atheistic, anticlerical state to deal with religions because it can totally ignore them, but a state which is truly neutral and negatively secularistic cannot do that.

Americans have contrived some very clever accommodations.[8] One of the neatest relates to the official act of marriage. Marriage, of course, is a contract under law; but in witnessing and performing of marriage, the government leaves it to the conscience of the individuals involved to determine whether they want a Catholic marriage, a Protestant marriage, a Jewish marriage, or a nonreligious marriage by a justice of the peace, and confers upon the Catholic priest, the Protestant minister, or the rabbi a legal status as the official who signs the marriage license and reports the proper performance of the ceremony to the state. This solves the problem that has plagued many countries where the state insists that the legal ceremony be completely nonreligious.

When we arrive at the negatively secular state, we must clearly distinguish between the total concrete society (or community) and the political state as such. The distinction is clearly implied or expressed in the U.S. Constitution that "We the people" is different from the government of limited powers. Thus, the Supreme Court can say that ours is a religious society although our government has no intrinsic religious commitment.

Thus far in this chapter I have made six distinctions, namely: natural law, normative ethics, accepted morality of a given society, concrete totality of a society, and political structure of a society. I now turn to the central thesis: political pluralism in the United States.

The diversity and pluralism of political views in U.S. society is neither profound nor great. While we all have different opinions with regard to specific problems, there is a fairly universal commitment to the democratic process and to democratic institutions as established initially by the federal Constitution and the constitutions of the several states—subsequently extended by legislation and judicial interpretation. Our two major parties are not ideological parties; we do not have a religious party or a Christian Democratic party. What ideological parties we do have—namely the Communist, the Socialist, and a few others—are comparatively tiny and insignificant. The great mass of Americans have joined in a general consensus which does not call for a total restructuring of government or a rejection of traditional institutions. Even regarding the rivalry between the two dominant parties, there is not much difference between "liberal" Republicans and "conservative" Democrats.

It is true that we have an increasing number of militant special-interest groups; but, for the most part, they operate within the democratic political process by persuasion, propaganda, and political activism. We can see our political consensus more clearly when we compare our political activism to that of countries (such as some of those in Central and South America) in which division is so fundamental that different parties cannot coexist peacefully and where the political push for power is often violent. We pension and generally show great respect to our former Presidents, even the bad ones; we don't shoot them. Only once in our country's history have we faced a pluralistic issue that only war could resolve. The general firm consensus regarding the democratic process and our political and legal institutions is of key importance for understanding the peaceful coexistence of diverse elements and factors in our society.

It is said that Americans no longer have a consensus concerning morality. The old rules covering sexual behavior, temperance, private and public decency, and family have broken down. The Judaeo-Christian tradition which has been a major component in the accepted morality of the West since the conversion of the Roman Empire has been slowly eroded and consciously rejected by numerous persons.

Traditionally, ethical acts have been classified in reference to formally distinct virtues. Four cardinal virtues were identified by Aristotle and have been current in our culture ever since. These are prudence, temperance, fortitude, and justice. These virtues are not neatly correlative. Prudence is the acquired skill of judging aright the morality of individual cases of human conduct as such. The habit of prudence is essential to the other virtues and has no independent field of its own. Temperance and fortitude refer to personal acts of the individual and relate, for temperance, to control of the appetites (e.g., for drink, food, or sex), and, for fortitude, to individual self-control in face of what is arduous or dangerous. One therefore cannot judge acts of temperance and fortitude except in relation to the internal disposition of the individual.

There is an objectivity about justice that is lacking in the other virtues. In commutative justice—the right relationship between persons with regard to goods and services—the equality in a sale or contract can be objectively judged. Overpricing is unjust regardless of the attitude or internal state of the pricer.

Upon applying the four virtues to ethical pluralism in America, temperance-related issues predominate. Regarding *justice,* however, we have a broad consensus which has actually increased. For example, the general view of interracial justice is far different than it was sixty years ago. The violation of human rights, whether at home or abroad, arouses our indignation. Statutes and the common law have produced rules which are in full accord with natural justice, and the courts by and large have produced decisions which are prudential applications of the principles of natural justice. Of course, natural justice as seen from the moral standpoint is not incorporated into the civil law in its totality. This can never be the case; civil law has limitations which make its applications much more restricted than the applications of natural law and normative ethics.

Issues such as racial justice, murder, and abortion all fall under justice and can be pursued in accordance with the principles of natural justice and legal justice. That is why, in the public debate, the principles governing the decision to legalize or not to legalize abortion are not principles relating to sexual morality or to religious morality. The principles relate to justice. There is no question but that when we are considering the basic rights of human beings, which include the primary right—the right to live—we are dealing with a matter which comes under natural and legal justice.

Pro-choice advocates constantly tie the abortion issue to woman's "reproduction rights," to the use of contraceptives, and to the woman's right to do as she wishes with her own body.[9] We must constantly make clear that the issue does not lie within the area of sexual morality or women's rights. It must clearly be placed within the area of justice. When the problem is thus properly posed, the primary moral and legal principles invoked in the abortion debate are not in controversy.[10] Almost everyone agrees that it is morally wrong to kill an innocent human being without adequate cause. It is generally accepted that the law should protect innocent human beings from violence, oppression, and killing.

In *Roe v. Wade* the Supreme Court has established the legal principle:

> If this suggestion of personhood is established, the appellant's case, of course, collapses for the fetus' right to life is then guaranteed specifically by the Amendment.[11]

The Court went on to stress the compelling interest of the state in protecting human life (even "potential human life"—whatever that means). Therefore, if there is a living human being in the womb, the state must give it legal personhood and, since the most fundamental right of legal personhood is the right to life, the state must protect that life. This is the crux of the abortion debate.

Philosophers and theologians have wrestled with the definition of personhood down through the centuries, and no significant consensus has been reached within either discipline. Regardless, neither the primary metaphysical perspectives of the philosophers nor the essentially spiritual perspectives of the theologians are particularly relevant to legal justice. Unfortunately, the U.S. Supreme Court in 1973, after reiterating the 5th and 14th amendments' establishment of the rights of all "persons" to life, chose not to clearly extend personhood to the unborn, in large part owing to disagreement among the philosophers and theologians—thereby opening the door to abortion on demand based on the decision that the rights of the mother must in nearly every case prevail.

Dr. Leon Rosenberg, in his testimony before Senator East's committee, stated that the question of when life begins cannot be answered by science, since it is a metaphysical question involving ethical and value judgments. On the contrary, the question presented to science is simply a biological one. Even Dr. Rosenberg admits that the zygote-embryo-fetus is actually living and self-actuating. He seems to argue, however, that its dependence on the mother for nourishment and an appropriate environment reduces *all* the actuality of its life. Personhood based upon the degree of dependence on the mother is specious if not hostile to offspring regardless of their state of development. For example, a newborn baby is actually *more* dependent on its mother than the nearly full-term fetus since it is now more vulnerable and must also depend much more on its mother's competence and responsibility.

A legal person, in the strict sense, is simply a subject of rights. However, the legal recognition of rights does not consist in recognizing a neat array of rights to be given to all human beings on the simple basis of their existence. The assignment of legal rights is a matter of distributive justice and so may be judged on a reasonable proportionality. Thus, the right to life is proportionate simply to existing as a living human being—whether the human being is an infant, an imbecile, an insane person, a normal adult, a comatose person, or a fetus. The right to life cannot be divided. A person cannot have a 40 percent or a 60 percent right to life, although other rights may be proportionate to different levels of development and so be divisible. For example, a day-old infant can inherit but cannot vote or make a contract. A young teenager can campaign for the candidate of his choice but cannot vote. Or a nineteen-year-old may vote for President but cannot run for the office. Viewed in this light, the Supreme Court's finding that the law had never recognized the zygote-embryo-fetus as a (legal) person in the *full* sense becomes irrelevant.

One might argue that the legal person has all these rights from the beginning but is restricted in his *exercise* of them. This is irrelevant to the present argument, first, because the Supreme Court itself made a distinction between personhood in the full sense and lesser personhood, and second, because to be denied the exercise of the right to life is equivalent to having no rights at all.

I submit that the basic question here is a factual one. The fact as to the existence of an actual (not potential) living independent human being from the moment of fertilization is a scientific question for which the scientific evidence is overwhelmingly affirmative. Only medical science can determine the first moment of human life, just as it alone determines the fact of death. Doctors need not know the intimate essence of man to make these determinations. On the other hand, no theologian is competent to sign a death certificate or pronounce a woman pregnant. The fact that some courts have ignored the scientific evidence or refused to consider it does not destroy the massive scientific evidence that has established the existence of an actual living independent human being in the womb. As five of the six scientists appearing before Senator East's committee affirmed, it is a commonplace of modern embryology that the individual human being comes into existence from the beginning moment of fertilization of the ovum. One has only to read a standard medical textbook.[12]

It should be pointed out that it was the medical profession that first realized the full force of scientific evidence. From about 1860 on, the American medical profession urged ministers and priests to inform their people that abortion at any point was murder. The medical doctors were, for the most part, responsible for the nineteenth-century state laws against abortion.

The health of the mother was in fact not the prime objective of the vigorous antiabortion drive led by the American Medical Association in the nineteenth century. As a modern historian puts it, educated

> physicians "objected strongly to snuffing out life in the making." What he describes as "the physician's crusade against abortion" began with the work of Dr. Horatio R. Storer of Boston. His report to the AMA in 1859 on behalf of its Committee on Criminal Abortion objected to the unscientific distinction between the status of the unborn before and after quickening and noted how the distinction permitted abortion in early pregnancy. Storer called for new legislation to stop "such unwarrantable destruction of human life." Throughout the next twenty years, as American statutes tightened, it was the physicians who led the defense of human life in the womb.[13]

That many physicians have since come around to a pro-choice position is in no way supported by subsequent scientific evidence that might prove Dr. Storer wrong. The most up-to-date scientific evidence does overwhelmingly support, however, that an intrinsically independent, actually living, self-developing entity of the species *homo sapiens* exists from the first moment of fertilization. The question of justice, therefore, is whether every human being, be he or she born or yet to be born, must be protected in legal justice—that is, granted at least minimum legal personhood. Both natural and legal justice affirms this principle.

Since the Supreme Court has chosen to ignore the preponderance of scientific evidence, those who advocate the right to life of the unborn must be active in a three-element program.

First, we must promote the general acceptance of Judaeo-Christian ideals and moral standards. I believe this requires a religious revitalization and a united religious effort. We must also promote and support basic moral training in the primary and secondary schools and the formal study of systematic normative ethics in colleges and seminaries.

Second, we must make ourselves, and Americans generally, aware of modern embryology (and the horror of what abortion, particularly in the second and third trimesters, can be) and go on from there to counter the massive pro-choice propaganda that seeks (often through deception) to minimize the humanness of the unborn while at the same time promoting issues such as women's rights and the costs of welfare as if the unborn were nothing more than "tissue" hostile to the best interests of mothers in particular and to society in general. Proving the living, self-developing, and intrinsically independent personhood of the unborn is first and paramount. Arguing that the issue, then, is one of *justice* (both natural and legal) logically follows.

Third, we must champion social programs designed to eliminate or reduce the causes that bring women to the tragic decision to abort their babies. Viable alternatives to abortion must be provided and made to be acceptable.

A human life amendment will not outlaw those cases of *indirect* and *unintended* killing of a fetus which have been allowed by both moral theologians and jurists. I refer to the removal of a diseased uterus, of an ectopic pregnancy, and so on. In fact, these are not abortions in the technical sense. Abortion properly defined is the *direct* killing of the fetus.

Abortions generally can be separated into two categories: those for which no putative justification proportionate to the right of life can be offered, and those in which there is some semblance of a justifying cause (such as the danger to the mother's life or indications of a horribly deformed baby). Regarding the first, an amendment should clearly state that from the beginning of fertilization the entity in the womb is a human being and must be accorded legal personhood in the meaning of the 14th Amendment. Lawyers should put this into foolproof language.

The second category of abortions consists of a loosely defined group of cases, generally held by Catholic moralists to be unjustified but which, in the view of many people—even those who accept the right-to-life position—are licit and perhaps morally obligatory.

Recalling two principles is appropriate before a discussion of these cases. First, the natural law does not require that all immoral actions be prohibited by civil law; and second, civil law has to accommodate to the society for which it is made. St. Thomas succinctly commented on both these principles:

> Wherefore human laws do not forbid all vices, from which the virtuous abstain, but only the more grievous vices . . . chiefly those that are to the hurt of others, without the prohibition of which human society could not be maintained. . . .
>
> . . . The natural law is a participation in us of the eternal law . . . human law does not prohibit everything that is forbidden by natural law.
>
> . . . [citing Isadore] law should be possible both according to nature, and according to the customs of the country.[14]

All the indications of public opinion that I have studied show that the majority of Americans are opposed to abortion-on-demand but believe that some exceptions should be made. Most of the polls support this view. The history of efforts (prior to *Roe v. Wade*) to change the state laws as well as the published positions of most religious bodies confirm it.[15] There is no uniform list of desired exceptions, though the saving of the mother's life is almost universally mentioned. Others include rape, incest, and horrible deformity of the fetus.

I am not advocating or morally justifying any of these. I do believe, however, that in view of the relationship between accepted morality and legal justice and the principles stated above, a human life amendment must allow for the possibility of exceptions. However, I do not believe that an amendment should list all possible[16] exceptions, as has been proposed for the case of saving the mother's life. To do so would be bad jurisprudence and would open the way for endless judicial extensions by analogy.

I have tried to develop a wording for a general policy statement and have been unsuccessful. The best I have to offer at this time is: "Provided, however, that nothing in this article shall prohibit a law permitting, as a last resort, an abortion in order to preserve a value as valuable as human life itself." Some such general statement would clearly permit legislation allowing the direct killing of the fetus, if necessary to save the mother's life.[17] It would also allow an argument to be made for the other generally proposed exceptions: rape, incest, and horribly deformed fetuses. But the argument would be in the state legislatures, not in the courts. Moreover, these latter arguments would be difficult to mount. By making these arguments difficult, further extension would be almost foreclosed.

3

CONSEQUENCES OF ABORTION ON DEMAND

Chapter Five

THE FAMILIAL CONTEXT OF INDUCED ABORTION

Vincent M. Rue

Abortion, unlike any other dimension of human consideration, has within a decade become nothing less than a national fissure. With equal velocity for both opponents and proponents, the agony of abortion has broadened the gnawing schism between the meanings of life and death; between the rights of the individual versus those of another; between the relations of wife and husband, daughter and parents, sister and siblings, lover and lover; and between the psychology of individualism and the cultural context of traditional values. Contrary to current beliefs, expectations, and public pronouncements, abortion is neither simple nor singular in its nature, context, or consequences. This chapter seeks to examine those complex issues germane to the familial and/or relational context in which abortion occurs.

Abortion in Macro Context

No longer an individual solution to an individual problem, abortion has gone mainstream.[1] From the Supreme Court[2] to the states,[3] from the 1980 White House Conference on Families[4] to family values,[5] abortion has become a national headache that does not go away. Originally heralded as a remedy for problem or unwanted pregnancies, has abortion become more of a problem escalator than a problem alleviator? With 29.7 percent of pregnancies terminated by abortion in 1979,[6] abortion is becoming an increasingly common form of fertility control.[7] While one-third of all abortions were concentrated on women under nineteen years of age,[8] and with four out of ten girls in this age group expected to become pregnant at least once,[9] in the period of 1971 to 1976, teenage sexual behavior actually increased by 41 percent and teenage pregnancy by 45 percent.[10] Hence, abortion in its social context seemingly solves fewer problems than it creates. Perhaps surmising this dilemma, societal attitudes favoring abortion are waning.[11]

Vincent M. Rue, Ph.D., is associate professor in human relations, California State University at Los Angeles, and president and executive director, Sir Thomas More Marriage and Family Clinics of Southern California. He is a coauthor of PARENTING AND FAMILY EDUCATION (1979).

In its psychocultural context, abortion has gained prominence at a time when the psychologies of affluence and self-fulfillment have reigned supreme. The typical self-fulfillment strategy presupposes economic well-being as a virtual right,[12] including the right to be free of economic strain and the burden of responsibility for a problem pregnancy and subsequent childbearing. The presumption of an ever-expanding affluence is also rapidly colliding with a new awareness of diminished resources, material and individual limitations, and expectational downsizing. This search for self-fulfillment has in the words of Lasch evolved into a "culture of narcissism" characterized by the "liberated personality" and typified by pseudoawareness, promiscuous pansexuality, and shallow protectiveness.[13]

In 1973 the Supreme Court in its *Roe v. Wade* ruling gave women the absolute procreative right for self-fulfillment.[14] And yet, female disillusionment as evidenced by relational dissolutions, husband abuse, child abuse, female violent crime, psychological complaints, female alcohol and drug abuse, abortion, and female suicide are all on the increase.

Neglected in research, presumed to be nonsignificant in the process of abortion decision making, and more powerful than any Planned Parenthood or Department of Health and Human Services, the family is emerging as a major force to be reckoned with in the delivery of health care services and the development of individual well-being. Every year abortion impacts nearly one and a half million women,[15] their partners, their relationships, and their families. What then are the emotional and relational risks, the risks for future heterosexual relationships, the risks for sexual decision making, the risks for subsequent pregnancies, the risks of value congruency, the risks of marital and family fragmentation and alienation, and the risks of self-alienation?

The Family and Crisis Management

Beyond a doubt, the family is the most adaptable institution known to man. Over the centuries, families have changed form, structure, membership, even functions, and yet have survived better than any nation or institution. Such a perception is derived from the family's ability to expand and contract with the development and recision of problems and/or needs. Reuben Hill said it well:

> In a society of rapid social change, problems outnumber solutions, and the resulting uncertainties are absorbed by the members of society, who

> for the most part are also members of families. Because the family is the bottleneck through which all troubles pass, no other association so reflects the strains and stresses of life. The family today is not only the focal point of frustration and tensions, but also the source for resolving frustrations and tensions. . . . Through its capacity for sympathy, understanding, and unlimited support, the family habilitates personalities bruised in the course of competitive daily living.[16]

This is no less true with the challenges and responsibilities posed by a problem pregnancy.

And yet, in *Planned Parenthood of Missouri v. Danforth*[17] the Supreme Court held that a father or a husband or a parent has no rights in the abortion area other than those which the state might have and which the state deigns to delegate. In effect, then, in pregnancy deliberations, the roles of father, husband, or parent are deleted. As the shrouds of secrecy and absolute female autonomy regarding pregnancy resolution are positioned, the traditional structure and functions of the family are truncated and subverted. This is clearly in violation of an abundant body of tradition, research and clinical knowledge that affirms the family as a powerful and effective problem-solving unit.[18]

Three systems of classification of family problems have been used by investigators in cataloging crises: by source (i.e., intra- or extrafamilial), by effects upon the family configuration, and by type of event impinging on the family. In the first classification, abortion is both intra- and extrafamilial. It is an individual family member's pregnancy combined with a socially sanctioned solution imposed from outside the family for an intrafamily conflict. The second type of classification, first suggested by Eliot[19] and later expanded by Hill,[20] involves the combination of the loss of a family member (dismemberment) or addition of an unprepared-for member (accession), or both, and the loss of morale and family unity (demoralization). According to this framework, a problem pregnancy commences as an accession conflict, seeking resolution in abortion and concomitant dismemberment (of the aborted child or perhaps the aborted child *and* the aborting mother), concluding with considerable demoralization.

Clearly, the consumption of abortion services normally has profound impact on families. It self-evidently prevents increases in family size and it prevents or delays family formation by those who might otherwise choose a forced-marriage solution or start, by default, a single-parent family. Correspondingly, abortion also impacts on family communication, parental roles, spousal roles, individual and family problem-solving abilities, self-perceptions, and future family relations. In particular, the decision-making process involving an unwanted pregnancy and consequent abortion serves to illustrate well the centrality of the family and the significance of the relational context.

Abortion Decision Making: The Micro Context

Abortion and the problems of decision making associated with it have all too often placed the highest value on the individual over relational priorities, focusing on the pregnant woman in her urgent need to make a decision. Emerging from the position that a woman has total control over her own body, women's advocates have failed to differentiate between a woman's body and the fetus that is the product of the relationship between two people and their relationship to their families. To ideological advocates of women's rights, the woman is assumed to be the sole factor in decision making. While this may be understandable in light of archaic ideologies that have traditionally excluded and still exclude women's rights and needs from forthright consideration, nevertheless, this position is an overreaction. Paradoxically, such a posture runs the risk of becoming ideologically rigid and counterproductive to women in their long-term relationships to men, and relationally negating for men in their relationships with women. As Cotroneo and Krasner[21] have noted, it is impossible to lift a pregnant woman out of her primary loyalty system—that is, her present and future family network—for the purpose of decision making without manifesting a complementary therapeutic concern for the relationship fallout of her decision on her mate, parents, children (born and unborn), siblings, grandparents, and other significant relationships. Their findings have suggested the long-term wisdom of facing the implications of each person's situation within their relationship system especially as crises are generated by unanticipated events like problem pregnancies.

A primary therapeutic goal, then, ought to be to help the pregnant woman face the impact of her relational legacies on her present capacity to make decisions. In this sense, the present and past do indeed have consequences for the future. Therapeutically, it is not optimum to reinforce relational evasion by family members, nor is it desirable to promote the fantasy that decision making can occur in a relational vacuum. Likewise, often ignored is the woman's unspoken wish to face her parents or mate with her ambivalence and to draw on their support, even when it comes in the form of disagreement or conflict.[22]

Then too, the pregnancy decision-making drama unfolds quickly. Perhaps a pregnant woman has made a firm decision that abortion is her answer to the problem pregnancy, and perhaps she is fully accepting of that decision. However, she is apt to have made that decision under extreme pressure. Probably shocked by the knowledge that she is pregnant and realizing there is very little time to make up her mind about the abortion, she may well overreact with intense anxiety and impulsivity to her situation. To exclude communication with her mate or parents at this vital point is to deprive her unnecessarily of the resources of the family bond. Wilson[23] found that appropriate communication at this time is invaluable, helping to explore feelings, values, options, and resources.

Understanding the nature of crisis and appropriate crisis intervention is also important. Typically, an individual negotiates problems by employing a variety of problem-solving mechanisms, one of which hopefully generates an answer. Before the solution occurs, the person is in a state of tension or disequilibrium, which usually does not become excessive if the state is short-lived and if the person is accustomed to such periods of tension. In a crisis, however, the tension is much greater, not only because the problem is more significant but also because the individual's usual way of dealing with the problem offers no solution. This is particularly true in the case of a minor with a pregnancy since very often there has been no prior problem-solving experience of this nature or magnitude.

The Pregnant Minor and Parental Roles

In a major review of adolescent sexuality, Chilman[24] noted that the uncomfortable state in which the pregnant minor finds herself is of a much longer duration than it is in her usual problem-solving activities and that she develops a feeling of helplessness and ineffectiveness. These feelings are often associated with some functional disorganization which may consist either of attempts at discharging inner tension or trial-and-error attempts to solve the problem. Through this mechanism the pregnant minor may either develop new methods of dealing with her problem or fail and simply avoid a solution. The new methods of problem solving developed during the crisis are typically added to her repertoire of behaviors and, if effective, will be likely to reoccur in the future. The inability to deal with the problem, or an inadequate understanding of the nature of the problem and its causes, and/or a poor solution will considerably impair future coping abilities of the pregnant minor.

Halpern and others[25] take this one step further in their systems approach to family treatment. From their perspective, at the more general systems level a system in crisis may be best defined as a system under such a high degree of environmental stress that both the system's ability to adapt and its ability to maintain its steady state are overwhelmed, resulting in a disorganization of the system. Following such disorganization the system will reorganize itself, but the potential for change is much greater in the reorganizing system than had the crisis not occurred. Thus, the potential exists that the family will be more functional after crises have been identified, verbalized, discussed, and resolved than if secrecy had prevailed. Mandersheid, Silbergeld, and Dager[26] have further elaborated on the resulting stresses from a crisis situation and the corresponding alienation and dysfunction in perception that can accompany fragmented and insulated crisis decision making.

So much more than a child yet so much less than an adult, an adolescent with a problem pregnancy deserves far more careful analysis and assistance than she has been afforded. All teenagers are at risk because they are in a critical stage of psychosexual development and interpersonal relationships.[27] They are socially, psychologically, and educationally ill equipped to meet the demands of adult responsibility, especially those of marriage and parenthood. Insecure about their identities as men and women and only at the beginning of heterosexual interaction, it becomes easy to discern the enormous havoc a nonmarital pregnancy injects into their lives. These adolescents are ashamed, frightened, alone, and unable to communicate their predicament to others, largely because of their own fears and self-disapproval. Sometimes the victims of their own destructive game playing with their parents,[28] they find the crisis changes everything: relationships within the community and with parents, siblings, friends, and God, as well as their attitude toward themselves. The loss of self-esteem can be monumental, demanding much attention and empathy. Why must this loss be irreparable within the family of origin? And why, at a time when adolescents most need potential guidance and assistance, should they be robbed of this invaluable resource?

From a number of different sources, a questioning attitude regarding parental exclusion is becoming more prevalent. The Sex Information and Education Council of the United States clearly stated: "As an isolated approach, abortion does little to help the individual work out basic conflicts about herself and may add to feelings of guilt and depression."[29] Hence, it is not unusual to see teenagers who have had an abortion return without counseling a year later with another unwanted pregnancy. Sarrel[30] has noted that the occurrence of a pregnancy often indicates a psychological need to become pregnant which is greater than the need not to be pregnant; and unless a therapeutic approach addresses itself to an understanding of that need and an adjustment of basic life situations, the need will persist and abortion will accomplish little with respect to the well-being of the individual. The same observation, of course, could be made of adoption or of marriage because of pregnancy or of keeping the baby without marriage. Indeed, if the basic factors which led to the pregnancy are not understood and are not altered, then the problem is likely to persist. Aguirre[31] underscores this point in his findings, which demonstrated the centrality of man-woman relations for a thorough understanding of repeat abortion behavior.

Without a doubt, the pregnant minor needs help in developing a "realistic plan" which takes into account her relationship with her family and the characteristics of her current living situation.[32] Foster[33] surveyed four hundred pregnant minors and concluded that this can best be done through actual home visits and family conferences. From her perception, parental involvement becomes all the more important when the girl's own family is a single-parent family.

To attempt to eliminate parental involvement from a pregnant minor's decision-making process is both unrealistic and unnatural. It promotes a false sense of independence and a misguided notion of personal freedom. Adamek[34] has asserted that personal freedom is only enhanced by helping people appreciate the facts of the situations they find themselves in and encouraging them to deal with the facts in ways which permit self-acceptance and personal growth *toward* others.

Cobliner, Schulman, and Romney,[35] reporting on a clinical study of pregnant adolescents, found many of the adolescent patients examined were restricted in their self-awareness, rather mechanical in their attitudes toward the expression of sex, basically lonely and isolated although members of peer groups, frequently hurt by their partner's disinterest in the pregnancy and lack of communication in the relationship, often in poor communication with their parents, and lacking a realistic appraisal of what it means to care for a baby. When patients consented, interviews were held with their mothers. These interviews were often helpful in establishing much better parent-daughter communication and in working out an appropriate variety of plans for handling the pregnancy.

Chilman[36] found that a number of small studies have shown that abortions are less distressing to the young woman if she has the psychological and financial support of both her parents and her partner. She also noted that case studies, rarely reported in the literature, have shown that the young woman often feels that her parents would not be able to accept her situation and that her partner would be unwilling to help her. In many cases, however, she is mistaken in this assumption. Though parents may be shocked and upset by their daughter's pregnancy, Chilman feels that usually they adapt to the situation. It is her concerted opinion that whatever decision the young woman, her parents, and her partner make together, the sharing they have had in the situation would probably have beneficial effects in most instances. According to Chilman, a secret abortion, without this prior sharing, would seem to create a psychological burden for the young woman and a barrier to her future relationships with those people in her life who are most significant to her.

In dealing with problem pregnancies the Consortium on Early Childbearing and Childrearing of the Child Welfare League of America has asserted that "[p]arents have a primary influence on their children's development of feelings of self-worth and ego strength. Parents are motivated to seek help in a crisis." According to the consortium, opening lines of communication between parent and child is seen as one of the important goals of sex and parenting education programs. They added: "Although young people are often asked how they think their parents feel about it [sexuality], parents themselves are seldom asked." In communication about adolescent sexuality, the consortium felt that often the experience provides "both parent and teenager with his or her first realization of the other as a sexual being. Frequently, parents are reassured that young people are not as 'far out' as they thought, and the young people often find their parents' values more liberal than they had anticipated."[37]

Perhaps the most comprehensive and current assessment of teenage problem pregnancies has recently been undertaken by the Family Impact Seminar of the Institute for Educational Leadership at George Washington University. One of the participants, Greer Litton Fox, writing on the role of the family, concluded:

> With regard to policies concerning teenage sexuality, the evidence from existing research suggests a rather simple cardinal principle: ways of involving the parent or parents of teens must be developed; implemented as a core component of the program; and evaluated, whether the specific program is primary prevention, sex education, contraceptive service provision, or pregnancy and post-partum assistance. Policies that ignore familial support, and undermine, rather than supplement, the efforts and *effectiveness* of parents are likely to yield programs that are wasteful, inefficient, and ineffective; and, what is more serious, are likely to do a considerable disservice to the teenagers about whom we are so concerned.[38]

Furstenberg, another participant, reviewed the kinship roles of families in dealing with a problem pregnancy and strongly criticized pregnancy counseling for not involving parents and perhaps other interested relatives or parties in the decision. In his words, "if they are not consulted, or at least considered, the decision reached may be disruptive, unrealistic, or perhaps even destructive to the interests of both the adolescent and her family."[39]

And finally, T. Ooms, who was the deputy director and report editor of the seminar, developed eight family-impact principles based on the findings of the contributors, two of which are germane here:

> #3. Policies should recognize that an adolescent's pregnancy and childbearing can have profound effects on other members of her family, and that the family, therefore, has an interest in being consulted about the decisions she makes about her pregnancy. . . .
> #6. Policies should reflect an understanding that families with adolescents are in a stage of transition in which parents' and children's roles and responsibilities undergo a process of negotiation and readjustment. Some disputes between them are to be expected as a natural part of this process.[40]

Maternal Role and Sibling Role Modeling

To exclude parental involvement from a daughter's pregnancy crisis is at best naive and at worst detrimental for future familial and interpersonal relationships. Parents are the primary reference group for most adolescents.[41] As Honig[42] has noted, clinical and research evidence make it abundantly clear that the heritage of parent-child relationships that a young person carries into and through adolescence can have impact on how she feels about herself and others. In order for an adolescent to develop into a reasonably self-reliant, adaptable, creative, and self-disciplined person there must be many opportunities to learn these patterns during the years of growing up.

Mothers in particular play a critical role in their daughters' sexuality. According to Inazu and Fox,[43] mothers can be expected to influence their daughter's sex behavior indirectly through their presence and their availability in providing socioemotional support. They found that daughters whose socioemotional needs are met at home are less likely to become involved in intimate relationships outside the home to fulfill these needs. Evidence from numerous studies suggests that nonvirgins are more likely to have poorer communication with their mothers,[44] to experience less parental involvement,[45] and to have less affectional relationships with their mothers.[46] Studies by Card[47] and Presser[48] have even shown that teenage mothers are more prone to have daughters who themselves become teenage mothers. Hence, the mother's role, be it positive or negative, is incontrovertible in her daughter's sexual development.

The multigenerational context of families is another key aspect which has received little attention in the abortion literature. The abortion decision interfaces directly with the developmental agenda of both daughters and mothers. Eriksonian developmental theory postulates adolescent growth spanning various stages: autonomy and separation, the establishment or consolidation of one's identity, the establishment of appropriate attachments to people outside the realm of the family, and self-mastery over impulses, including the ability to anticipate future consequences of present actions. Abortion subverts each of these stages in its overemphasis on the individual and its separation from the relational context. It impacts negatively on self-identity mainly through guilt production, which is especially unnecessary and damaging at this stage of development. Abortion fosters pseudotrust and attachment with abortion personnel and aligns the individual with those who hold concurrent opinions. And lastly, abortion reinforces impulsivity, secrecy, and denial, increasing the probability of future dysfunctional problem solving.

The demanding roles of a mother and her developmental agenda interact concurrently with her daughter's stages of growth. According to Litton Fox,[49] the parent of a maturing daughter must serve as both protector of the daughter-as-child and as guide for the daughter-as-woman. Abortion confounds these roles in that it can be a "silent solution" with no parental awareness or involvement, or the roles may be mistakenly interchanged. In addition, abortion impacts upon the mother's stages of development: the crises of being (finding meaning beyond the maternal role), doing (accomplishment of reentry into nonfamilial activities or responsibilities), and aging (coping with the loss of culturally valued youthfulness and beauty). Abortion not only voids motherhood, but it also deifies "me-ism" and promotes insecurity via mother-daughter competitiveness.

In their latest research, Inazu and Fox,[50] after studying over four hundred mothers and their fourteen- to sixteen-year-old daughters, concluded:

> The mother's presence as a role model for her daughter, both in terms of her salience as a significant other in her daughter's life and in terms of her own non-marital sexual experiences, was significantly related to the daughter's sexual status . . . this study would suggest that policies which are directed at strengthening family functioning through undergirding

adult family members in their roles as parents are as likely to be fruitful as policies targeted directly at teenagers.

This research, similar to the growing body of related studies, underscores the ultimate importance of the family unit as the primary context within which individual behavior is defined, developed, and differentiated.

And yet, how many teenagers involve their parents in their sexual decision making, including abortion? One study of fourteen hundred parents in Cleveland suggested that most teenagers do not;[51] and on abortion, estimates vary from one out of five to maybe half who do.[52]

In spite of fears raised as to parental condemnation, it should be realized that open and honest communication is a requisite for maturity and healthy personality development. Hence, it is not only expected that a problem pregnancy be disruptive of family dynamics, but it is desirable, since it is away from this familial context that the minor daughter has turned, and where ultimately she must return and be accountable for her choice. On the other hand, it seems unfair to minimize the responsible concern of significant persons in a woman's life, or as a matter of course to act on the assumption that they are unconcerned, indifferent, or hostile. Helping agents or family members who overlook relationship considerations in favor of unilateral prerogatives evade the basic human issues of mutuality and fairness and injure the possibilities of future trusting relationships.

For those adolescents who involve their parents in abortion decision making, the initial emotional risks are high: fear of parental rejection; hurt; embarrassment; and loss of approval, privileges and/or freedom. And yet, the potential for maturity, intimacy, and future familial and relational closeness is also high. For those who do exclude their parents, there is a plethora of possible negative consequences: excessive guilt, intrapsychic conflict, alienation, self-rejection, damaged interactional abilities, increased fears, depression, loss of identity, and the likelihood of repeat abortions with their attendant physiological sequelae.

To think, then, in terms of crisis decision making within the context of a relational vacuum is to program failure. Abortion as a crisis should be equivalently added to the list of other crises family members encounter and need familial assistance in resolving: for example, identity crises, rape, suicide, rejection, drug addiction, school problems, sibling hostility, phobias, death of a family member, emotional disturbances, and so on. Rueveni[53] and many others have advocated family network intervention—that is, mobilizing support for families in crisis. Umbarger and White[54] further illustrate the need for redefining the problem away from the notion of individual "symptom bearer" to the healing of the family system as a whole.

Males and Abortion: The Double Standard Revised

Extensive research has focused on abortion and women, while men have largely been legally, psychologically, and medically bypassed. In interviews with over four hundred males at an eastern abortion clinic, Milling[55] found that, while most of the males involved in the pregnancy were consulted regarding the abortion, most of the romantic relationships (70 percent) failed one month post abortion.

Shostak[56] observed that a sizable minority of males find their abortion experience more frustrating, trying, and emotionally costly than public and academic neglect of this subject would suggest. He also noted that three out of four male partner respondents stated that they had a difficult time with the abortion experience; that most relationships did not survive the abortion stresses; and that a sizable minority reported persistent dreams, both day and night, about the child-that-never-was, as well as considerable guilt, remorse, and sadness. While most males deny negative or emotional consequences from abortion, research by Jaffee,[57] Luker,[58] Luscutoff and Elms,[59] Smetana,[60] and Zorabedian[61] suggest that a distinct minority of those men studied have found the abortion experience to be bewildering and painful beyond their coping abilities.

Becoming a father is, of course, far more complex than intromission and conception. Rather, it is an ongoing process begun long before the actual entrance into fatherhood signaled by pregnancy and childbirth. This process includes the development of certain personal qualities, goals, attitudes, self-representations, expectations, roles, object relationships, conflicts, and defense mechanisms. For men as well as women, abortion abruptly arrests this process and creates a role vacuum in which confusion, ambivalence, guilt, and hostility abound.

Francke,[62] in part drawing on her own abortion experience, which nearly ended her marriage, warned of considerable role conflict for males in that they are so eager to protect the female's well-being that they tended to discount or suppress their own needs—a realization that added to their unexpressed guilt and anger, which can fester for months afterward. Francke found men devastated—that is, the ones who cared. While legally the right to abdicate future motherhood is guaranteed, the right to insist on future fatherhood is not. This alone is very disturbing and unfair to many men. This societal impotency has for a number of men produced sexual impotency, typified by a feeling of helplessness and hostility. In addition, Francke found men to be "silent sufferers, bewildered and frustrated by their emotional responses" to abortion. Furthermore, she concluded that abortion is a far greater dilemma for men than researchers, counselors, and women have even begun to realize.[63]

For men who do not care about the women they impregnate, abortion is a neat disposal system of the evidence of their sexuality and a rather conclusive abdication of caretaking responsibilities.[64] This, too, typifies the cultural imperative of self-fulfillment and "me-ism," thereby denigrating human sexual interaction to the level of secrecy, denial, irresponsibility, and future problematic relationships and pregnancies.

In a very real sense, the double standard has been revisited and revised with abortion. Consider the following examples.

1. While women may choose motherhood, men may not choose fatherhood.[65]
2. If women choose motherhood, men are obligated in paternity action.
3. While women may choose an abortion over the male's objection, men typically shoulder the bulk of the financial cost.
4. When men promote abortion for their partners, it is typified as coercion, lack of caring, abdication of traditional male roles, insensitivity, and selfishness—whereas when women choose abortion it is the exclamation of women's rights, an affirmation of the right to health and freedom from male oppression, and a confirmation of sovereign territoriality over the female body and reproductive functions.[66]
5. Abortion is granted *ipso facto* for the woman, insuring a continuance of "normalcy" in prepregnancy relationships with parents, peers, and significant others, yet typically negating the relationship with her sexual partner without his consideration.[67]
6. When sexual partners, be they married or not, have different religious orientations, regardless of the male's beliefs of traditionalism or religious affiliation which may condemn abortion or his accompanying religious estrangement, the woman may proceed with the abortion.[68]
7. In the resolution of a problem pregnancy, both male and female have equal rights with respect to adoption, but not to abortion. In both adoption and abortion, at least one parent wishes to terminate involvement of parental rights and responsibilities. Such a termination, in either case, completely forecloses the rights of both parents. Hence, when the

parents' interests in the child conflict, the determination of rights in one conflict should have a significant application to the other. Therefore, if due process and equal protection are guaranteed for the male in adoption, parallel provisions should—but do not—exist in abortion.[69]

8. While a child is allowed recovery for the wrongful death of the putative father, the unwed father has not been allowed to recover for the wrongful death of his aborted illegitimate child.[70]

To state the case succinctly, the Supreme Court, in protecting the privacy of the mother in abortion, may well have violated the constitutional rights of the father, married or not.

Abortion and Its Psychological Consequences

Beyond legalities, the abortion experience confronts the very nature of a woman's identity. Countless authors have exclaimed the merits of this medical procedure and asserted only temporary, nonpathological, and limited adverse emotional sequelae.[71] And yet, the only consistent positive reaction reported in an exhaustive literature review is that of *relief.* Virtually no study reported additional positive feelings, void of negative reactions. However, rank-ordered negative feelings may include: guilt, anxiety, depression, a sense of loss, anger, relational changes with partner, crying, a feeling of being misled by misinformation or lack of information, deterioration of self-image, regret or remorse, nightmares, anxiety about possible infertility, loneliness/alienation, marital disruption, physical concerns, disturbance in sleep patterns, imagining the aborted child, flashbacks, psychotic reactions, hopelessness, helplessness, powerlessness, and changes in significant relationships.[72] According to Illsley and Hall,[73] guilt and abortion have virtually become synonymous: "It is superfluous to ask whether patients experience guilt—it is axiomatic that they will."

Correspondingly, it is becoming increasingly clear that abortion is a far more physiologically complicated procedure than was previously thought.[74] Psychologically, the negative potential reactions span anxiety and depression to psychosis and suicide. It is beyond the scope of this discussion to provide an in-depth analysis of this phenomenon. However, in Table 1, thirty-four studies concerning these negative reactions are briefly reported.

That there are so few studies and that negative reactions are typified as "minority reports" might be partially explained in the following manner. First, a number of investigations have been funded by organizations or agencies dedicated to abortion, and

Table 1
Major Studies on Psychological Ill Effects of Induced Abortion

Study	Date	Major Findings
Sim[75]	1963	Abortion is poor treatment for mental illness or prevention.
White[76]	1966	Abortion increases bitterness toward men, especially the father.
Pare and Hermione[77]	1970	More motherly and more mature women feel more postabortion guilt.
Colman and Colman[78]	1971	The stress from previous abortions can delay preparation for subsequent childbearing and retard mother-child bond formation.
Calef[79]	1972	Postabortion anxiety and disruption of marital sexual relations were suggested.
Bracken and Suigar[80]	1972	Self-reported negative abortion reactions were associated with being single, young, and lacking in support from partner and parents.
Osofsky and Osofsky[81]	1972	Sixteen percent of abortion patients were judged unhappy and 25 percent expressed guilt.
Perez-Reyes and Falk[82]	1973	Fifteen percent of postabortion adolescents expressed adverse feelings of depression, guilt, anger, and anxiety.
Kaltreider[83]	1973	Increased emotional difficulties exist in midtrimester abortion patients; those women who perceived the fetus as a human being, i.e., baby, felt guilty or sad.
Ewing and Rouse[84]	1973	Nineteen percent of postabortion patients expressed immediate negative reactions, especially if there was prior history of emotional disturbance.

Table 1—*Continued*

Study	Date	Major Findings
Hutcherson[85]	1973	Women who abort were found to be low in self-esteem.
Lawrence[86]	1973	Abortion does little to reduce anxiety, especially in second-trimester saline procedures.
Barglow and Weinstein[87]	1973	Postabortion mourning period was correlated with heavy decision influence by parents, peers, and partners.
Martin[88]	1973	Negative abortion adjustment was related to emotional involvement in pregnancy, few close friends, poor parental relations, and no support from sex partner.
Moore-Caver[89]	1974	Review of abortion literature found severe guilt in 2 to 23 percent of patients.
Bracken, Hachamovitch, and Grossman[90]	1974	Lack of parental emotional support to aborting daughters or pressure by parents for abortion were associated with negative reactions.
Blumberg, Golbus, and Hanson[91]	1975	Higher rate of depression was reported for genetic versus elective abortion, plus postabortion family disharmony and flashbacks.
Adler[92]	1975	Some postabortion patients experienced relief and happiness with guilt, shame, fear, loss, anger, resentment, depression, or remorse.
Evans, Selstad, and Welcher[93]	1976	Twenty percent regretted the abortion experience. Conservatism, religious affiliation, pressure to abort were highly related.

Table 1—*Continued*

Study	Date	Major Findings
Lipper and Feigenbaum[94]	1976	Repeat aborters experienced acute obsessive-compulsive reactions to viewing the limp fetus.
Greenglass[95]	1976	Twelve percent of aborted women experienced negative psychological reactions with 3 percent attempting suicide. Preabortion psychiatric patients were three times as likely to require therapy postabortion.
Jacobsen, Perris, and Espvall[96]	1977	Psychological profile of women who had aborted identified traits of dominance, aggressiveness, and autonomy suggesting a sado-masochistic orientation.
Kent[97]	1977	Abortion in patients' histories were major precipitants in seeking psychotherapy.
Burkle[98]	1977	Abortion patients typically utilized denial of aggressiveness and projection onto unborn child.
Bracken[99]	1978	Being married was highly correlated with a difficult abortion decision. Fifteen percent of the sample experienced a difficult abortion decision, anxiety, depression, and pain.
Blumenfield[100]	1978	Evidence was found of underlying psychological conflict in women seeking abortion; 34 percent had underlying conflictual wish to be pregnant.
Spaulding and Cavenar[101]	1978	Postabortion guilt and psychoses, and consternation and anniversary reactions were reported.

Table 1—*Continued*

Study	Date	Major Findings
Cavenar, Maltbie, and Sullivan[102]	1978	Psychiatric sequelae of abortion in potential grandparents and other family members were described, in addition to post-abortion psychogenic problems for some women for twenty years after the procedure.
Cavenar[103]	1978	Reports were cited of psychogenic abdominal pain after abortion and anniversary reactions.
Brewer[104]	1978	Twenty percent of sample reported negative psychic trauma.
Fisher[105]	1979	Abortion patients in therapy experienced poor relationships with men, poor impulse control, and masochistic tendencies.
Shusterman[106]	1979	Positive abortion reactions were related to satisfaction with decision to abort, nonupset over pregnancy, and sharing with their partner. Negative reactions were related to the inverse.
Cavenar, Spaulding, and Sullivan[107]	1979	Impact of abortion on family members was reported; in particular, the intrapsychic conflict experienced by children whose mother had aborted a pregnancy known to them.
Liebman and Zimmer[108]	1979	Twenty-four immediate and long term postabortion aberrations affecting self-image, relationships, and future coping abilities were reported.

many investigators have personally favored abortion, which can create a potential systematic bias in design, execution, and reporting of the findings.[109] Second, American women have known relatively little about the physiological and/or psychological dangers of abortion and, rather, have focused primarily on the immediacy of problem-pregnancy solution. In a very real sense, then, if there is no awareness or concern, there is little or no verbalization. Third, with greater publicity of the fetal stages of development and greater controversy over abortion, American women are beginning to realize that abortion does indeed destroy human life and that negative reactions to this dehumanization are appropriate and legitimate. Fourth, and inversely, with societal sanctioning of abortion, there has been a "mainstream effect" of pressuring women to deny negative postabortion feelings because they are unacceptable and incompatible with social and peer perceptions favoring the procedure. Fifth, women participating in research frequently feel the pressure of conformity to conventional and acceptable postabortion responses and are perhaps even fearful of the loss of confidentiality and the reporting of any negative sequelae in order to avoid any stigma of deviancy.[110] Sixth, few long-term longitudinal studies have been conducted which assess personal, relational, and familial consequences. Such durational investigations are needed in order to examine validly the actual extent of relational disruption. And seventh, there is evidence to suggest that only in-depth postabortion interviews with a trusted person truly reveal the personal agony and relational trauma that abortion induces;[111] questionnaires may then be of dubious value because of the complexity and ambivalence of human attitudes and because answers to survey questions are notoriously sensitive to the wording of the questions.[112]

Abortion as a Social Problem

Promoted by social, judicial, and political engineers, abortion has been heralded as the solution for problem pregnancies. Additionally, there are those who advocate induced abortion as cure for poverty,[113] elixir for marital and self-fulfillment,[114] remedy for defective humans,[115] treatment for mental health,[116] antidote for sexual inequality,[117] and prevention for child abuse.[118] Evidence presented here would suggest otherwise. Abortion in itself solves nothing; in fact, it often regenerates failure in increasing risks for repeated abortions.[119]

Like the Trojan horse, abortion is only beginning to be seen for what it truly is and does. There is evidence to suggest that induced abortion promotes "mystification and masking" within the family which is dysfunctional for the individual in every context.[120] In relationships, abortion provides "pseudohomeostasis"—that is, a stability through nonadjustment rather than through readjustment, which promotes even more serious relational disequilibrium, particularly for parents and daughters.[121] For men it provides relief, alienation, role conflict, and masculine insecurity. For women it provides relief, but it also induces a heavy burden of guilt, secrecy, and intrapsychic conflict. Clinically, if an unwanted pregnancy is a mistake or a problem, then abortion becomes a denial of the problem. Psychologically, abortion then reinforces defective problem-solving behavior.

Of much interest recently has been the relationship between child abuse and abortion. If violence begets violence,[122] and abortion is the violent truncation of life, then to what extent does abortion actually enable child abuse? Even the language of abortion has been typified as "dehumanizing" as it refers to fetal removal as "pieces of tissue" or a "clump of cells."[123] Ney[124] examined demographic data and found that abortion was increasing as rapidly as child abuse and reported that unrestricted abortion diminishes restraint against rage, the taboo against aggressing the defenseless young, and the value of children while it increases hostility between generations, escalates the battle of the sexes, and breaks down the pair-bonding ability in mothers with their infants and, hence, promotes child abuse. Studies by Calef[125] and Kumar and Robson[126] lend corroboration to these findings.

Abuse, of course, is a behavior that manifests itself in degrees. Abortion as a process of elimination or termination likewise is accomplished in varying degrees from the initial crisis decision making to the postabortion sequelae. Both child abuse and abortion exist because of denial, hostility, frustration, the elevation of self, and the negation of life. Even if at the present time it cannot be empirically demonstrated that abortion "causes" child abuse, abortion does cause personal and relational abuse.

It may also be said that abortion weakens the marital structure. In the case of an interfaith or varying-degrees-of-religiosity marriage, the decision to abort by the spouse with the less conservative belief system necessarily collides with that of the other partner.[127] Abortion may even be antithetical to marriage in that it eliminates procreative responsibility and occurs most frequently among those who cohabit.[128] One study found that 75 percent of the abortion respondents asserted that "a child at this time would interfere with my career, education, or personal freedom."[129] Abortion also disguises and increases marital dysfunction in that a problem pregnancy from an extramarital affair can be secretly disposed. In short, being married is frequently referred to as the dominant sociodemographic correlate of a difficult abortion decision.[130]

With the recent psychocultural obsession with self, faulty thinking has led to faulty social rules. Abortion is one of the more painful social lessons to learn. From the imperative of compulsive self-fulfillment, each of us has become his or her own object of worship. As selves, we have been culturally commanded to "do our own thing," liberate ourselves from repressive traditionalism, concentrate on our feelings, potentials, needs, wants, and desires. The pied piper of "me-ism" has nearly led us to our demise, for nothing has subverted self-fulfillment more thoroughly than self-indulgence. Yankelovitch said it well:

> Even moderate forms of the assumption that selves are culture-free and wholly autonomous run the risk of alienation, loneliness, meaninglessness, and futility. We are not our own work of art. We do not create ourselves as an artist paints a picture or writes a novel. Constant changes in commitments and outlook are not the route to real self-fulfillment. Suppression of needs is not always bad; in fact, some suppression is required if one is to avoid becoming a blob of contradictions.[131]

In a broader sense, selfhood is integrated with caring, even intuitively. When one ceases to care—about family, children, the future, the helpless, friends, the world—the meaningfulness of experience vanishes and so does the essence of selfhood and individual fulfillment.

Abortion, then, is an undesirable symptom of a far greater problem. There is, of course, a benefit to abortion. It provides relief, which in turn feels good. But at the core of abortion there is a moral and social absurdity. Desires are morally sanctioned which do not contribute to either the individual's or society's well-being. At this core there is no discrimination between socially valuable and socially destructive desires, and there is no principle other than hedonism for interpreting human sexuality and the sacrifices inherent in human reproductive functioning.

Abortion shreds the soul of humanity and the fabric of relationships. It exists *for* women, yet it is *against* women, men, and children. Like an anesthesia, abortion comfortably numbs all from experiencing the burden of pregnancy. Abortion has become a social eraser, individually, quickly, and secretly eliminating all traces of the problem that is pregnancy. And yet, traces always remain. Within the depths of humankind, the indelible marks of violation appear.

4

CONSEQUENCES OF A HUMAN LIFE AMENDMENT

Chapter Six

MEDICAL TREATMENT FOR PREGNANT WOMEN

Denis Cavanagh

Before discussing some of the medical complications of a human life amendment, it is appropriate to review some of the arguments touching on medical and/or scientific aspects that served as a basis for the Supreme Court's sweeping abortion decisions handed down in 1973.[1]

First, "one's philosophy, one's experience. . . . (and) in addition, population growth, pollution, poverty and racial overtones tend to complicate and not to simplify the problem"[2]—thus, social problems in our society apparently played some part in the decision.

Second, Justice Blackmun mentions the Hippocratic Oath but then dismisses this argument against abortion by stating that "the Oath was not uncontested even in Hippocrates's day."[3] (It is of some interest that since 1973 the standard Hippocratic Oath has been modified in many medical school graduations so as to be more in keeping with the Supreme Court decision.)

Third, Justice Blackmun points out that, at the common law, abortion performed before "quickening" (sixteenth to eighteenth week) was not an indictable offense. He thus prepares the way for the justification of abortion prior to the sixteenth week. He does this without pointing out that before modern technology was available there was no way of appreciating that the fetus was alive except through the report of fetal movements by the mother. The state abortion laws were therefore written on the basis of the best information available.

Whereas quickening reported by the mother was acceptable in the past as the indication of life, we now know that fetal movements can be observed much earlier than this by ultrasonography and fetoscopy. In fact, fetal brain activity has been picked up as early as forty-three days into the pregnancy by electroencephalography and fetal heart sounds at eight weeks by ultrasonic techniques. But Blackmun excluded this scientific information in writing the majority opinion, because he apparently wanted to avoid support for the inconvenient conclusion that even in the first trimester the fetus is alive.

Denis Cavanagh, M.D., is professor of obstetrics and gynecology, University of South Florida College of Medicine. He is a coauthor of several medical textbooks, including Obstetric Emergencies (1978).

Fourth, Justice Blackmun, in a poor attempt at *reductio ad absurdum,* pulls in the old long-abandoned theological concept of mediate animation with the statement, "Canon law came to fix the point of animation at forty days for a male and eighty days for a female,"[4] in an obvious attempt to win friends in the feminist movement and at the same time create a credibility gap as far as Christian teaching on abortion is concerned.[5] The fact is that there was little knowledge of embryology at the time these laws were developed; and even intellectuals like Thomas Aquinas, because of lack of scientific information, came to conclusions that now appear to be ridiculous. For his errors, Blackmun does not have that excuse.

Fifth, Justice Blackmun mentions the British case *Rex v. Bourne* to support the view that an abortion may be done if there is "a serious and permanent threat to the mother's health."[6] He fails to mention that Dr. Alec Bourne, the obstetrician-gynecologist who established this view, became so disgusted at the abuse of the "mother's health" indication that before he died he became a member of the Society for the Protection of Unborn Children and was ultimately violently opposed to the British Abortion Act of 1967. Again, this very pertinent information was either unknown to the majority of Supreme Court Justices because the subject was poorly researched, or it was deliberately omitted in the development of their legal opinion.

Sixth, Justice Blackmun, in an effort to establish that social abortion can be countenanced as a contribution to reducing maternal mortality rates, stated that "[m]ortality rates for women undergoing early abortions, where the procedure is legal, appear to be as low as or lower than the rates for normal childbirth."[7] In justification of this he quotes the well-known pro-abortionists Potts and Tietze[8] and omits balancing testimony which could have been obtained had it really been desired.

Seventh, Justice Blackmun writes of "high mortality rates at illegal abortion mills"[9] and gives no reference, although it is now well established that, instead of the ten thousand illegal abortion deaths per year which pro-abortionists had claimed, there were less than one hundred deaths from all types of abortion in the entire United States in 1967.[10] Here again, we see evidence of deliberate misrepresentation of the facts, or of very sloppy preparation, in what has turned out to be a landmark Supreme Court decision.

Eighth, Justice Blackmun, writing of the fetus, takes the view that conception is synonymous with fertilization, ignoring the possibility that conception might be synonymous with implantation of the fertilized ovum in the uterine wall (blastocyst stage). At the International Conference on Abortion held in Washington, D.C., in 1967, while there was some disagreement as to whether human life began at fertilization or at implantation, the ethicists (Protestant, Catholic, and Jewish) at that conference agreed that, on the basis of the medical evidence presented, life was present at least from the blastocyst stage.[11] The practical point is that, as soon as the woman misses her next menstrual period and realizes she is pregnant, human life is known to be present and represents a biological continuum to adult personhood. Even by the most modern tests, pregnancy is not detectable with any degree of accuracy before nine days after fertilization. Again, the selection of fertilization as the beginning is interesting and may have been a way of getting more support for the majority opinion from people who find the use of "minidose" oral contraceptives and intrauterine contraceptive devices morally acceptable.

Justice Blackmun used other data which could be analyzed and shown wanting, but I will comment further only on the crux of the matter: Justice Blackmun states that there is disagreement about when human life begins and that "[w]e need not resolve the difficult question of when life begins."[12] I suggest that, by considering a few fundamental facts with regard to reproductive physiology and fetal growth, the Supreme Court Justices could have decided when human life began and that, if they had done so, they could not possibly have reached the conclusion that a woman's right to privacy was more fundamental than the fetal right to life.

It is clear from the scientific facts that there is no disagreement about when human life begins. It is clear that the fetus is human because its parents are human. It is clear that it is alive from conception. There is no real disagreement as to the scientific facts, but only as to the ethics of the situation.

In support of this statement, I quote an excerpt from an editorial entitled "A New Ethic for Medicine and Society," from *California Medicine,* September 1970. *California Medicine* is the official journal of the California Medical Association, and the article was written by a pro-abortionist with reference to the campaign mounted to move from liberalized abortion to unbridled reproductive freedom with abortion as a woman's right.

> [S]ince the old ethic has not yet been fully displaced it has been necessary to separate the idea of abortion from the idea of killing, which continues to be socially abhorrent. The result has been a curious avoidance of the scientific fact, which everyone really knows, that human life begins at conception and is continuous, whether intra or extra-uterine, until death. The very considerable semantic gymnastics, which are required to rationalize abortion as anything but taking a human life, would be

ludicrous if they were not often put forth under socially impeccable auspices.[13]

The deliberate termination of a pregnancy, at whatever stage in pregnancy prior to viability, is the same procedure. Attempts to determine an artificial dividing line before which an established pregnancy may be ethically terminated are complete nonsense. A fetus of twelve weeks is not essentially different from one of twenty-four weeks, or one of twenty-four weeks from one of thirty-six weeks. It may be safer medically to terminate pregnancies at eight rather than sixteen weeks, but the procedure is no more justified if the indication is a nonmedical one. If society gives sanction to the destruction of innocent human life in the fetal stage, then why not in the newborn, the insane, or the senile? After all, society in the past has sanctioned all of these practices, and already in the United States children with abnormalities have been allowed to die when remediable measures were available.[14]

Many physicians support the current abortion law because of patient pressure and the enormous sums of money which can be made for little work. Many medical school departments of obstetrics and gynecology in this country derive a large portion of faculty income from abortions, and private abortion clinics and organizations such as Planned Parenthood have a vested interest in seeing that the 1973 Supreme Court decisions constitutionalizing virtual abortion on demand are upheld. Additionally, there are the "seduced idealists" of the 1980s who genuinely feel that they are building a better world for all of us. Hence it is not difficult to find "experts" to testify in support of the Supreme Court decisions of 1973, and any attempt to reverse those decisions will be met with vocal, well-organized, and well-funded opposition.

However, an increasing number of Americans are beginning to realize that the medical facts have been distorted to justify abortion for social reasons; and increasing numbers of Americans are realizing that the fetus is not a potential human being, but rather a human being with potential. For this reason, there is now a strong movement to find a solution to the problem of abortion on demand.

Predictably, the introduction of the human life amendments has led to a counterattack by the pro-choice lobby. In the forefront of the opposition to a human life amendment is the American Civil Liberties Union, which in 1981 published a report entitled *The So-called Human Life Amendment—The Most Critical Threat to Our Privacy.*[15] The report states first that the Supreme Court decisions guarantee each woman the right to decide, with her physician and without governmental interference, whether to have a child or to obtain an abortion, at least within the first three months of pregnancy. The fact is that the Supreme Court decisions are so sweeping that they give a woman the right to have an abortion on the basis of her physical or mental health up to full term if a sympathetic consultant can be found. Second, the authors emphasize that the fertilized egg would be a "person" under the Constitution, although it is obvious that a woman in whom fertilization has just taken place would have no idea that she was pregnant. In fact, by the time the patient realizes she is pregnant, the fetus is well formed and well deserving of the title of "human being with potential" rather than "potential human being." Third, the specter is raised that an amendment would make an abortion a crime probably equal to murder and would give the unborn more rights than the born. This statement is difficult to understand considering the fact that state abortion laws prior to 1973 were designed to protect both the mother and the fetus; and, even with a human life amendment, in any circumstance in which there was a serious threat to the mother's life or health, the fetus may die as a result of the medical treatment of the mother. I can think of no circumstance where the life of the mother would be sacrificed for the sake of the fetus. With a well-written human life amendment, every effort would be made to save the fetus *except* when that effort clearly endangers the life of the mother. Fourth, "above all it would establish a primarily religious belief—that a fertilized egg is a human being from the moment of fertilization."[16] If this is to be interpreted as a religious belief, then is it not also a religious belief that life begins at birth? Embryologically and physiologically the latter is certainly a less tenable view because at that time the fetus merely adapts its respiratory, cardiovascular, nutritional, and endocrine systems to its new extrauterine environment.

Perhaps I as an obstetrician should be flattered by the view of the Supreme Court and the ACLU that a full-term fetus is not alive until I see fit to perform a cesarean section and grant it the gift of life. It may be convenient for some to popularize the myth, but the fetus is just as alive at the minute before it is delivered as at the minute after it is delivered. The denial of intrauterine fetal life is simply a convenient rationalization, and there is no connection between these arguments and religion.

Abnormal Pregnancies

Pro-choice advocates have charged that because of fear of litigation a physician could not give adequate care to a woman under a number of circumstances including spontaneous abortion, incompetent cervix, ectopic pregnancy, hydatidiform mole, obstetrical complications of pregnancy (e.g., toxemia of pregnancy, placenta previa, and abruptio placentae), and pregnancy complicated by medical conditions (e.g., heart disease and diabetes). Most of these objections have little substance, but in the formulation of a human life amendment they must be addressed. In this chapter I analyze these situations and assess whether a human life amendment would pose a serious threat to the life or health of pregnant women.

Spontaneous Abortion

Approximately 10 percent of all pregnancies end spontaneously—90 percent in the first twelve weeks. A spontaneous abortion may be threatened, inevitable, incomplete, or complete. These conditions are easily differentiated by the average physician from the patient's history and the findings on physical examination as summarized in Table 1.[17] If a patient has a *threatened* abortion, and there is no evidence of intrauterine infection, the patient is treated with bedrest and supportive measures. If the abortion is *inevitable* or *incomplete,* however, the uterus should be evacuated promptly as soon as the diagnosis is made. Even if the patient has a threatened abortion, if severe intrauterine infection

Table 1
Spontaneous Abortion by Type

Abortion	Bleeding	Tissue Passed Vaginally	Tissue in Vagina	Status of Internal Cervical Os	Uterine Size
Threatened	Slight	None	None	Closed	Commensurate with "dates"
Inevitable	Moderate	None	None	Open with membranes or tissue bulging	Commensurate with "dates"
Incomplete	Severe	Placental or fetal tissue	Possibly	Open with tissue in cervical canal	Smaller than "dates"
Complete	Minimal	Complete placenta and fetus	Possibly	Closed with no tissue in cervical canal	Smaller than "dates"

Source: Revised from D. Cavanagh, R. Woods & T. O'Connor, Obstetric Emergencies (1978) (reprinted with permission). Note: The differential diagnosis of first-trimester abortion is usually easy. The amount of bleeding, the size of the uterus, the status of the internal cervical os, and the presence or absence of tissue in the vagina usually give the diagnosis.

is present this poses a significant threat to the life of the mother, and correct medical management calls for intravenous administration of the appropriate antibiotics and the evacuation of the uterus. In 1981 Grimes, Cates, and Selik reported on fatal septic abortions in the United States over the period 1975–77 and found that thirty-six women died.[18] The infection was associated with legal abortion in twelve cases, spontaneous abortion in fifteen, and illegal abortion in eight; one case was unclassified. It is important that physicians realize the importance of evacuating the uterus promptly under these circumstances. Here the death of the fetus is a secondary effect of the proper medical management of the mother. These cases are clear-cut and the decisions are usually simple. In the presence of a human life amendment the correct medical management would be no different from what it is now, and most people would agree that the physician more concerned about litigation than about the danger to his patient should not be practicing medicine.

Incompetent Cervical os

In cases of incompetent cervical os the fetus is usually lost in the second or third trimester. The patient usually has a history of previous second-trimester abortions or premature deliveries in which there was a gush of fluid and a relatively painless delivery with little bleeding. If recognized during pregnancy, this condition can be treated by the placement of a synthetic band around the cervix to keep it closed until the fetus is sufficiently mature for delivery. The principles of this procedure for incompetent cervical os are described elsewhere.[19] Contraindications to performing the operation are the presence of ruptured membranes and dilatation of the cervix over 4 cm. These contraindications apply in the presence or the absence of a human life amendment, so the plan of management would be unaffected and the risk to the mother would not be altered, except where the physician is incapable of making the appropriate decision.

Ectopic Pregnancy

Ectopic pregnancy is still an important cause of maternal death in the United States.[20] In over 90 percent of cases the pregnancy is in the tube and as soon as the diagnosis is made the patient should be treated surgically for removal of the tubal pregnancy. If the patient is in shock, general supportive measures are taken and blood loss immediately replaced. Again, this constitutes good medical care for the mother, and the loss of the fetus is an undesirable secondary effect. It is sometimes argued that an advanced ectopic pregnancy, especially an abdominal pregnancy, may go to full term and the baby may be born alive. However, a successful outcome is very rare and it is in the best interests of the mother to advise her to be treated immediately if a diagnosis of ectopic pregnancy is made. This is a life-threatening situation for the mother and the decision of the physician would certainly not be affected by the passage of a human life amendment.

Hydatidiform Mole

Incredible as it might seem, it has been suggested that if a human life amendment were passed a physician would find it difficult to treat a patient with a hydatidiform mole. This complicates one in two thousand pregnancies in the United States. It is a condition in which the fetus does not develop because of cystic degeneration of the primitive placenta. Any competent obstetrician-gynecologist knows that the correct treatment consists of evacuating the uterus as soon as the diagnosis is made. Further management will depend upon whether the patient has an "invasive mole" or the more malignant trophoblastic variety of the disease called choriocarcinoma. Organized fetal tissue cannot be identified in these cases unless a twin pregnancy is present. In any event, the correct treatment for the mother is prompt evacuation of the uterus, and the risk to the mother would not be increased if any of the proposed human life amendments are passed.

Obstetrical Complications of Pregnancy

Obstetrical complications have not generally been mentioned in association with the abortion controversy until Justice Blackmun saw fit to abandon the twenty-week and/or 500-gram limit adhered to in the standard medical definition of abortion.[21] As a result, potential obstetrical complications are discussed below.

Toxemia of Pregnancy

Dr. George M. Ryan, Jr., president of the American College of Obstetricians and Gynecologists, in his statement on May 30, 1981, before the Separation of Powers Subcommittee opposing the Human Life Bill, saw fit to present toxemia of pregnancy as one of the problem areas if abortion is outlawed. He is reported as stating that prevention of the more severe effects of this disease involves early delivery with concomitant risk to the baby. Apparently, he further stated that failure to act in this situation for fear of abridging the rights of the fetus could result in death of the mother and the fetus. To be sure, in the management of severe toxemia of pregnancy, medical measures to control the disease may fail and early delivery may be indicated. However, with good medical management, the toxemic process can usually be controlled, even with relatively simple measures, until the fetus is viable.[22] In any event, if proper medical guidelines are followed, the risk to the mother would be no greater in the presence of a human life amendment. The most important factor in the protection of the mother with toxemia of pregnancy is to see that she is referred to a competent obstetrician.

Placentae Previa

Placentae previa is a condition which is associated with bleeding in late pregnancy.[23] In this situation the placenta, instead of lying at the fundus of the uterus, is lying between the fetal presenting part and the vagina. Thus, as the lower uterine segment of the uterus begins to develop, painless vaginal bleeding occurs. If the diagnosis is made before the fetus is mature enough for delivery, the patient is treated conservatively with bedrest, preferably in the hospital, until about the thirty-sixth week of pregnancy. However, if bleeding becomes a threat to the mother's life at any time an immediate cesarean section should be performed. With any significant degree of placentae previa, cesarean section is usually the best method of delivery for both the mother and the baby. In this condition, too, the treatment would be the same if a human life amendment had been passed and there would no increased risk to the mother.

Abruptio Placentae

The premature separation of a normally placed placenta in late pregnancy results in abruptio placentae. In its most severe form, the condition causes abdominal pain with heavy vaginal bleeding. Shock may supervene and the fetus may die as a result of separation of the placenta. Whether the fetus is alive or dead, the mother is best treated by vaginal delivery or cesarean section to empty the uterus and by early and adequate replacement of blood loss. Again, the passage of a human life amendment would make no difference to the proper care of the mother.

Disorders Complicated by Pregnancy

There is now general agreement that abortion does not contribute to success in the management of the patient with severe mental illness.[24] I therefore concentrate on the more tangible problem of severe organic disease in the mother, complicated by pregnancy. Because a human life amendment is under consideration, we must examine its effect on pregnant women with serious intercurrent disease. It is rare that the termination of pregnancy is a direct contribution to the care of a woman whose pregnancy is complicated by an intercurrent medical problem. However, as long as it affects even a few women, it must be given careful consideration. There are no accurate figures available as to how many of the approximately 1.5 million legal abortions which are being carried out annually would come under this heading. However, if we consider the report by Hall[25] in 1965, it is reasonable to assume an abortion-delivery ratio of no more than 1:429 justified medically in 1983 (see table 2). This would mean that a maximum of approximately 3,500 abortions per year would have to be performed because pregnancy posed a serious threat to the life or health of the mother. It would be reasonable to assume that even this figure is high, because it is likely that many of the patients who had abortions done could have been carried through pregnancy successfully without significant danger to life or health because of advances in medicine since then.

Table 2
Therapeutic Abortions, Sloane Hospital, New York, 1950–60

	Abortion/Delivery Ratio	
	Ward	Private
1950–55	1:141	1:37
1956–60	1:429	1:111

Situations with regard to serious organic diseases and their management during pregnancy are below summarized, with particular reference to the effect of a human life amendment on maternal mortality (table 3). In addition to diseases which are specific to pregnancy, such as those listed above, a pregnant woman is subject to any of the many disorders which may occur in a nonpregnant woman. Thus, it will be possible to comment here on more serious disorders only. As a preliminary statement, a rule that overarches the possible problem of disorders complicated by pregnancy is that, if the obstetrician takes good care of the mother, she will take good care of the fetus and abortion is unnecessary. Due to continuing progress in medical knowledge, there are fewer medical indications for abortion every year; and even in these cases, resort to abortion is often an admission of medical inadequacy.

Heart Disease

Heart disease is a major cause of maternal death in the United States; but if maternal disability is minimal, both maternal and perinatal mortality are only slightly increased. With marked degrees of heart disease, the maternal death rate is in the region of 2 percent but perinatal mortality may reach 50 percent. Under

Table 3
Disorders Complicated by Pregnancy

Disorder	Medical Indication for Abortion
Heart Disease	
Rheumatic heart disease	Rarely, with adequate treatment
Congenital heart disease	Rarely, with adequate treatment
Hypertensive heart disease	Very rarely, with adequate treatment
Coronary artery disease	Rarely, with adequate treatment
Cardiac arrhythmias	Very rarely, with adequate treatment
Cardiac surgery and pregnancy	Very rarely, with adequate treatment (cardiac surgery may be a substitute for abortion)
Vascular Disease	
Essential hypertension	Very rarely
Coarctation of the aorta	Very rarely
Arterial aneurysms	Very rarely
Varicose veins	None
Thromboembolic disease	Very rarely
Respiratory Disease	
Tuberculosis	Very rarely
Bronchiectasis	Very rarely
Sarcoidosis	Very rarely
Asthma	Very rarely
Cystic fibrosis	Very rarely
Blood Diseases in Pregnancy	
Anemia in pregnancy	Very rarely (e.g., aplastic)
Hemoglobinopathies in pregnancy	Rarely (e.g., patients with sickle-cell anemia and sickle-cell disease)
Thrombocytopenic purpura	Rarely
Clotting disorders in pregnancy	Very rarely
Myeloproliferative diseases	Very rarely (e.g., polycythemia vera, leukemia, lymphoma)
Diseases of the Endocrine System	
Diabetes mellitus	Very rarely if well controlled
Thyroid disease	Very rarely in hypo- or hyperthyroidism
Parathyroid disease	Very rarely
Pituitary disease	Very rarely
Adrenal disease	Very rarely (especially in phaeochromocytoma)

Table 3—*Continued*

Disorder	Medical Indication for Abortion
Diseases of the Nervous System	
Cerebral vascular accidents	Rarely
Epilepsy	Very, very rarely
Chorea gravidarum	None
Multiple sclerosis	None
Myasthenia gravis	None
Tetany	Very rarely
Obstetrical paralysis	None
Peripheral neuropathies	None
Diseases of the Gastrointestinal System	
Liver disorders	Very rarely (e.g., acute yellow atrophy)
Cholecystitis and cholelithiasis	None
Pancreatitis	None
Disorders of the gastro-intestinal tract	Rarely (e.g., ulcerative colitis, regional enteritis)
Kidney and Urinary Tract Disease	
Acute glomerulonephritis	Very rarely
Chronic glomerulonephritis	Rarely
Nephrosis	Very rarely
Acute renal failure	Rarely (depends on the cause)
Anomalies of the urinary tract	
Unilateral renal agenesis	Rarely
Ectopic kidney	Very rarely
Polycystic kidney disease	Rarely
Pregnancy after renal transplantation	Rarely
Urinary tract calculi	Very rarely
Urinary tract infection	Very, very rarely
Connective Tissue Diseases	
Systemic lupus erythematosus	Very rarely
Rheumatoid arthritis	Very, very rarely
Scleroderma	Very rarely
Periarteritis nodosa	Very rarely
Marfan's syndrome	No benefit to mother
Infectious Diseases	
Bacterial infections	Very rarely (e.g., septic shock due to endometritis)
Viral infections	Very rarely (e.g., encephalitis, brain stem polio, cardiomyopathy)
Spirochetal and protozoal infections	Very rarely (e.g., toxoplasmosis with cardiomyopathy)

Table 3—*Continued*

Disorder	Medical Indication for Abortion
Skeletal Disorders	
Osteogenesis imperfecta	None
Chondrodystrophy	None
Skin Disease	
Skin diseases related to pregnancy	
Prurigo gestationis	None
Herpes gestationis	None
Impetigo herpetiformis	Very, very rarely
Skin diseases complicated by pregnancy	
Psoriasis	None
Pemphigus	None
Discoid lupus erythematosus	None
Cancer	
Carcinoma of the breast	Very rarely
Carcinoma of the uterine cervix	Almost always
Cancer of the ovary	Almost always
Cancer of the vulva and vagina	Sometimes
Leukemia and lymphoma	Very rarely
Melanoma	Very rarely, some disagreement
Carcinoma of the thyroid	Very rarely
Cancer of the gastrointestinal tract	Very rarely (e.g., colorectal cancer)
Tumors of the central nervous system	Rarely unless acute intracranial pressure during pregnancy

optimal conditions of diagnosis and management, involving the obstetrician, cardiologist, and occasionally a cardiac surgeon, there is almost no cardiac complication so severe as to require abortion to save the life of the mother. Occasionally, cardiac surgery may be an alternative to abortion and provide the mother with definitive treatment at the same time.

The functional capacity of the heart is the best single indicator of the patient's prognosis, and the New York Heart Association Classification (1964) is a useful guide.

Class I. Normal physical activity causes no discomfort.

Class II. Normal activity causes discomfort and slight dyspnea.

Class III. Less than normal activity causes discomfort or dyspnea.

Class IV. Any physical activity is impossible, and the patient is dyspneic at rest.

About 85 percent of maternal deaths in women with heart disease occur with Class III or Class IV disease, and patients in these two classes constitute only about 15 percent of those with heart disease. It is especially important to watch the patients who are pregnant for evidence of heart failure. Even a mild respiratory infection may precipitate cardiac decompensation. Because of the altered circulatory hemodynamics of pregnancy, left heart failure is more common than right heart failure in the pregnant patient, and the most common manifestation is acute pulmonary edema.

Prevention of Problems

Appropriate medical and obstetric measures in the patients at risk will help to prevent pulmonary edema. Appropriate obstetric measures follow:

- Give adequate analgesia. Avoid scopolamine, and use morphine, 10 mg, in preference to meperidine.
- Use pudendal nerve block or conduction anesthesia for delivery.
- Give oxygen freely during labor and immediately postpartum.
- Shorten the second stage of labor by forceps delivery to save the patient the effort of bearing down.
- Unusual care should be taken to avoid excessive postpartum bleeding. Unless there is significant postpartum hemorrhage, oxytocics should not be given.
- If possible, deliver the patient in the left lateral position. Avoid cesarean section unless a definite obstetric indication is present. If the patient is delivered in the lithotomy position, lower the legs promptly after delivery to reduce drainage of blood into the general circulation. At that time, even a volume of 700 ml might be critical.
- Discourage the patient with Class III or IV cardiac disease from breastfeeding her infant.
- Keep the patient in the hospital for at least one week after delivery. Give her appropriate advice with regard to contraception if she desires it. Make appropriate arrangements for home help before the patient is discharged from the hospital.

Diagnosis of Pulmonary Edema

This is readily made because of the onset of severe dyspnea. The patient frequently has a coughing episode, and frothy pink fluid appears at her lips. She is cyanotic and anxious. Tachycardia is present, and the neck veins are usually distended.

Treatment of Pulmonary Edema

The following procedures should be instituted.

- Place the patient in the sitting position with legs down.
- Give oxygen, 100 percent, by mask with mechanical positive-pressure ventilation.
- Inject morphine, 10 to 15 mg, intravenously.
- Inject digoxin, 0.5 mg, intravenously; follow it with 0.25 mg every 6 hours for two doses.
- Slowly inject aminophyllin, 0.5 g, intravenously.
- Inject furosemide, 40 mg, intravenously.
- Carry out physiologic venesection, using tourniquets on three of four limbs and rotating them every 15 minutes.
- In an acute emergency, perform a phlebotomy and remove up to 500 ml of blood to reduce the load on the heart.

When the acute episode is over, follow-up therapy will include completion of digitalization with a maintenance dose of digoxin, 0.25 mg, daily, and placement on a low-sodium diet. An oral diuretic should be given if it is required. For purposes of further care, any patient who develops heart failure should be considered henceforth to have heart disease, Class IV, and appropriate measures should be taken with limitation of patient activity and good medical care being essential to reduce risk. Unfortunately, a patient with severe heart disease is sometimes aborted to "solve the problem" and then dies because of inadequate attention to her heart disease. On the other hand, patients who elect to continue with their pregnancy sometimes receive superior care from their physicians who are now forced to "sweat out" the pregnancy with their patients.

Asthma

The pregnant woman who is having an acute asthmatic attack presents a very difficult problem. Again, abortion is very rarely necessary, and good medical management is more important. The patient who is admitted in labor with bronchospasm should receive vigorous therapy for relief of symptoms. Patients being treated for asthma should have this continued throughout pregnancy and labor.

Diagnosis

A history of previous asthmatic attacks related to allergy, bronchitis, or anxiety may be obtained. Physical examination reveals respiratory distress with inspiratory retraction, prolonged expiration, and prominent rhonchi diffusely over both lung fields. Laboratory findings in these patients may contribute little. However, in severe asthmatic attacks, arterial blood gases may show decreased arterial oxygen tension, an increase in arterial carbon dioxide tension, and acidosis.

Management

Even in the emergency situations treatment can be initiated during preparation for delivery.

- Start positive-pressure treatments, using epinephrine nebulization.
- Give a subcutaneous injection of 0.2 ml epinephrine (1:1,000 solution). This is contraindicated for use with trichloroethylene, cyclopropane, or halothane anesthesia. Alternatively, aminophylline, 250–500 mg, in 500 ml 5 percent dextrose in water, may be given as an intravenous infusion.
- Give hydrocortisone, 100–200 mg, intravenously as an initial dose. Follow this with 100 mg in a liter of 5 percent dextrose in water every 8 hours.
- If metabolic acidosis develops, correct it with 1 ampule (44.6 mEq) of sodium bicarbonate intravenously. Take care in administering sodium bicarbonate in the presence of a high carbon dioxide tension in arterial blood.
- Give antibiotics if there appears to be an initiating or perpetuating infectious factor.
- Administer oxygen liberally to the patient during labor to maintain good arterial oxygen tension.
- Anesthesia for delivery should, preferably, be pudendal block, although a major conduction anesthetic given by an experienced anesthesiologist is very satisfactory. General anesthesia is best avoided in the obstetric patient with asthma.

Sickle-cell Disease

Sickle-cell conditions typically appear in black women. Patients with the sickle-cell trait (SA) are at little risk. Patients with sickle-cell anemia (SS) or patients with sickle-cell disease (SC) are in an entirely different category and pregnancy can be very dangerous for both mother and baby. In either of these two conditions a sickle-cell crisis may occur.

The problem is very serious. The maternal mortality ranges in various series from 0 to 25 percent and the perinatal mortality from 25 to 50 percent. Therapeutic abortion and sterilization are medically indicated in some patients. If refused, careful observation is mandatory.

A crisis is manifested by attacks of headache and abdominal, joint, or bone pains lasting from several hours to several days. The hemoglobin level remains relatively unchanged despite a hemolytic crisis. Numerous nucleated red cells may be present in the peripheral blood, and leukocytosis is almost always present. X-rays of the bones may reveal cortical thinning and diffuse osteoporosis with thickening of trabecular markings on x-ray films. The sickle-cell smear is diagnostic for both sickle-cell trait (SA) and sickle-cell anemia (SS). Hemoglobin electrophoresis will identify other hemoglobinopathies such as SC disease and S-thalassemia.

Bone and joint pains resemble those of rheumatic fever. The presence of a rigid, tender abdomen may suggest an acute surgical emergency, but bowel sounds are normal. Headache, convulsions, and paralysis due to cerebral thrombosis may be mistaken for a variety of conditions, including preeclampsia or eclampsia. Splenomegaly is a feature of SC disease but rarely occurs in sickle-cell anemia. In sickle-cell anemia the picture is often compounded by the presence of iron deficiency anemia. Complications such as hematuria, pyelonephritis, osteomyelitis, leg ulcers, and gallstones are not uncommon.

Management of Sickle-cell Crisis

- Give oxygen (100 percent) by face mask.
- Give analgesia. Because of the severity of the pain, morphine sulfate 10 mg every 4 hours may be required.
- Correct acidosis with sodium bicarbonate, 1 ampule (44.6 mEq), added to intravenous fluids.
- Treat complications such as pyelonephritis.
- Consider giving a partial exchange transfusion.

Indications for an exchange transfusion are painful crisis pregnancy at twenty-eight weeks with a previous clinical course indicating severe hemoglobinopathy, or previous partial exchange transfusion with hematocrit under 25 percent or hemoglobin A less than 40 percent. The procedure involves a series of phlebotomies with each liter of blood removed being replaced with fresh, washed, packed cells from a hemoglobin AA donor, and the balance of the patient's blood volume being reconstituted with lactated Ringer's solution. The phlebotomy and infusions may be performed alternately or simultaneously. The plan of treatment follows:

- For every 500 ml of blood removed, infuse two units of packed red cells and 100–200 ml lactated Ringer's solution, with careful monitoring for hypotension, circulatory overload, and transfusion reaction.
- Obtain a hematocrit after the third exchange transfusion is completed.
- Repeat the procedure until an equilibrated hematocrit of 35 percent is reached. Most patients will require phlebotomy of

1,500 ml of blood to achieve an adequate hemoglobin AA concentration and maximum benefit from the procedure.

- Follow-up should include: (1) serial hematocrits (should be maintained at greater than 25 percent; (2) serial reticulocyte counts (this should remain at 0–1 percent to demonstrate marrow suppression); (3) serial hemoglobin electrophoresis, to demonstrate hemoglobin A of greater than 40 percent; (4) folic acid, 1 mg per os daily; (5) iron therapy if indicated by serum iron studies; (6) microscopic examination of urine for evidence of infection on each visit; (7) close monitoring of the patient for early signs of preeclampsia, to which these patients are predisposed; and (8) close monitoring for signs of chronic fetal distress in view of the high perinatal mortality rate associated with this condition.

Diabetes Mellitus

Diabetes mellitus occurs as a complication of one in every 300 pregnancies in the United States. Although maternal deaths are now rare because of improved treatment, the fetal mortality remains in the region of 20 percent. Pregnant diabetics are classified as follows:

Class A. Diabetic status based only on an abnormal glucose tolerance test.

Class B. Onset of diabetes after age twenty; duration of diabetes less than ten years; no vascular disease.

Class C. Onset of diabetes between ages ten and nineteen; duration of diabetes ten to nineteen years; no vascular disease.

Class D. Onset of diabetes under age ten; duration of diabetes twenty or more years; vascular disease, including calcification of leg vessels; diabetic retinopathy.

Class E. Same as Class D, plus calcification of pelvic vessels.

Class F. Diabetic nephropathy (often Kimmelstiel-Wilson intercapillary nephrosclerosis).

Patients with severe diabetic retinitis and nephropathy who are in danger of death or blindness may be candidates for therapeutic abortion. Still, many of the emergency situations involving diabetes mellitus in pregnancy can be avoided if the patient is seen jointly by the obstetrician and the internist at least every two weeks throughout pregnancy. Overt diabetics usually require insulin and, as a rule, the requirement is greater during pregnancy. Blood glucose determinations should be used for regulation of diet and insulin. Sepsis, toxemia, and hemorrhage are the most common causes of maternal death, and all of these are more common in the pregnant diabetic. If they occur, they must be dealt with vigorously.

Delivery

The patient with any significant degree of diabetes mellitus should be admitted to the hospital at about the thirty-sixth week. She may have to be admitted earlier if she has toxemia of pregnancy or polyhydramnios, or if her diabetes cannot be controlled on an outpatient basis. If a patient is taking insulin for diabetes, it is generally advisable to deliver her before the thirty-eighth week. In a patient with severe diabetes, delivery may be desirable as early as the thirty-fourth week. However, other factors must be considered when this decision is being made; and serial urinary estriols, ultrasonography, L/S ratios, and stress tests for the fetus are all useful aids. As a general rule, patients should be delivered vaginally; but if this is not practical, cesarean section should be carried out.

When the decision has been made to deliver a patient with severe diabetes mellitus, the following procedures are appropriate.

- In the case of a patient whose cervix is 50 percent effaced and 1–2 cm dilated, with a presenting part at station 0, the membranes should be ruptured and an oxytocin infusion begun at a rate of 4 mU/min. The dosage is increased as necessary. Continuous monitoring of contractions and fetal heart tones is mandatory.
- If the cervix is thick and closed, and pointing posteriorly, then delivery is unlikely to occur within 12 hours, so elective cesarean section would be the best method for delivery. If a patient has significant diabetes mellitus and a decision has been made to deliver her vaginally, it is important that a 12-hour trial of labor be given. If there is no significant progress by this time, then cesarean section should be performed.

Thyrotoxicosis

Thyrotoxicosis is a serious problem for both mother and fetus, principally because it tends to be overtreated, resulting in the development of a hypothyroid state in the mother and her baby. During the first and early second trimester, this may result in fetal maldevelopment, cretinism, or goiter. Unless in very exceptional circumstances, however, there is no medical indication for a therapeutic abortion. Still, all pregnant women with thyrotoxicosis should be hospitalized and management carefully planned in consultation with an internist and surgeon. Therapy is individualized according to the degree of thyrotoxicosis and the duration of pregnancy. The prognosis is generally excellent for mother and fetus if normal thyroid function can be achieved promptly and then maintained either by medical or surgical measures or a combination of both. The most useful laboratory tests are those of total T_4 and T_5 resin uptake.

Thyroid Crisis

Thyroid crisis is an acute exacerbation of all symptoms of thyrotoxicosis, accompanied by fever, cardiac arrhythmia, and extreme tachycardia. Heart failure may occur, and the outcome may be fatal. Nausea, vomiting, diarrhea, hepatomegaly, jaundice, tremors, and delirium are all part of the clinical picture. The "thyroid storm" may be precipitated by infections, unusual emotional stress, or labor. Most often, however, it is precipitated by surgery in a patient who has not been adequately prepared medically. Management consists of the following:

- Give sodium iodide, 1 g/day, intravenously, to inhibit the release of thyroid hormones.
- Give oxygen.
- Give propylthiouracil, 1,200 mg/day, orally, in divided doses.
- Give reserpine, 2.5 mg, intramuscularly every 6 hours; or propranolol, 1–2 mg, intravenously, then 20 mg every 6 hours orally to control the maternal heart rate with direct monitoring by EKG.
- Hydrocortisone, 300 mg, intravenously every 24 hours is useful; and digitalis and diuretics are used in conventional doses.
- Intravenous fluids, 6,000–7,000 ml, may be necessary to combat dehydration; and replacement of electrolytes is an essential supportive measure. Hypothermia may be necessary for the hyperpyrexia, and phenothiazines have been suggested for use in the presence of severe hyperpyrexia.

Cerebrovascular Accidents

Pregnant women have a higher incidence of cerebrovascular accidents than nonpregnant women. Recurrent subarachnoid hemorrhage or the chance thereof may be an indication for cesarean section. It is unwise to allow a patient to bear down in the second stage if she is known to have a congenital aneurysm of the circle of Willis. The problem is rarely recognized early enough for abortion to be considered.

Hypertension associated with eclamptogenic toxemia, especially in the presence of disseminated intravascular coagulation and increased intracranial pressure due to "bearing down" in the second stage of labor, may cause rupture of congenital cerebral aneurysms, arteriovenous malformation, thrombosis of cerebral veins, or bleeding from any weakened cerebral arteries. Some of these cerebrovascular accidents could be avoided postpartum if oxytocics were avoided in patients with hypertensive disease in pregnancy. A massive intracerebral hemorrhage may occur in a pregnant woman, especially if she is hypertensive. This condition is managed in the same way in pregnant and nonpregnant women.

Subarachnoid Hemorrhage

When cerebral arterial rupture occurs in pregnancy, the mortality is two to three times that in the nonpregnant woman. The condition may be detected prior to rupture if a careful physical examination is made. Ocular palsies, diplopia, squint, and facial pain due to pressure on the third, fourth, fifth, and sixth cranial nerves may be present. Visual loss and a bitemporal field defect signify pressure on the optic chiasma. Pressure on the optic tract produces homonymous hemianopia. Sudden severe headache with nausea and vomiting follows rupture. The patient may become semicomatose or even comatose. Nuchal rigidity and bilateral positive Babinski signs are present. On spinal tap the cerebrospinal fluid is bloody and under increased pressure.

Cerebral angiography is the best diagnostic means. All four cerebral vessels should be inspected because several aneurysms may be present, and rupture will result in subarachnoid hemorrhage.

With cessation of active hemorrhage, the cerebrospinal fluid gradually clears and the pressure returns to normal in about three weeks. The mortality from the first hemorrhage is about 35 percent, while an additional 15 percent of patients die from a subsequent arterial rupture in the first few weeks. A second rupture after six months is relatively uncommon. In general, the prognosis is poor with cerebral aneurysms but better with bleeding from arteriovenous malformations. The prognosis is best when no lesions are discovered with four-vessel arteriography.

The patient should be kept at rest and exertion should be avoided. Surgical measures designed to trap or obliterate the aneurysm are gaining in popularity, and results are improving. It is difficult to evaluate the results of surgical treatment, however, because patients with the worst prognosis are not candidates for surgery, and the patients who do best after surgery are those whose prognosis would be relatively good in any case. Nevertheless, because of the danger of recurrent bleeding, surgery should be tried if an aneurysm can be identified.

Gastrointestinal Disorders

Ulcerative Colitis

Most authorities consider that therapeutic abortion is medically justified in cases of acute, fulminating, treatment-resistant ulcerative colitis that is exacerbated by pregnancy. In an acute fulminating episode, the patient suddenly develops violent diarrhea, vomiting, cramps, high fever, and profound toxemia. The stools are watery and contain foul fecal matter mixed with mucus, pus, and often gross blood. The diagnosis is confirmed by procto-sigmoidoscopy or colonoscopy. As far as management is concerned:

- There is no specific treatment for ulcerative colitis. Strict bedrest and fluid and electrolyte replacement are the prime features of management. When anemia is severe, transfusion with compatible blood is indicated.
- Diphenoxylate, 2.5–5 mg, orally four times daily, or a combination of deodorized opium tincture (0.6–1.5 ml) and belladonna tincture (0.6 ml) orally every 4 hours are effective in reducing cramps and stool frequency. Anticholinergic drugs and opiates should be given at regular intervals rather than according to the number of stools. In severe cases none of these agents are very effective in controlling the number of bowel movements. Severely ill, toxic patients with a high fever are in danger of perforation of the bowel and should be given antibiotics effective against the intestinal flora. The placement of a gastrointestinal tube is useful for the administration of antibiotics, and suction can be used as necessary. In seriously ill patients, it is worthwhile to give hydrocortisone, 100 mg, intravenously, three times daily. Although not curative, glucocorticoids induce remission in over 60 percent of patients.

Surgery is indicated for ulcerative colitis under the following circumstances: (1) failure to respond to medical measures, (2) progressive abdominal distension with innumerable stools and anemia, (3) massive hemorrhage, (4) colonic obstruction, and (5) suspected carçinoma. The most effective surgical measure is total proctocolectomy with establishment of a permanent ileostomy.

Renal Disease

Acute Glomerulonephritis

An initial attack of acute glomerulonephritis is rare during pregnancy; most obstetric problems relating to glomerulonephritis involve transitional, chronic forms of the disease. Nephritis causes hypertension, predisposes to eclamptogenic toxemia, and contributes to an increase in perinatal mortality and morbidity. The treatment of glomerulonephritis in pregnancy is the same as that in the nonpregnant patient. The disease may be an indication for cesarean section when placental dysmaturity or eclamptogenic toxemia occurs. If azotemia is present in the patient with acute glomerulonephritis, dietary protein is restricted. Sodium and water intake are restricted only when edema or severe hypertension are present. Diuretics such as furosemide are sometimes helpful in the management of marked edema or severe hypertension. Hypertensive encephalopathy may require parenteral therapy with antihypertensive agents, such as methyldopa in a dosage of 250–500 mg four times daily. Approximately 5 percent of patients with acute glomerulonephritis fail to respond to treatment and progress to renal failure, cardiac failure, and death. The presence of the pregnancy in these few patients may be a contributing factor, and so therapeutic abortion should be considered as part of maternal care.

Chronic Glomerulonephritis

Approximately 10 percent of patients with acute glomerulonephritis develop chronic glomerulonephritis, and some of these patients will become pregnant. Although this situation is rare it is very serious. In the presence of retinitis, the fetal mortality rate is almost 100 percent. In about 50 percent of cases, pregnancy leads to permanent deterioration in the condition of the mother. This is one of the very few genuine medical indications for a therapeutic abortion. If a patient elects to continue with her pregnancy, all of these factors must be carefully monitored and she should generally be delivered as soon as the fetus is sufficiently mature to survive.

Nephrosis

In cases of nephrosis, pregnancy does not usually cause progression of the underlying renal disease, and so therapeutic abortion is very rarely indicated.

Pregnancy and Cancer

Pregnancy and cancer rarely coexist, but when they do the emotional effect is very great and deserves special mention. Pregnant patients may develop cancer but more commonly cancer patients become pregnant. In one report of approximately seven hundred cases of cancer in pregnancy the order of frequency of the cancers was breast, leukemia, and lymphomas as a group; melanoma; gynecologic cancer; and bone tumors.[26] With better obstetrical care in the past two decades, deaths from hemorrhage, sepsis, and toxemia, although still the most common causes, have been decreasing; but cancer as a cause of death in the pregnant patient is on the relative increase. Cancer in pregnancy creates three special problems: first, in pregnancy, changes in such structures as the breast may mask the development of an early cancer; second, increased vascularity of the breasts and pelvic organs may contribute to early dissemination of cancers of these organs; and third, malignancies subject to endocrine influences are most suspect for exacerbation with pregnancy.

Breast Cancer

The most common cancer associated with pregnancy is breast cancer, although it occurs only once in approximately three thousand pregnancies. However, pregnancy coexists with breast cancer in approximately one of every thirty-three patients with breast cancer. Whereas the overall five-year survival rates in the U.S. are 40–50 percent in patients treated with radical mastectomy with or without pre- or postoperative X-ray therapy, when the disease is associated with pregnancy or lactation, five-year survival rates vary from 0 to 40 percent. At this time a number of clinical conclusions seem justified:

1. If axillary nodes are not involved, survival is comparable for pregnant and nonpregnant women.
2. More pregnant women have positive axillary nodes at radical mastectomy than do nonpregnant women.
3. When comparing pregnant and nonpregnant groups, there appears to be significantly decreased survival probability among pregnant patients once axillary nodes are positive.
4. There are no data suggesting increased likelihood of cure because of therapeutic abortion, whether nodes are positive or negative. On the other hand, there is evidence to support the view that, if the primary tumor is inoperable, the removal of the uterus and fetus together with the tubes and ovaries as part of an estrogen ablation procedure is worthwhile for palliation. Some suggest that this procedure should also be offered to patients with axillary metastasis; but in this case the hope is for increasing the free interval rather than effecting cure. In these serious life-threatening situations, it is the obstetrician's duty to advise the patient of the information available, and the patient's decision will be tempered by her attitude toward the pregnancy.
5. Although postpartum sterilization or contraception is usually offered to patients with breast cancer, it should be noted that pregnancy subsequent to radical mastectomy does not seem to alter the prognosis, although many people assume that it does. There is general agreement that if the primary treatment fails the patient will eventually die of breast cancer regardless of a simultaneous or subsequent pregnancy. However, if the cancer has been completely removed, there is no good evidence of added risk to the patient because of coexistent or future pregnancies.

Cancer of the Uterine Cervix and Corpus Uteri

Cervical dysplasia and carcinoma *in situ* are diagnosed quite frequently in the course of pregnancy. These patients require careful observation but can be delivered vaginally unless there is an obstetrical indication for cesarean section. They should be followed carefully postpartum and offered a hysterectomy if severe dysplasia or carcinoma *in situ* persist at three months postpartum. Invasive carcinoma of the cervix requires immediate treatment. If it is diagnosed in the first or second trimester, it should be treated without regard for the pregnancy, either by radical surgery or radiotherapy, because it poses a serious threat to the mother's life. If diagnosed in the third trimester, or occasionally in the late second trimester, abdominal delivery by cesarean section may be delayed at the patient's request so that the fetus has adequate maturity.

In general, management of invasive cancer of the cervix during pregnancy is the same as in the nonpregnant patient. In stage I and stage IIA carcinoma of the cervix, radical abdominal hysterectomy with pelvic lymphadenectomy gives excellent recovery rates, and the fetus can be removed from the uterus by classical cesarean section prior to the procedure being performed. For other stages of invasive disease, radiation therapy is generally used. External therapy is usually given up to about 4,000 rads tumor dose to the whole pelvis, and this usually results in radiation placentitis and spontaneous abortion. Thereafter, two radium insertions are usually done to complete the treatment. In the presence of invasive carcinoma of the cervix there is an acute threat to the mother's life and the threat is a real one, and so there should be no delay in treating the patient, although the fetus will often die in the process. Carcinoma of the uterine corpus is extremely rarely complicated by pregnancy; but treatment is on the same lines as for cervical carcinoma, with the patient being advised to have prompt treatment. This is how patients were treated who were given good care prior to liberalization of the abortion laws. What is outlined here is the correct treatment for the mother, and so the passage of a human life amendment will carry no added risk for the mother.

Ovarian Cancer

Ovarian cancer coexists with pregnancy once in approximately fifteen thousand cases. The malignancy is usually present prior to conception and pregnancy has no adverse effect on the course of the malignancy. The management follows the principle of the management of ovarian cancer in the nonpregnant patient. This consists of a total abdominal hysterectomy with removal of both tubes and both ovaries and the omentum. In some very early cases of ovarian cancer affecting only one ovary, or in patients with certain special tumors, it may be possible to remove only the affected tube and ovary and allow the pregnancy to continue. In general, however, the pregnant patient with ovarian cancer should be treated as though she were not pregnant. Again, if the simple principles of good medical care are extended to the patient, a human life amendment will have no adverse effect on maternal health.

Carcinoma of the Vulva

Carcinoma of the vulva is managed in the pregnant patient essentially in the same way as it is managed in the nonpregnant patient. Even patients treated by radical vulvectomy and bilateral groin dissection in early pregnancy may continue with the pregnancy and be delivered vaginally. If there is excessive scarring, cesarean section may be necessary.

Leukemia and Lymphoma

These conditions are treated as in a nonpregnant patient. Pregnancy has no direct effect on the course of leukemia or lymphoma and therapeutic abortion does not affect the patient's prognosis. However, pregnancy is not a reason to delay any application of standard treatment measures to the woman with acute leukemia. Cytotoxic agents form the basis for the treatment of leukemia. Alkylating agents such as myleran, triethylenemelamine, chlorambucil and cyclophosphamide are not particularly harmful to the fetus.[27] In general, the pregnant patient with leukemia should be treated for her disease as though she were not pregnant. For both the mother and the fetus, uncontrolled leukemia is more dangerous than any of the therapeutic agents to be employed in management. Thus, the passage of a human life amendment would not increase the risk to the mother.

Melanoma

The treatment of melanoma in the pregnant woman is essentially the same as in the nonpregnant patient. The general view is that termination of pregnancy is not therapeutic. Recently, Shin and associates,[28] in a review of 251 cases of early-stage melanoma, concluded that although the course of stage I melanoma is not altered by pregnancy, patients with stage II disease have significantly shorter survival if pregnant. Thus, there may be an indication of benefit to the mother of therapeutic abortion in a stage II disease. In any event there is no question that this condition is a serious threat to the mother's life and therapeutic abortion would not be proscribed by the human life amendment should the obstetrician feel that this was in the best interests of the patient as far as treatment of her disease was concerned.

Carcinoma of the Thyroid

Carcinoma of the thyroid gland is rarely seen with pregnancy. Data appear to support the concept that concurrent or subsequent pregnancy does not influence the course of thyroid cancers and that its presence is not an indication for termination of the pregnancy. If isotope studies are considered necessary during the pregnancy, an iodine isotope with a short half-life should be used—such as ^{123}I or ^{132}I, if available, rather than ^{131}I.

Cancer of the Gastrointestinal Tract

Cancers of the gastrointestinal tract are not influenced by pregnancy. The most frequent cancers are of the rectum and colon. In the first and second trimesters the cancer is treated as though the patient were not pregnant. In the third trimester the infant should be delivered by cesarean section and the cancer managed according to the standard treatment technique. Unfortunately, gastrointestinal cancers are not usually diagnosed until late because the pregnant patient is already subject to vomiting, sluggish bowel movements, and hemorrhoids with blood in the stools. Thus, signs and symptoms of cancer are often missed during pregnancy. Therapeutic abortion has no place in the management of gastrointestinal cancer except when the uterus is removed as part of the radical resection.[29]

Tumors of the Central Nervous System

Although there is a general feeling that therapeutic abortion and sterilization should be carried out in patients with brain tumors, there is in fact little support for the idea that these measures affect prognosis. A conservative approach is often feasible, and some neurosurgeons prefer to delay definitive neurological surgery until postpartum because of increased risk to both mother and fetus. However, if there is a rapid increase in intracranial pressure, intervention before then will be required. With regard to delivery, most multiparas are delivered vaginally and most primigravidas are delivered by cesarean section.

In summary, with regard to organic medical complications, pregnancy is an intercurrent, transient condition which rarely poses a significant threat to a woman's life or health in the United States today. However, in addition to diseases which are specific to pregnancy (obstetrical complications), a woman is subject to any of the disorders which may occur in nonpregnant women (medical complications). The health of the fetus is often affected by the disorder, and the treatment necessary for the mother may affect the fetus. On occasions, the treatment necessary to preserve the life of the mother may result in the death of the fetus. In these cases the death of the fetus is a secondary effect of the proper medical management of a mother with a serious disease and would not, therefore, be affected by a human life amendment.

* * *

One problem of which we must be aware is the tendency by some to regard repeated assumptions as facts. For example, it is assumed by many that the Supreme Court decisions of 1973 have contributed significantly to lowering the maternal death rate in this country. As already mentioned, I submit that there is no evidence for this. Indeed, when each five-year period is considered, there was a smaller fall from 1973 through 1977 (from 15.2 per 100,000 live births to 11.2 per 100,000 live births)[30] than there was

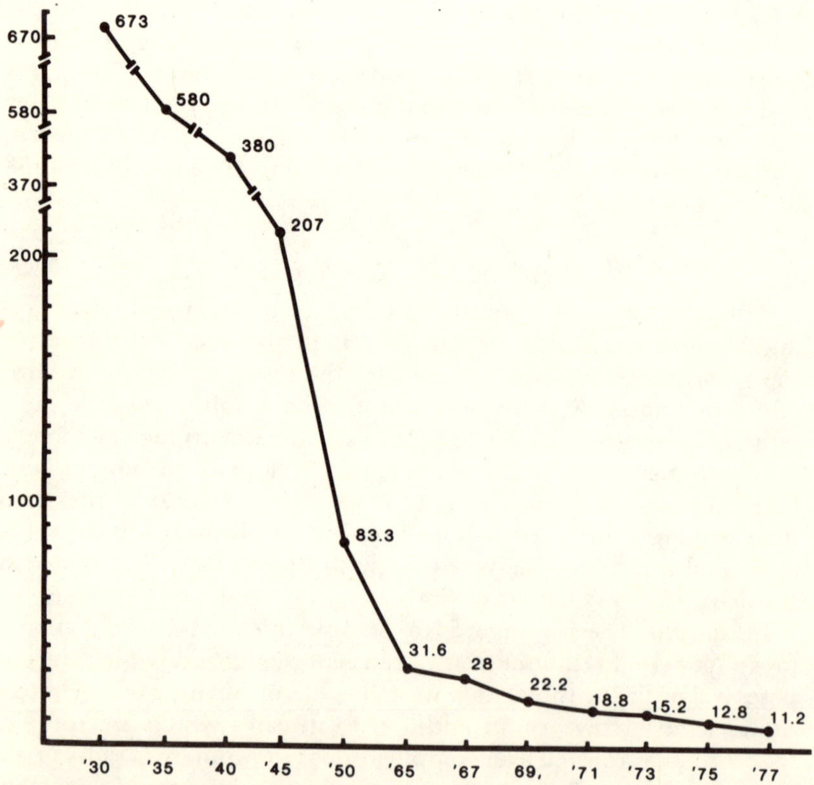

Fig. 1. Maternal deaths per 100,000 live births in the United States, 1930–77.

from 1969 through 1973 (22.2 per 100,000 live births to 15.2 per 100,000 live births) (fig. 1).

Another example of this phenomenon is the assumption that, when federal funds for abortion were restricted in August 1977, abortion morbidity and mortality would rise. According to the Center for Disease Control, morbidity and mortality did not increase.[31] Data on women coming to obstetric acute-care facilities were collected from twenty-four institutions located in the District of Columbia and thirteen states across the country from October 10, 1977, through June 10, 1978. Ten institutions were located in states in which legal abortions might be less available because of the absence of public funds, and fourteen were in states which were continuing to use state funds to finance Medicaid abortions. Out of the 3,157 abortion complications reported through this hospital surveillance project, seven occurred after admitted illegally induced procedures. In three other instances in which complications occurred the women did not name the cause of the abortion. For analytic purposes it was assumed that these women also underwent an illegal or self-induced abortion. None of these ten complications occurred in women reported to be a Medicaid recipient. No abortion deaths related to either illegal or legal abortions were detected through the hospital surveillance study. There was also no significant difference between the institutions in funded and nonfunded states or in the proportion of Medicaid women with abortion complications over the eight-month period. These examples show how important it will be for legislators to scrutinize the data presented—because, unfortunately, some "experts" use statistics much as drunken men use lamp-posts: for support rather than illumination.

* * *

Looking at the abortion situation from the point of view of an obstetrician-gynecologist, I feel that the following steps should be taken:

1. A human life amendment which affords protection to the unborn without significant danger to the life or health of the mother should be voted on in the Congress as soon as possible.
2. The human life amendment proposed must be one which will ensure the broad base of support required to obtain a two-thirds majority in both houses of Congress and ratification by three-quarters (38) of the state legislatures. Thus, it must be the most medically defensible amendment which we can devise. Either the NRLC or Hatch Federalism amendment would be most likely to succeed from a medical point of view.

The aim of a human life amendment is to nullify the effect of the ill-conceived Supreme Court decision of January 1973. The arguments that a human life amendment will lead to charges of murder being brought against users of DES, the oral contraceptives, the "minipill," and even the IUD are preposterous, because no charge of illegal abortion could be brought unless the patient could be *proven* to be pregnant at the time of use.[32] Even the most sensitive pregnancy tests are not 100 percent accurate, and even the most recently devised serum pregnancy tests are not positive until the ninth day after fertilization, at which time the conceptus is implanted in the endometrial lining of the uterus.[33] In any event, there certainly will be no *corpus delicti.* These facts are surely known to physicians opposing a human life amendment. Thus, it seems fair to assume that by failing to mention them they hope to undermine support for a human life amendment among the millions of Americans who believe that conception is synonymous with implantation rather than fertilization, and to whom the use of these contraceptive agents is therefore morally acceptable. I personally believe that human life begins with the formation of the unique genetic package at fertilization. However, there is great disagreement on the percentage of fertilized ova lost spontaneously, with some such as Hilgers[34] placing the loss at 1 to 3 percent and others such as Boué placing it at 85 percent.[35] Implantation is certainly the first firm rung in the ladder of life. After all, as some have argued despite the best efforts of Steptoe and Edwards, the "fertilized ovum" now known as Louise Brown could not have gone much further in a test tube. Certainly, once the "fertilized ovum" has reached the blastocyst stage and become implanted in the uterine wall, its presence is legally verifiable and—given good fortune, nutrition, and time—it will become as one of us.

While the view that a decision on abortion should be left to the woman and her doctor is being strongly advocated by the American Medical Association and the American College of Obstetricians and Gynecologists, I feel that the "track record" of physicians in this area leaves much to be desired. Lest I be acccused of bias in this statement I will again use an example given by the well-known abortion advocate Dr. Robert Hall.[36] On September 1, 1955, a therapeutic abortion board was formed at the Sloane Hospital for Women in New York. At that time this teaching hospital of Columbia University College of Physicians and Surgeons was felt to be one of the most academically outstanding and best-run hospitals in the United States. Prior to this date, the mechanism had been based on the now-much-touted idea that the therapeutic "abortion decision should be left to the woman and her doctor," but with the additional precaution of approval by the chief-of-service. It was found that the abortion rate was higher among the private patients than among the ward patients, despite the fact that there were more high-risk obstetrical patients among the poor. Thus, closer supervision was undertaken from September 1, 1955. From that date a three-member board composed of a senior obstetrician, an internist, and a psychiatrist reviewed all abortion applications. The effect of more careful evaluation was to reduce the therapeutic abortion/delivery ratio from 1 in 69 to 1 in 225, even though psychiatric indications continued to be included. It will be noted from table 3 that, even after this change in supervisory approval, abortions were performed four times more frequently on the private service than on the ward service. This suggests that the rules were still being "bent" more frequently when payment for the abortion was involved. In data collected by Hall[37] from sixty outstanding American hospitals, the same pattern was evident, with the abortion/delivery ratio being 3.6 times higher among private patients than among ward patients. The situation in this respect has certainly not improved in 1981; so, unless the life of the fetus is to be taken with impunity, the decision should *not* be left up to the two people under most pressure—namely, the woman and her doctor.

In 1973, the Supreme Court decided that it was *not* necessary to "resolve the difficult question of when life begins." The result has been a fetal holocaust in the interest of social convenience. This fact alone supports the view that it is imperative for Congress and the states to consider passage of a human life amendment at this time.

Chapter Seven

THE MEDICAL ASPECTS OF BIRTH CONTROL

James D. Madden

Relatively efficient, problem-free, and reversible contraception is only a few decades old, and anyone familiar with contemporary contraception would acknowledge that all methods and agents used for contraception have disadvantages—some significant. Contraception has cost more than a few women their lives, although contraception advocates are quick to point out that the deaths due to contraception are far fewer than would be expected as a consequence of maternal mortality in unrestrained reproduction. It would seem that, for the first time in the history of womankind, biology is no longer determining destiny in that relatively effective and safe contraception is available. Large numbers of women in the United States have chosen—for a variety of reasons—to circumvent by artificial means, temporarily or permanently, the natural reproductive mechanisms. They have chosen in general not to use natural methods such as lactation. Using contemporary contraception, they become pregnant only if and when they choose. This emancipation of the human female is unprecedented, being enjoyed by women in general, and will likely not be relinquished. The risks of using contraception appear to be small, particularly when compared with more dangerous everyday activities such as driving an automobile.[1] It would be an unfortunate irony if legislation against contraception led to an increase in overt abortion within or outside the law.

The human is perhaps the most infertile of all species. Unlike most mammals, the human female does not experience "heat," thereby conveying to the male that she is at a "fertile time." Nor is ovulation induced by intercourse as in some other mammals. Moreover, there are no artificial or natural selection pressures which would tend to "eliminate" human females and males who are poor breeders. In the only prospective study of its kind, Miller found the incidence of early spontaneous abortion in the human female to be 42 percent.[2] This is likely a considerable underestimate of early fetal wastage, since the design of the study

James D. Madden, M.D., is clinical associate professor of obstetrics and gynecology, University of Texas Health Science Center, Southwestern Medical School, Dallas. He is author of numerous medical papers.

allowed detection of pregnancy only after implantation. Those human blastocysts that never achieved implantation during the week following fertilization would have gone undetected in the study. It should not be surprising that even subtle environmental influences such as tobacco smoking and moderate alcohol intake are known to lead to an increased incidence of spontaneous abortion.[3]

Ovulation is the process whereby an ovum matures and is released from the ovary. This maturation and release is controlled by hormones originating in the brain (hypothalamus and pituitary). The ovum is retrieved by the oviduct. Within the oviduct, the ovum is nourished until fertilization by a sperm occurs. The conceptus remains in the oviduct for two to three days, apparently for maturation, and then the early pregnancy moves on to the uterine cavity. Now the human blastocyst (consisting of about one hundred cells) floats freely in the uterine cavity for nearly four days before beginning to implant in the uterine lining (endometrium). The endometrium has been prepared for this event by postovulatory hormone secretions from the ovary (corpus luteum). The implanting blastocyst produces and secretes into the maternal bloodstream a hormonal signal (human chorionic gonadotropin—HCG) that notifies the mother's body that a pregnancy has occurred. The appearance of this hormone will cause the mother's ovary to continue to produce hormones (progesterone, estrogen) to sustain the pregnancy for the first six weeks. Thereafter a fetal tissue, the placenta, will supply these hormones. HCG can be detected in the pregnant woman's blood eight days after ovulation. The detection of HCG in a woman's blood or urine is the basis for all pregnancy tests.

From purely biological considerations it is reasonable to assume that human life begins with the fertilization of a human egg by a human sperm. It does remain conjectural, in my estimation, at what point in the multifaceted subcellular process of fertilization human life may be considered to have begun. In recent times, by medical convention the term "contraception" has come to mean any device or method that interferes with biological events that would otherwise eventuate in pregnancy perceived by the mother or physician. This would, of course, include all those permanent or temporary manipulations of the male or female reproductive systems which actually prevent conception *and* those prohibiting implantation of the blastocyst or leading to its early demise.

Legislation that aims to protect human life must be specific regarding the stage of human life it seeks to protect. The following is a summary of the presumed modes of action of various methods of contraception. What impact a human life amendment would have on various methods of contraception currently in use will in general be self-evident. A caution at this point is appropriate, however. In many instances the efficacy of a contraceptive method depends on its capacity to interfere with reproductive efficiency at more than one site. I will attempt to specify the primary mode of action of such contraceptives, but it is important to state first that knowledge of molecular mechanisms in reproduction is not complete. Additionally, or consequently, the mechanisms of action of contraceptives are not fully understood.

An argument (at least theoretical) can be made to support almost any position in the controversy over how various contraceptive methods exert their effects. For example, while all would agree that total sexual abstinence is truly contraceptive, it has been argued that *periodic* sexual abstinence (rhythm) may lead to increased frequency of spontaneous abortion[4] and congenital malformation[5] due to fertilization by "aging sperm" or fertilization of "overripe eggs." There is by no means compelling evidence that this is true, but on the other hand it cannot be determined for certain that there is no such risk.

More certain is that vasectomy, tubal ligation, and coitus interruptus are truly contraceptive. The same may probably be said of the barrier methods (condom, diaphragm, and cervical cap) in that they also mechanically interfere with the joining of sperm to ovum. However, spermicidal agents are typically used in conjunction with the abovementioned barrier methods. These agents are chemicals designed to arrest the metabolism of spermatozoa while they are still in the vagina. In a recent study the use of these agents has been implicated as causing an increase in spontaneous abortion and certain congenital malformations and fetal neoplasms.[6] Overall, the frequency of congenital disorders was 2.2 percent for the group using spermicidal foam, jelly, and cream and 1 percent for the control population. This is a small difference; but as the study was well designed and involved a large sample (4,772 pregnant women), the results are statistically significant. Still, whether these abnormalities are induced by alterations in the sperm, ovum, or embryo is unknown and the authors of the study state that their results should be considered tentative until confirmed by other data.

Ovulation (the release of an egg from the ovary) is dependent on the production and highly orchestrated release of hormone signals originating in centers (hypothalamus and pituitary) in the brain. The principal mode of action of the classical oral contraceptives (combination of synthetic estrogen and progestin) is to suppress production and release of these signals.[7] During the years since the oral contraceptive was first marketed (in 1970), it has become apparent that reducing the estrogen and progestin content by as much as 65 and 90 percent respectively does not lead to an appreciable increase in contraceptive failure rate. Lowering the dose of these hormones has been laudable from a medical standpoint, as it appears to reduce side effects and health risks. For example, it is thought that the incidence of deep-vein thrombosis in the leg is reduced by about 25 percent when 50 μgm of synthetic estrogen formulations are used instead of higher doses.[8] This is important, since deep-vein thrombosis could lead to a pulmonary embolism, a potentially lethal consequence.

Although the frequency of ovulation is uncertain when these lower dose preparations are used,[9] it is likely that the lower (and safer) the dose of hormone, the greater the likelihood that secondary contraceptive effects of the pill must be relied on for pregnancy prevention.

The minipill, an oral preparation containing a progestin only, is used for contraception by a very small number of women in this country. This is primarily because of a higher contraceptive failure rate in addition to a very high incidence of abnormal bleeding. Three brands of minipill in the market (Micronor, Nor Q-D, Ovrette) have U.S. Food and Drug Administration approval. Contraception appears to depend on a combination of mechanisms which vary according to the particular progestin, dosage, and user.[10] Unlike combined estrogen-progestin contraceptives, which almost always prevent ovulation, minipills apparently inhibit ovulation in only 15 to 40 percent of cycles. Likely, they interfere with ovulation in a manner identical to what was described for the classical oral contraceptive. Progestin alters the function of the oviduct in that ovum transport through the oviducts may be accelerated, thereby reducing the likelihood of fertilization or depriving a fertilized ovum sufficient time to develop for implantation. Also, a normally functioning corpus luteum may fail to develop from the ovarian follicle after ovulation. This would preclude hormonal maintenance of the early pregnancy. Midcycle thinning and other changes in cervical mucus, which are present in an untreated cycle and facilitate the passage of sperm to the vagina and on to the uterine cavity, do not occur in women taking the minipill. Further, there are conspicuous histologic changes in the endometrium which are presumed detrimental to blastocyst survival and implantation.

During the 1960s there was a resurgence of interest in the use of intrauterine contraceptive devices (IUDs) for control of reproduction. Polyethylene devices of many configurations were developed which contained small amounts of barium sulfate to render them radiopaque. More recently, medications (such as copper and progesterone) have been added to improve contraceptive efficiency and decrease adverse effects. Currently marketed in the United States are the Lippes Loop, Saf-T-Coil, Cu 7, and Progestasert. The U.S. Food and Drug Administration report of 1978[11] summarizes the current status of the IUD from a medical standpoint as follows:

> Currently marketed IUD's have a net pregnancy rate of approximately one to six per one hundred women users at the end of the first year. Expulsion rates are reported to range from four to eighteen, and removals for medical reasons due to adverse side effects twelve to sixteen at the end of one year. . . .
>
> In general, morbidity and mortality rates associated with the use of IUD's remain low. In the United States, the current mortality rate is estimated to be somewhere between one to ten deaths per million woman-years of use. Furthermore, IUD's are believed to be associated with a higher morbidity rate but a lower mortality rate than oral contraceptives.
>
> While IUD's are considered to be generally safe and effective, increased risks of spontaneous abortion, septic midsemester abortion, and premature delivery pose potential problems in the face of a low but persistent pregnancy rate. Moreover, there is continued and growing concern about the problem of infection resulting from the use of the intrauterine contraceptive device and its possible effects on future fertility particularly among the nulligravid.

The numerous cellular and biochemical alterations induced in the endometrium by the IUD are believed to be responsible for the contraceptive effect. All devices stimulate an inflammatory or foreign-body reaction within the uterus. After IUD insertion, numerous polymorphonuclear leukocytes (white blood cells) appear in the endometrium and uterine fluids, followed by foreign-body giant cells and macrophages. These cells may literally engulf or consume the spermatozoa or the fertilized ovum by the process of phagocytosis. Medicated IUD's (using copper and progesterone) further alter the metabolism of the endometrial cell, thereby decreasing the likelihood of successful blastocyst implantation. Some studies have shown transient increases of human chorionic gonadotropin in the blood of women wearing an IUD.[12] However, the best studies to date suggest that implantation never progresses to the stage where fetal human chorionic gonadotropin production can be detected.[13] There is no evidence that IUDs (even those containing progesterone) interfere with ovulation.

Whether the IUD consistently prevents sperm from reaching the site of fertilization remains under question, although sperm have been found in both the oviducts and uteruses of women wearing IUDs.[14] However, apparently IUDs at least reduce the number of sperm reaching the site of fertilization. (The IUD string, attached to aid in removal, often creates inflammation in the cervix and may thereby also limit sperm movement through the female reproductive tract.)

In 1978 the U.S. Food and Drug Administration concluded that "IUD's are generally safe, effective, and a useful form of birth control."[15] That statement is essentially accurate, and it is reasonable to speculate that IUDs will continue to be used as contraceptives in this country, subject to some controls. For example, removal from the market of IUDs with configurations most prone to medical complications can be expected, as well as advisories discouraging their use particularly by women who have never reproduced.

Diethylstilbestrol (DES), an estrogen compound, is the prototype of a class of agents which have been called "interceptives," since their principal mode of action appears to be interference with implantation.[16] The mechanism of action remains unclear. Estrogens neither interfere with ovulation or fertilization nor interrupt an implantation that has been established prior to estrogen contact. Modification of tubal transport of eggs, alteration of tubal or uterine environment, and/or interference with post-ovulation ovarian hormone production are possible modes of action, but most remarkable are the dramatic changes in the architecture and secretions of the endometrium that make it inhospitable to a blastocyst attempting implantation. DES is dangerous, however. The FDA considers the use of that agent for contraceptive purposes to be safe only as an emergency measure and explicitly warns against its use as a routine contraceptive.

Prostaglandins will likely be used in the future for pregnancy prevention. The exact mode of action will depend on the time of the cycle in which the drug is administered. Prostaglandins are readily absorbed from the vagina and successfully induce menstruation within a few days after the first missed menstrual period. The side effects of these agents (vomiting and diarrhea) have minimized use to date.

Chapter Eight

FERTILITY CONTROL

Dennis J. Horan

In its June 1974 report to the NRLC Board, the legal committee tasked with drafting the Garn Amendment stressed that to overcome the burden of *Roe v. Wade*[1] a human life amendment must: (1) define the word "person" in the 5th and 14th amendments to include the unborn; (2) prohibit, by reaching private action, the private performance of abortion; (3) contain an exception to allow medical procedures which were necessary to save the life of the mother but which might also be classified as abortions; and (4) allow both Congress and the states to enforce the amendment through appropriate legislation.

The third provision was the most controversial and has continued to spark controversy among right-to-life advocates to the present. The legal committee's intent was to create the strongest possible amendment. By allowing only one exception for a narrowly limited circumstance, the committee was of the opinion that the amendment foreclosed the courts from adding further exceptions by way of judicial interpretation. An amendment without exceptions, which was assumed to allow by judicial interpretation the same such medical procedures, was felt to present an open invitation to the courts to create other exceptions. An amendment with one narrowly stated exception was thus considered to be stronger than an amendment with no stated exception at all.

Further, the committee stressed that any amendment will need state and federal legislative support. This is so because the United States Constitution, even when it contains provisions that restrict private conduct, is not a criminal code or a regulatory statute. Even when the specific provision involved is self-executing, the Constitution prohibits but does not punish. Without the necessary state or federal legislation, the broad public policy that the Constitution announces may remain simply that—a hortatory expression of goals to be achieved. This additional point is central to the discussion of the proposed Garn Amendment that follows.

Dennis J. Horan, J.D., is chairman, Americans United for Life. He is past chairman, American Bar Association Committee on Medicine and Law. He is a coeditor of DEATH, DYING AND EUTHANASIA (1977), NEW PERSPECTIVES ON HUMAN ABORTION (1981), and INFANTICIDE AND THE HANDICAPPED NEWBORN (1982).

Section 1 of the Garn Amendment makes the unborn a person for purposes of the 5th and 14th amendments of the Constitution. What effect would the personhood of the unborn have on current fertility practices? In and of itself, it would have little or no effect other than to authorize supportive legislation under the enforcement clause that could prohibit the manufacture and sale of abortifacients—that is, drugs and devices that clearly cause fetal death. The amendment would not ban, but would make "bannable," those drugs and devices.

A constitutional amendment is not a criminal statute; a practice that is contrary to the intent or spirit of an amendment does not become a crime simply by virtue of the existence of the amendment. Criminal statutes and regulatory controls must be *separately* enacted through state and federal legislatures. The Garn Amendment in and of itself would not criminalize private fertility control practice, whether abortive or contraceptive. In the absence of criminal and regulatory legislation, performance of an abortion and the production or use of abortifacients would be as immune from punitive state action the day after the Garn Amendment became effective as the day before.

Purely contraceptive practices—meaning those drugs and devices that act as pure contraceptives by preventing the union of sperm and ovum but not causing fetal death—would not and could not be banned by this or any other section of the amendment. This is so because the Supreme Court's holdings recognizing a constitutional right to practice contraception, beginning with *Griswold v. Connecticut*[2] and continuing through *Eisenstadt v. Baird,*[3] would not be changed by this amendment, which affects only *Roe v. Wade,*[4] *Doe v. Bolton,*[5] and their progeny. The purpose of the right-to-life movement is to save unborn lives from destruction. Contraceptive practices become of interest to the movement only where they also entail fetal destruction.

Nor can it be presumed that the proposed amendment would, by its own force, result necessarily in enactment of state criminal or regulatory legislation that would proscribe conduct that is known to cause fetal death. Receptive legislatures would pass such legislation but others would need right-to-life prodding and, thereafter, constant surveillance. Even if some criminal and regulatory antiabortion legislation would arise from legislative action, it does not follow that such legislation would necessarily affect the use, much less the production or sale, of abortifacient fertility control drugs and devices.

If a state chose to treat abortion within the homicide code by defining the "individual" subject to various forms of homicidal conduct to include the human fetus—thereby removing any inference that the state may have denied the unborn child equal protection of criminal law with respect to his or her right to life—it would still be necessary to show that a person charged with homicidal conduct caused the death of a certain human being in a certain manner with a statutorily requisite state of mind in order to convict the person of the crime. In view of this, it is difficult to see how anyone could reasonably be charged with, much less convicted of, any form of criminal homicide for using drugs and devices that might act by discouraging implantation of a fertilized ovum in the uterus. The prior existence and death of such a fertilized ovum could not be proved since it would be difficult, if not impossible, to prove a causal connection between the death of a specific fertilized ovum and the use of the anti-implantant drug or device. Since most (if not all) alleged anti-implantants have contraceptive effects as well, and are used for that purpose, it would be nearly impossible to prove that the individual charged with the crime had the "evil" state of mind necessary to prove that death of a fertilized ovum was intended or even within the contemplation of the individual charged with the crime. Nor would reckless disregard for the outcome support the requisite intent without proof of the demise of a specific victim.

Similar observations are valid to a somewhat lesser degree with regard to the use of drugs or devices that cause fetal death after implantation (abortifacients), at least when they are employed without prior knowledge that the woman is pregnant. The prior existence and death of the fetus, a causal connection between the use of a particular drug or device and fetal death, and the state of mind of an individual who used a drug or device with any use other than to cause fetal death would be difficult and, in most cases, impossible to prove.

Thus, even in a situation where there is perfect symmetry in the protection that the criminal law provides the human fetus and born human beings, it is highly improbable that *use* of anti-implantants and early abortifacients would be subject to any effective control by any homicide law mandated by the Garn Amendment.

It must be concluded, therefore, that the *use* of fertility control drugs and devices that might, arguably, prevent implantation or that cause early abortion would not be proscribed by any homicide law generated solely by virtue of the recognition of "personhood" of the unborn for purposes of equal protection. Whether or not such drugs or devices are to be subject to any other criminal law will almost certainly be totally a matter of the discretion of the various legislatures.

Nor does it follow that, because there exist statutes against homicide, the production or sale of the instruments of homicide become illegal. A law forbidding murder does not, by reason of that prohibition, ban handguns in the streets or knives in the kitchen. Legislative action specifically to control the manufacture and distribution of abortifacients and anti-implantants would be necessary in order to forbid such drugs and devices from entering the chain of commerce.

Section 2 of the Garn Amendment provides: "No unborn person shall be deprived of life by any person." A specific "life of the mother" exception, permitting laws that allow abortions to be performed when necessary to prevent maternal death, is appended to this general prohibition.

This section is intended to reach both "private" and "public" abortions—abortions performed with and without governmental assistance or participation. Its language tracks the already existing prohibition against deprivation of life found in the 5th and 14th amendments. The word "deprived" has caused no jurisprudential confusion in the past. It refers to a deliberate act of killing. It does not include fetal death caused by auto accidents or budget reduction in maternal care programs. Nor was it intended in June 1974 that the mere existence of a personhood human life amendment including this private action section would support private injunctive or damage actions when the amendment was violated.[6] In June 1974, *Bivens v. Six Unknown Named Agents* and its progeny were not well understood; and the legal committee of the NRLC did not intend that an important section of the Garn Amendment depend on *Bivens* for its vitality, although it might unwittingly authorize such a conclusion.

Bivens and its progeny, which helped create the cause of action based directly on the Constitution, seem to be limited to correcting abuses or wrongs by federal officials which cause deprivation of constitutional rights. In other words, this new cause of action, based on *Bivens,* seems to be limited to playing the same role against federal officials as the Civil Rights Act plays against state officials.[7] This is so because the Bill of Rights, generally speaking, applies against the federal government. *Bivens, David v. Passman,* and their progeny, however, would support wholly private actions by one citizen against another without involving the intertwined activities of a federal official when based on an amendment that clearly reaches private action, as does the Garn Amendment. Therefore, the possibility of right-to-life advocates enforcing the amendment through private litigation exists, but there is little precedent for guidance. Additionally, an unreceptive judiciary makes the legislative solutions preferable. Where legislatures will not act, then private action may be the only viable alternative.

There is a strong difference, nevertheless, between what the committee intended in its draft and what it may have unwittingly authorized. The committee intended to make it absolutely clear that *legislation* passed pursuant to this amendment could prohibit private persons from procuring abortions. If private actions are brought in addition, so much the better. The committee, however, did not intend that under Section 2 someone with a grievance against the tobacco industry could seek injunctive relief against the manufacture of cigarettes because smoking them might, in some rare cases, cause harm or even death to an unborn child. Prudence in the drive for goals seems warranted.

Moreover, Section 2 standing alone would not directly affect contraceptive practices. Nor would it even if those fertility control practices carried with them incidental acts of fetal death. As we previously concluded with regard to Section 1, state or federal legislation would be necessary.

The phrase "no unborn child" in Section 2 of the Garn Amendment would almost certainly be interpreted by legislators to permit the section to apply through state criminal legislation only when an unborn child is known to be in existence. When no identifiable individual unborn child can be said to certainly exist or to have existed—as in cases involving the use of anti-implantants and many early abortifacients—Section 2 legislation could not be invoked as a homicide sanction because it could not be shown that any person has extinguished or threatens to extinguish a life in being. However, regulatory legislation directly aimed at the production and licensing of contraceptives which are also abortifacients would be appropriate under this section.

Specific legislation by the appropriate legislative body, carefully drawn, would be necessary to carve out and extinguish those fertility control practices that are known to cause fetal death from contraceptive practices that do not.

Because the Garn Amendment makes the unborn child a "person" from fertilization and explicitly prohibits any person from depriving an unborn person of life, the amendment clearly permits state and federal governments to enact criminal and regulatory legislation intended to protect unborn life throughout all of pregnancy. The amendment would authorize legislation that prohibits and penalizes, either civilly or criminally, the performance or the attempted performance of any procedure intended to cause the death of an unborn child known to exist at the time the procedure is performed.[8]

Certainly, therefore, anyone who uses any drug, device, or object—whether a curette, a suppository, a fist, or a pill—to cause the death of an unborn child in existence could be penalized by law. Moreover, the state might legitimately choose to regulate or to proscribe any drug or device with abortifacient or anti-implantant effects (whether an IUD, a pill, or a prostaglandin suppository) on the same basis as it might choose to ban handguns or regulate automobile manufacturing to assure passenger safety: to protect the lives of human persons subject to its jurisdiction from the potential effects of the use or abuse of certain products.

There are, however, legal and public policy limitations on the state's power to regulate potentially anti-implantant and abortifacient products. First, the Garn Amendment does not purport to affect the fundamental right to prevent conception. Thus, any regulatory scheme that in any sense burdens or infringes on the right to practice contraception would still need to be justified by a compelling state interest and to be narrowly drawn only to protect that interest. A compelling interest in the protection of prenatal life would exist under the amendment. However, any regulatory scheme must be drawn to avoid infringing on the right to contracept. Thus, the regulation must very carefully sort out the abortifacient or anti-implantant element in any fertility control drug or device and eliminate only that aspect, or provide for an almost equal alternative. This would be most difficult.[9]

Second, any attempt to ban or regulate the use of a specific multifunction fertility-control product would be subject to criticism based on the fact that other products not intended to control fertility, but nevertheless also potentially abortifacient or anti-implantant, were not banned or regulated. If it is made a crime, for example, to prescribe certain birth control pills or IUDs on account of their potential anti-implantant effects, why would it not also be a crime, some might argue, to sell alcoholic beverages or tobacco, which are potential abortifacients, to pregnant or potentially pregnant women? A difficult problem in drafting any such legislation would be in distinguishing the degree to which a contraceptive or other effect of a product predominates over an unintended, but statistically possible, anti-implantant or abortifacient effect. When and under what conditions should a contraceptive product, which may also have abortifacient effects, be banned or regulated? When does prudence in service to the unborn dictate caution?

In the case of the IUD, it might be argued that a specific prohibition is justified because the IUD is manufactured with intent to produce an anti-implantant effect in order to accomplish its intended purpose; its anti-implantant effect is not merely a by-product of its intended purpose. On the same ground, regulation or prohibition of the production and sale of some other multifunction fertility control drugs and devices would be appropriate. Certainly, in the case of single-function products, as the prostaglandin suppository appears to be, such controls would seem to be absolutely necessary. It is, however, important to clarify what the public policy goal of regulation of multifunction fertility control and other multifunction drugs or devices might be. A discussion of anti-abortifacient or anti-implantant effects of such products—based on consideration of whether or not these effects are primary, secondary, or included in the normal, customary, and intended use for which the product is manufactured—can be seen by the public as directed at deciding if the product can be used without "evil" intent or is somehow evil in itself. These are issues that go far beyond customary public policy alternatives. Such considerations may be useful in determining the ethical character or legal intent of conduct that contemplates the use of such products, but they bear no necessary relationship to the number of unborn lives lost through their use. A public policy directed at minimizing the number of unborn lives lost, rather than at simply imposing legal sanctions on certain drugs or devices perceived by some to be manufactured or prescribed with evil intent, would not be concerned solely, or even primarily, with regulation of multipurpose fertility control products. Additionally, the extreme care that must be taken in drafting such legislation in order to prevent it from falling before the scythe of the fundamental right to contracept would make the task of the legislature doubly difficult and complex.

In sum, with passage of either the Garn or NRLC amendment, the various legislatures would certainly have the authority to proscribe conduct intended to cause fetal death regardless of the instrument used to achieve that end. The various legislatures would also have the power to proscribe or to regulate the production, sale, and prescription of single and multifunction fertility control products, as well as to proscribe and to regulate all other nonfertility control products that have abortifacient or anti-implantant effects. Development of a consistent public policy on the manner in which and the extent to which such products should be regulated, however, runs directly into another public policy that provides a fundamental right to use contraceptives. It would therefore, upon passage of either the Garn or NRLC amendments, fall to the several legislatures the careful and complex weighing of these potentially opposing policies in the balance.

Chapter Nine

PREGNANCY DUE TO RAPE AND INCEST

Basile J. Uddo

Rape! The very word conjures up the most frightening images of violence and personal violation. It underscores the physical vulnerability of women and the perverseness to which an admixture of sex and violence can be carried. Rape leaves deep, often long-lasting scars on the body and the mind of the victim—scars that have often been exacerbated by the culture in which the victim lives and by the people and institutions to which she turns. Rape, an age-old violation frightening in all its aspects and growing in its frequency, has imported its ugliness into the already dismal abortion debate—because, among the debilitating fears associated with rape, pregnancy ranks among the highest.[1]

To make the problems even worse, rape is inextricable from a historical interspersion of racism. Susan Brownmiller has aptly described this complicating relationship:

> No single event ticks off America's political schizophrenia with greater certainty than the case of a black man accused of raping a white woman. Facts are irrelevant to the public imagination. Objectivity is thrown out the window. A maze of angled mirrors buried deep within the individual psyche rises to confront the perceiver and distort the vision. What is the truth? Upon hearing the bare outlines of such a case—no, upon merely learning the race of the defendant and victim—a convulsive reaction sets in. Part of the public screams guilty while another part, equally vociferous, equally certain, screams innocent, a frame-up. Racism and sexism and the fight against both converge at the point of interracial rape, the baffling crossroads of an authentic, peculiarly American dilemma.[2]

As if rape alone were not emotional and complex enough, every discussion of rape must contend also with the reality of racism.

Incest, by comparison, is a topic less widely discussed and somewhat beyond the immediate attention of the general public. But rather than interpreting this as an indication that incest is less frightening, emotional, or repulsive, it is more likely an indication that it is so frightening, emotional, and repulsive that people cannot bring themselves to face it and discuss it. One of the oldest

Basile J. Uddo, J.D., is Associate Professor of Law, Loyola University School of Law, New Orleans.

and most rigid taboos, incest touches upon all of the same raw nerves as rape, and then some. For, in addition to the violation of the victim, there is the incomprehensible awareness that the perpetrator is not some stranger lurking in the shadows, but a relative, most often a father, whom our culture perceives and promotes as the protector and defender of his children. In incest, that image, most often true, is turned inside out and the protector becomes the abuser.

Again, adding the possibility of pregnancy to all of the emotional, psychological, and physical harm that incest can cause, the intensity of emotion becomes overwhelming, especially in light of the popular notion that children of incestuous relationships are likely to be mentally or physically defective.[3] Consequently, it must be admitted that, if abortion is the most emotion-charged issue of our time, the response to rape- or incest-induced pregnancies is a very close second.

Similarly, it must be admitted that whatever consensus exists in opposition to abortion rapidly dissipates in the face of the question of rape and incest exceptions to any anti-abortion legislation.[4] Even among those who identify themselves as right-to-life advocates, rape and incest cause consternation. In fact, several generally right-to-life moralists become concerned and accommodating when the pregnancy in question is rape or incest induced.[5] It seems evident, however, that much of the controversy over rape and incest exceptions stems from misinformation and exaggerated fears of pregnancy. Ignorance about fertility patterns and factors influencing the possibility of conception, along with pro-choice rhetoric, have created a baseless fear that pregnancy is far more likely than in fact it is.[6]

This chapter is intended to correct some of the misconceptions and to put the issue in proper perspective. To do this, the nature of the problem of rape/incest-induced pregnancies is examined, as are the possible responses to that problem—including legal abortion. Finally, the effect of the proposed wording of the Garn and NRLC amendments on treatment of rape and incest, and resulting pregnancies, is assessed.

The interworkings of either the Garn or NRLC amendment and the issues of rape and incest raise two separate and distinct problems. Usually, when discussions of rape and incest exceptions are raised, the reference is to an explicit recognition that surgical abortion would be legally permitted to terminate an already established pregnancy that resulted from rape or incest. Such proposals tend to be bold admissions that as a matter of public policy the children of rape or incest should not enjoy the protection that would be afforded other unborn children. Typically, the proposal is less grounded in theory—despite occasional attempts to rationalize the pregnancies of rape and incest as continuing aggression—than in utility, the utility being the easy destruction of a growing reminder of an unpleasant, probably repulsive, experience.

Oddly enough, the rape/incest exception is often referred to as the ethical or humanitarian basis for permitting abortion. As one writer explains it:

> Where there is no doubt that rape has occurred consensus of opinion is that termination should be performed, both to save the mother the long months of animosity to her growing fetus, and to save the baby from being born only to find itself abhorrent as a constant reminder of its conception and of its father.[7]

This statement is typical of the candor that generally prohibits proponents of rape/incest exceptions from masking the "need" for abortion in medical or physical terms.

The second and distinct problem raised by rape and incest vis-à-vis a human life amendment is the more immediate crisis treatment that rape/incest victims receive. Here the treatment is generally chemical, as with the so-called morning-after pill, though occasionally surgical, as with a "preventative" D&C or menstrual extraction.[8] In most cases the treatment occurs without a confirmation of pregnancy, primarily because time would not allow a reliable pregnancy test. Obviously, the mode of action of these various treatments must be known before a determination can be made as to the effect of a human life amendment on them.

When rape and incest are raised as justifications for abortion of established pregnancies, it is generally done in a context that, first, emphasizes the emotional and prejudicial nature of the subject and, second, at least implies that the issue is real and that the frequency of rape/incest pregnancies is high enough to warrant special exceptions.[9] While this has typically been a successful rhetorical device, it does not correspond to reality. The facts are that rape and/or incest pregnancies are an extremely infrequent occurrence.

The more candid commentators, even those decidedly pro-abortion, have admitted to the unlikelihood of such pregnancies. For example: "A pregnancy conceived by forcible rape would probably head the list as the most often unwanted, but it is such an unlikely event that it is not really relevant to an understanding of the reasons why women define certain pregnancies as unwanted."[10] Clearly, the statistics support this conclusion. Great Britain has had legalized abortion long enough to have amassed some fairly dependable statistics. One report found that, of 54,000 abortions done in Britain in 1969, only eighty (0.15 percent) were done to end pregnancies resulting from rape.[11] A similar Czechoslovakian study found only twenty-two rape-induced pregnancies out of 86,000 (0.02 percent) consecutive induced abortions.[12]

The American experience confirms these foreign studies. A 1967 study in Chicago reported no pregnancies from confirmed rape in the prior nine years.[13] Similarly, only one pregnancy in more than 300 rape victims was reported in Washington, D.C., in 1968.[14] One very recent and excellent treatment of this topic has drawn together much of this data to conclude:

> The findings of pregnancy [from rape] vary from an incidence of none (0) to 2.2 percent of the victims involved. In four of the studies no pregnancies were documented. This included a large percentage of women at risk who for various reasons did *not* take any hormones such as DES. Of interest is the work of Hayman, co-author of by far the largest study—2,190 female victims; Hayman states that "a very small proportion of patients became pregnant as a result of the assault." Added significance can be attached to Dr. Hayman's not recommending estrogen therapy, on the basis of his experience, as a standard procedure in treating victims of sexual assault. Editorializing in the *Annals of Internal Medicine,* he summarized the statistics as follows: "The probability of becoming pregnant or contracting syphilis or gonorrhea is small, very roughly, from 1 in 200 to 1 in 50."[15]

So overwhelming are the statistics that a New Zealand commission on contraception, abortion, and sterilization, which suggested a significant liberalization of New Zealand's abortion law in 1977, recommended against allowing abortions for rape since the incidence of such pregnancies was too low and the likelihood of false reports too high to warrant a rape exception.[16]

There are several very sound reasons why rape so seldom results in pregnancy. Fundamental among these is the relatively low incidence of conception from *any* single unprotected act of intercourse. Christopher Tietze places the occurrence of such conceptions between 2 and 4 percent.[17] Rape conceptions would be even lower. This is true because not every legally defined rape—defined as penetration—results in ejaculation. Consequently, legal rape may occur without the presence of sperm. Further reducing the odds is the unlikelihood of an attack occurring during the one-to-three-day period in a victim's menstrual cycle when ripe ovum and viable sperm could produce conception. Moreover, even rape on the day of ovulation has only a one-in-ten chance of inducing pregnancy.[18] In addition to these already scant odds there exists the probability that the trauma of a sexual assault will inhibit ovulation even if it would otherwise have occurred. This finding was first suggested by a ghoulish Nazi experiment wherein women who were about to ovulate were subjected to realistic mock gas-chamber executions and then examined to see if the experience affected ovulation—which it did, very often inhibiting it altogether.[19]

Two other very significant factors support an incidence of rape pregnancy far below the Tietze data on unprotected intercourse. First, large numbers of victims are in fact protected in the sense that they may have been surgically sterilized, had a previous hysterectomy, were using some form of passive contraceptive, or were otherwise infertile. Drs. Mahkorn and Dolan have expanded on this factor:

> For example, in a study of 117 victims, no patients were known to have become pregnant as a result of the assault, despite only 17 of this number having been given anti-implantation medication such as DES. Reasons for this include the fact that 23 were taking oral contraceptives, had an IUD in place, or had previously had a tubal ligation. Moreover, another 49 had no medical risk of pregnancy because of an already present pregnancy, a previous hysterectomy, pelvic radiation, or because the victims were either postmenopausal or had not reached menarche.[20]

Finally, a growing body of data shows a high incidence of sexual dysfunction among sexual assailants, including erective and ejaculatory dysfunction, sufficient to minimize the likelihood of vaginal ejaculation.[21] Given these many and varied obstacles to conception, it is easy to understand the extremely low incidence of pregnancies conceived through rape.

Thus far the discussion has focused upon the incidence of rape-induced pregnancy without mention of incest. This is because incest presents a somewhat different problem, since it might often involve more than a single act of intercourse effected under assault circumstances. In fact, some incest relationships could involve numerous acts of intercourse over substantial periods of time. Yet the logical likelihood of more pregnancies is very difficult to substantiate, largely because there simply is not much reliable, pertinent data. The dearth of data is not surprising given the social opprobrium attached to incest and given the family ties involved. Unlike rape—where, although reporting may understate the problem, there remain enough reported cases to accurately assess the pregnancy problem—reported incest cases are too few to assess. For example, in an urban area the size of Chicago's Cook County only twelve indictments were entered for incest in 1966.[22] Consequently, much of the data on incest pregnancies is contradictory and largely dependent upon its date, sources, and methods of its collection. Despite the contradictions, there are several sound studies that suggest an incidence of pregnancy similar to rape in its infrequency.

Dr. George Maloof, for example, reports that "incest treatment programs uniformly marvel at the low incidence of pregnancies from incest."[23] He cites the experience of the Christopher Street program in Minneapolis, which reported a 1 percent pregnancy rate among 400 female incest victims.[24] Similarly, an incest treatment program in Santa Clara County, California, reported less than 1 percent incidence of pregnancies in 1,500 families treated.[25] A Washington State program reported no pregnancies.[26] Yet, as Dr. Maloof admits, some studies have found dramatically higher incidence of incest pregnancies, some as high as 18 to 20 percent.[27] The answer seems to lie in the age of the study. Older studies often draw on untreated cases of incest; new figures coming from incest treatment centers themselves show that current awareness of the problem and efforts to treat the causes have succeeded in ending incestuous relationships before pregnancy occurs. The older studies of untreated cases arose in a context where pregnancy was seen by the victim as a way to disclose the relationship and end it—an act of desperation rendered unnecessary by prompt intervention and treatment. As Dr. Maloof summarizes: "The [older] published studies may be considered as cases which have not been treated, and in which the incest may have progressed further than the average case in the treatment programs. Pregnancy is often a desperate measure taken to end the incest, and has been probably utilized more in the past, when the community was less sensitive to reacting to a possible incest situation and when treatment programs which allow families to work together were not available."[28] Consequently, in the modern treatment context the incidence of incest pregnancies is probably quite low. But even with a higher incidence there are many sound reasons against "treating" these pregnancies through use of abortion. These reasons are discussed below.

Historical Legal Treatment of Abortions for Rape and Incest

Given the traditional reverence for life underpinning the American legal system, and the rarity of rape or incest pregnancies, American law had historically not been persuaded to except these cases from anti-abortion laws. As late as 1967 no state or federal law recognized rape or incest as a justification for abortion. In fact, as late as 1967 the only widely accepted exception to anti-abortion laws was the preservation of the life of the mother, with several states also including the preservation of the mother's health.[29] Significantly, no American case ever granted a judicial exception for rape or incest, despite the temptation to do so after a British trial judge in 1938 flirted with the idea in *Rex v. Bourne.*[30]

In *Bourne* a fourteen-year-old girl was impregnated as the result of being raped by several soldiers. Dr. Bourne, the defendant, offered to perform an abortion on the girl, knowing he would violate the law. After doing so he turned himself over to police authorities and willingly invited prosecution—a prosecution that became a cause célèbre. The presiding judge—Macnaughten—essentially rewrote the British anti-abortion law and assured Dr. Bourne's acquittal. He did this by crafting jury charges that placed the burden on the Crown to prove Dr. Bourne's bad faith or lack of belief that the operation was necessary to preserve the girl's life. Additionally, he rewrote the "life of the mother" exception, equating it with a desire to prevent the girl's becoming a "physical wreck or a mental wreck."

There are any number of reasons why American courts did not seize upon *Bourne* to create judicial rape or incest exceptions prior to *Roe v. Wade.* Fundamental among these would have to be the traditional reverence for life which American courts have only recently begun to ignore. Additionally, *Bourne* is not a precedent. It is merely the jury instructions of a single, undistinguished trial judge based upon no legal authority and at odds with Anglo-American law. Even the most ardently pro-abortion jurist would be hard pressed to depend upon *Rex v. Bourne* as an indication of anything other than judicial caprice and lawmaking. As the *British Medical Journal* candidly said in an approving editorial: "It was less a criminal trial than a co-operative effort by judge, jury, counsel, and witness to create law out of strong but ill-defined feeling."[31]

But what the courts probably recognized as a uniquely baseless act of judicial legislation, the American Law Institute ultimately came to embrace. In its proposed official draft of the Model Penal Code, the institute suggested for the first time model abortion legislation that would justify abortion in cases of "rape, incest or other felonious intercourse."[32] The institute admitted that this was an "innovation in the written law in the United States"[33] but seemed to suggest that it enjoyed support because "it is evident from the dearth of reported American prosecutions in such cases and from the failure of prosecution in *Rex v. Bourne* . . . that abortion under these circumstances is not regarded as a secular antisocial act."[34] To say the least, the institute made a leap of faith to reach its secular conclusions. A dearth of prosecutions can be explained in many ways, including a dearth of illegal rape or incest abortions. Similarly, the failure of prosecution in *Bourne* due to the jury instructions of a single trial judge in an orchestrated prosecution hardly places the entire British Empire, much less the United States, on the side of rape and incest exceptions. Perhaps the best indication that the institute was wrong is in the small number of states that actually accepted the rape/incest suggestion between 1959, when it was first officially proposed, and 1973, when the Supreme Court mooted the issue.

By 1971 only ten states had adopted rape and incest exceptions of some kind.[35] Another three had adopted only rape exceptions,[36] while another four had legalized all early-term abortions.[37] To further demonstrate the overreaching of the institute, it is important to note that the Model Penal Code recommended no requirement that rape or incest abortions be clearly established as genuinely produced by rape or incest, nor did the code suggest that reports of the sex crimes be made to authorities prior to granting the abortion. Yet, virtually every state that granted such exceptions required some proof of the claim and/or some reporting to police authorities.[38]

Pro-abortion commentators seemed well aware that the Model Penal Code was, on most points, at odds with the American attitude toward abortion. With obvious frustration one such commentator concluded:

> However persuasive the arguments in support of the Model Penal Code provisions may be to those who are pre-disposed to favor liberalized abortion, they have so far been repudiated by state legislatures to which they have been submitted.[39]

Nonetheless, it is impossible to know how many more states would have been finally persuaded by the decidedly pro-abortion view of the Model Penal Code had not the Supreme Court stepped in. Similarly, it is difficult to predict how many states would try to create or preserve rape/incest exceptions under a human life amendment. Necessarily, that brings us to a consideration of what effect a human life amendment would have on such exceptions.

The Effect of a Human Life Amendment on Rape and Incest

In discussing this point it is important to note that the issue here is surgical[40] abortion for established pregnancies produced by rape and/or incest. The question of a human life amendment's effect on crisis treatment must be treated separately.

As to those abortions that would be done for what has become known as "humanitarian" reasons—rape and incest—both the

Garn and NRLC amendments would indeed have an effect: most likely absolute prohibition. The cautious phrase "most likely" is intentional. Constitutional amendments are not statutory laws and are therefore necessarily more general in their mandate. The prediction of what effect an amendment will have is therefore markedly riskier than predicting the effect of a statute or a detailed regulation. The complicating factor—in addition to the generality of amendments—is the ultimate dependence upon judicial interpretation, an undertaking that often produces surprising, and sometimes irrational, results. As late as 1972, for example, constitutional scholars would have balked at the possibility that the 14th Amendment says what *Roe v. Wade* decided it says.[41]

Nonetheless, prediction can become somewhat more dependable if certain assumptions can be made. I choose those of John T. Noonan, Jr.

> [T]he Constitution is not addressed to persons of bad will, but to persons—judges, legislators, office holders, citizens—who want to abide by its provisions. . . . No language can be made foolproof. There is no language that cannot be distorted by evil men or inverted by clever men. . . . The Constitution, and any amendment to it, speak to the understanding of those who with good will seek to comprehend the purposes of its framers. . . .[42]

Without these assumptions, prediction is impossible because, in a state where legislators, courts, prosecutors, and citizens are committed to a pro-choice philosophy, a human life amendment might have no effect—at least not without a long, grueling battle of national proportions.

But with these assumptions it seems clear that some safe predictions are possible. First, it is clear that by itself a human life amendment will do nothing: constitutional amendments simply are not self-executing. As one writer puts it: "Thus it cannot be argued that such a proposal, in and of itself, would make the taking of unborn human life murder. . . . [t]o argue otherwise would be akin to alleging that the thirteenth amendment makes the holding of slaves a felony by its terms, a proposition which finds no support in the cases."[43]

Consequently, it is also quite clear that someone would have to act, most obviously Congress and/or the state legislatures. What is significant, however, is that either the Garn or NRLC amendment would give these legislators the basis—the compelling interest denied in *Roe v. Wade*—necessary to act to prohibit all but death-preventing abortions. Most certainly, then, either amendment would supply the basis for prohibiting abortions performed for so-called humanitarian reasons—that is, rape and incest.

Without totally ignoring the assumptions made above, it is legitimate to ask two further questions. What if a state does not act to protect the unborn by statute? Or what if a state acts but creates broader exceptions, specifically those for rape and incest? The answer, it seems, is in the prohibition and enforcement sections of the Garn and NRLC amendments, wherein private action to take unborn life is proscribed and Congress and the states are empowered to act. Standard constitutional law would support the conclusion that these provisions form a basis for action on behalf of the unborn unprotected by a recalcitrant legislature. This action would likely be to enjoin all but death-preventing abortions. Consequently, an abortion sought on the basis of rape or incest could be enjoined as contrary to the mandate of the human life amendment in that it would take the life of one whose protection was assured in the amendment.

Admittedly, any number of questions (e.g., about technical rules of standing, guardianship, class actions, equitable remedies) could be raised at this point. However, it is my opinion that these problems would be the same in the human life amendment context as in any other and that they therefore need no special treatment here. The important point is that these procedures would be available, and quite likely effective—especially when the assumptions of good faith are reinserted. Also, it should be noted that rape and incest exceptions could create equal-protection problems; but on that point I defer to the chapter by Professor Wardle (chapter 2).

A final and virtually certain effect of either the Garn or NRLC amendment is the preclusion of state action in violation of the principles of the amendment. At a minimum this would preclude the use of state or federal funds or facilities for nonlifesaving abortions, including those performed as a result of rape or incest.

The Case Against a Rape/Incest Exception

Having discussed the infrequency of rape/incest pregnancies, the historical treatment of the problem, and the projected effect of a human life amendment, it might be asked: Is not the absolute prohibition too harsh, given the small number of pregnancies involved and the admitted difficulty that even one such pregnancy could produce for the woman involved? In short, it might be argued that, all things considered, a rape/incest exception might be a tolerable concession on a very controversial point. There are both moral and practical reasons why this argument is without merit.

Morally, the value of life should not be determined by the context of conception. As repelling as rape and incest are as crimes, the unborn child is not the criminal. As difficult as carrying the pregnancy might be, it is a lesser concern than the protection of life. Bernard Nathanson summarized the issue quite well in *Aborting America:*

> If a part of the human community were not at stake, no woman should be required to undergo the degradation of bearing a child in these circumstances, but even degradation, shame, and emotional disruption are not the moral equivalent of life. Only life is.[44]

While Nathanson may ignore creative ways of lessening the "degradation" he is on point concerning the moral principle.

Practically, a rape/incest exception is ill advised because it would undeniably be the thin edge of the wedge used for permitting many abortions beyond those specified. While the point has been overstated and has accounted for an unjustified callousness toward rape victims, rape is a difficult crime to establish. It is especially so when prompt reporting and examination are not made. Consequently, allowing abortion for rape invites a flood of bogus rape abortions.

The willingness of abortion providers to fudge on the indications for abortion has been well documented. One California study, done before that state liberalized its abortion law, showed a very high incidence of abortion availability in cases clearly not acceptable under the "life of the mother" law then in effect. In the study the researchers surveyed the chiefs of obstetrical services at twenty-nine hospitals in the San Francisco and Los Angeles areas. The hospitals included an array of public and private, denominational and nondenominational units. The researchers presented a series of cases and asked in each case whether the responding hospital would perform an abortion under the hypothetical circumstances, and, if not, did the respondent think an abortion would be available at some other reputable hospital in the area. One case dealt specifically with a rape-induced pregnancy. Clearly an abortion would have been illegal under prevailing state law. Yet fifteen hospitals said they would perform the abortion, while only seven said they would not; and of those seven, three thought the case would stand a good chance of approval at another reputable hospital. Even more disturbing was that twenty-seven of thirty-one individual respondents said they would approve of abortion in the stated case. This gave the rape case the third highest approval level of the eleven cases presented.[45] Obviously the restrictiveness of the law was readily ignored, and such could be anticipated with a rape or incest exception to a human life amendment.

This problem was underscored after California liberalized its abortion law and allowed rape as a justification. As one doctor put it: "Forcible rape is a problem at the present time in California because the presentation of false rape cases has increased. This is evidenced by the fact that among applications for therapeutic abortion for forcible rape in California, 19 percent were turned down by the committee in terms of their disbelief in the actuality of the forcible rape itself."[46] Presumably, the rejected cases were only the more blatant ones, and many others could not be filtered out.

It is safe to assume that a rape/incest exception could never be contained, especially given the mind set of many existing hospital staffs. This mind set was vividly portrayed at a pro-choice conference held in 1970 where one physician bemoaned the dramatic difference in abortion ratios between ward patients and private patients. His question was: "I am concerned as to whether we are really recruiting to make these services available to the poor."[47] Notice the word "recruiting"—apparently a common practice, as indicated by another conference participant: "Dr. Guttmacher has proudly referred to the nearly equal ward and private abortion rates at Mount Sinai Hospital. I would like to explain that as residents, we beat the bushes to get cases for that committee so that he could get the ward ratio higher."[48] Could one really depend upon these people to apply any kind of exception carefully, much less one as malleable as rape/incest?

A rape exception raises another significant question. How should rape be defined? For example, there is an enormous difference between forcible rape, wherein a woman or girl is brutally assaulted, and statutory rape, wherein a young girl is impregnated by her slightly older boyfriend in an act of consensual intercourse. Yet many proponents of a rape exception fail to distinguish these cases.

Finally, a rape exception also produces the possibility of aborting a child willingly conceived, even between a married couple several days before a rape. Physically, there would be no way to determine whether the child was already in existence at the time of the rape or was the product of the rape. Consequently, the child of a wholly licit and loving union could be destroyed under a rape exception.

Another, somewhat tangential, point should be considered in this regard. Few would doubt that the traditional difficulty in obtaining rape convictions, and in sensitizing the population to the crime of rape, has emanated from a suspicion about the veracity of the allegation of rape.[49] It is only recently that critics of these problems have begun to persuade prosecutors and the public that rape as a crime must be taken seriously. It is my opinion that a rape exception to a human life amendment would do damage to the progress made in this area. Such an exception would increase the motivation for and number of false accusations, thereby seriously damaging the credibility of genuine rape victims. This would be an unfortunate result of creating an exception for which there is very little need.

Most of the reasons against a rape exception would apply with equal force to one for incest. The moral arguments are the same, especially in light of data questioning the evidence of a correlation between incest and genetic defects.[50] The practical problems (e.g., false claims, difficulty of proof, etc.) would also be similar. The difference, however, is in the higher incidence of pregnancy due to incest, and the evidence that after-the-fact solutions such as abortion are no solution at all. At first blush it would seem that an incest exception would be more necessary because of the higher incidence of pregnancy; however, quite the opposite seems true.

First, despite the greater number of pregnancies, incest-afflicted families are extremely hesitant to admit to the occurrence of incest. As one recent comprehensive study puts it: "The adults in the family have a realistic fear of social shame and legal sanctions, while the involved child often feels too fearful of family dissolution or retaliation by the adults to risk disclosure to outside authorities."[51] Consequently, the view that incest victims will openly seek abortion, if such are allowed, is naive at best.[52]

The second and more important point, however, is that abortion is never a treatment for incest. In fact, the quick disposal of the evidence of incest could well subject the victim to continued exploitation. What incest demands is intervention and multifaceted treatment. As noted earlier, this approach not only treats causes rather than symptoms, but it could actually prevent pregnancies, thereby negating any need for an incest exception. Recall my earlier comments[53] about the discrepancies between the low pregnancy figures from incest treatment centers as compared with the higher figures from studies where early intervention and treatment seemed not to exist. In Dr. Maloof's opinion, pregnancies were more likely "when the community was less sensitive to reacting to a possible incest situation and when treatment programs which allow families to work together were not available."[54] Therefore, abortion does not stop the problem, while treatment can. Encouragement to treatment rather than abortion makes good sense.

Finally, when they do occur, incest pregnancies, unlike those induced by rape, are seldom revealed until the second trimester, when abortions become significantly more dangerous. Hence, an incest exception would invite the infliction of greater harm on an already traumatized victim.

Abortion is to rape and incest what morphine is to pain—a superficially appealing, temporarily relieving, woefully inadequate response to something serious. The immediate benefits only mask the deeper wounds, which can fester to the point of great injury. A physician would never "treat" his patient only with morphine unless his was a hopeless case. To "treat" rape and incest pregnancies with abortion is a way of saying these women are hopeless cases—violated, tainted, damaged goods, for whom abortion is a way to scrub away the "scarlet letter."[55]

This need not be the case. As horrible as these crimes may be, the victim need not be degraded by being asked to take life as a response. These women can be treated with dignity and love. They can be helped as whole persons, not simply as bearers of bad memories that must be extinguished. Sensitive counselors have dared to suggest that both rape and incest are problems larger than pregnancy, which call on us as creative, loving beings to find a better way to treat the victims of those crimes. That better way is a commitment to societal change that can stem the problem. Such change would include competent counseling; emotional, physical, and financial support; and development of dignified alternatives such as adoption.[56]

Crisis Treatment of Rape/Incest Victims

The other major question raised by the Garn or NRLC amendment is the effect they would have upon standard crisis treatment intended to prevent pregnancy in rape and, to a lesser extent, incest victims.

The treatment most often used is the estrogen diethylstilbestrol (DES), which must be administered within seventy-two hours of intercourse.[57] In order to predict the effect of the proposed amendments, it is necessary to understand the mode of operation of this treatment. That is, is it contraceptive or abortifacient?

DES is usually referred to as a postcoital contraceptive, its intended use always being after intercourse. It is more popularly known as the "morning-after" pill and is recommended only for "emergency " situations, since it carries unpleasant side effects in the short run and more serious risks in the long run.[58] As with most contraceptives, the mode of action is in some doubt, though there seems to be a consensus that DES most often prevents implantation of the fertilized ovum. In common parlance, this is thought of as an abortifacient effect—though some researchers prefer the term "interceptive," because it falls between contraception and abortion of an implanted pregnancy.[59]

One recent text concludes quite unequivocally that "the interceptive effect of estrogen is postovulatory rather than postcoital,"[60] suggesting that estrogen so administered always works upon fertilized ova. The author goes on to suggest that while there is doubt about how the anti-implantation effect occurs—whether due to changes in the motility in the fertilized ovum or in changes in the endometrium—there is no doubt that his data supports *only* a postovulatory effect.

On the other hand, some have suggested that DES also has an antiovulatory effect. In the case of rape, this effect would occur when DES was administered immediately after a rape and just before ovulation was "scheduled" to occur. This effect would, of course, be fortuitous and not planned. Whatever the case, however, the antiovulatory effect has not been adequately proven. In fact, one study seems to directly contradict it by concluding that "[p]ostcoital estrogens usually prevent uterine pregnancy but not ectopic implantation"[61]—an unlikely result if DES is primarily contraceptive. Consequently, the effect of a human life amendment on DES could not easily be predicted upon the assumption that it is primarily contraceptive. Even admitting to some uncertainty, the weight of evidence suggests that DES more often prevents implantation.

Given this conclusion, the effect of either of the proposed amendments can be assessed. The first and perhaps safest conclusion is that by itself neither amendment would have an effect upon the sale, manufacture, or use of DES. Again, constitutional amendments are not self-executing. The more important question, however, concerns the kinds of statutes the proposed amendments would require or allow.

As to required statutes, I think the answer is clearly none. The amendment's protection is of unborn persons. Nothing in the proposed wording requires protection of persons whose existence is not yet known or demonstrable. This is precisely the case with rape treatment, since DES is only effective within seventy-two hours of intercourse—too soon a period to confirm pregnancy. Consequently, there is no proof of the existence of a person at the time DES would be administered, and no mandate to protect. Additionally, without a confirmed pregnancy it seems incomprehensible that a guardian *ad litem* could ever be appointed to seek protection of persons not known to be in existence. Put simply, neither the Garn nor the NRLC amendment would require any state or Congress to prohibit the use of DES in rape treatment.

What sort of statute a state would be allowed to enact is a somewhat more difficult question. It seems certain that the manufacture, use, and sale of DES could never be prohibited on the basis of the proposed amendment because it has a variety of nonabortifacient uses. One text on the uses of drugs lists five principal uses of DES, not including rape treatment or pregnancy prevention.[62]

It would be *possible,* however, to prohibit the use of DES for rape treatment or other attempts at pregnancy prevention. Given the likelihood that when DES does prevent pregnancies it most often does it by preventing implantation, a state or Congress could decide to exercise extreme caution and prohibit its use in these cases. This is unlikely and probably unwise because, at least in the case of rape treatment, the incidence of pregnancy is so low that the occasions upon which DES would produce an abortion are minimal and perhaps nonexistent. Recall the Hayman study mentioned earlier,[63] which recommended that DES not even be used in rape cases because the chances of pregnancy are so slim. Clearly, legislative judgment and the political processes could be trusted to make a wise decision on this point.

Finally, it should be asked what effect standard statutes against abortifacients and abortion would have on DES. Pre-1973 abortifacient statutes would seem to have no effect upon DES because those statutes regulated only pure abortifacients that had no other medical or commercial use. As noted, this is not the case with DES.

Pre-1973 abortion statutes raised a more difficult question. Those statutes generally fell into two categories: those that required proof of pregnancy as an element of the crime, and those that only required an intent to produce an abortion or miscarriage without requiring proof of pregnancy. Clearly, those requiring proof of pregnancy would not affect the use of DES. However, those requiring only intent present a different problem in that it might be argued that administration of DES to a rape victim is done with the intent to produce an abortion. Given the statistics on conception from rape, however, this would be a questionable conclusion. It is just as likely that it could be proven that DES was given with the intent to ease the victim's mind with full knowledge that producing an abortion was highly unlikely.

This latter argument is buttressed by the judicial construction of the "mere" intent statutes prior to 1973. Many courts that faced the question required that the state prove that the defendant had knowledge or belief that the woman was pregnant at the time of the alleged abortive act.[64] Requiring this element of proof would allow the administration of DES to rape victims who are unlikely to be pregnant. Consequently, any state acting under either of the proposed amendments could preserve this element of proof to make unlikely the criminalization of DES use for rape victims.

Rape and incest are among the most controversial issues affected by a human life amendment. Yet, much of the controversy stems from ignorance and emotion rather than from reality. The significant problems that these crimes present are in no way ameliorated by the availability of abortion—in fact, abortion is a hindrance to more sensitive, caring, and integrated treatment. The human response to the real problems of rape and incest is complex and challenging. It requires understanding, care, and compassion; it substitutes lifegiving for death dealing; it treats the woman with respect, not embarrassment or revulsion.

No matter how few pregnancies result from these crimes, they must be viewed as the clearest examples of genuine "problem" pregnancies, tragedies which society has not well understood and for which it has not provided. A new attitude must emerge, emphasizing that the considerable difficulty involved in helping other human persons is well worth it—especially when, in every case, not only will a human life be spared but an innocent woman will be saved from further degradation.

Chapter Ten

INFANTICIDE, EUTHANASIA, IN VITRO FERTILIZATION, AND FETAL EXPERIMENTATION

Victor G. Rosenblum

Since the time of the introduction of the first version of a human life amendment[1] soon after the decision of the Supreme Court in *Roe v. Wade,*[2] it has been the stated intent of most amendment framers and proponents to go beyond the question of abortion—to strike at the heart of the evil of which abortion is a most visible part.[3]

That evil is discrimination: the discrimination that considers some human beings as "less equal" than others, a discrimination that culminates in defining some members of the human community out of our society and denying even their lives the protection of our laws. It is a discrimination based upon physical or mental condition, developmental status, or economic and physical dependency.[4]

The essence of the Garn Amendment, its spirit, is expressed in the majestic words of its first section declaring that "personhood"—the status which invokes the protection of our Constitution and laws—belongs "to all human beings, irrespective of age, health, function or condition of dependency."[5] This statement means, very simply, that because one is biologically a human being, an individual living organism of the species *homo sapiens,* one is a person. No sociological criteria based upon one's lack of productivity or independence and no physical or psychological criteria based upon one's incapacity, senility, inability to relate to others, or physical or mental handicap can deprive one of the rights and protections of membership in society.

Application of this great principle includes and transcends abortion, to which Section 2 and other parts of Section 1 more specifically relate.[6] It applies as well to infanticide, euthanasia, *in vitro* fertilization, and fetal experimentation.

There are four avenues through which the Garn Amendment can affect these practices.

Victor G. Rosenblum, Ph.D., J.D., is professor of law and political science, Northwestern University. He is former president of Reed College (1968–70). He is a coauthor of THE MAKING OF A PUBLIC PROFESSIONAL (1981).

The first is the least "legal," in a technical sense, but it may well be the most significant in a jurisprudential sense. It is the impact of the "spirit" of the amendment. Justice Brandeis correctly wrote, "Our government is the potent, the omnipresent teacher. For good or for ill, it teaches the whole people by its example."[7] Our country—indeed all of Western civilization—is now engaged in multiple struggles over whether the quality of one's life or simply one's existence as a human being is the prerequisite to constitutional recognition and protection. The ideals of a society are congealed in its laws, and especially in its fundamental law. When a human life amendment is enacted, representing the consent of two-thirds of Congress and three-quarters of the state legislatures, this will in part result from and in part create a national consensus in favor of the protection of human life based on its *existence* rather than on its quality. When our society enshrines this unconditional support of human life in all its forms and phases in the Constitution, the principle of the human life amendment will have the same status and aura as the Bill of Rights,[8] the ban on slavery,[9] and other central precepts of our constitutional system.

The other three avenues relate to the impact of a human life amendment on the criminal and civil law. They may be approached by answering three questions. With regard to infanticide, euthanasia, *in vitro* fertilization, and fetal experimentation, what will the human life amendment restrain the federal and state governments from doing? What will it require governments to do? What will it permit governments to do? As we shall see, the most significant question is the last since, to have genuine operative effect, a human life amendment—like nearly every constitutional amendment—must be joined by implementing legislation.

The Garn Amendment incorporates its biological standard of personhood into the 5th and 14th amendments to the Constitution. The 5th Amendment applies to the federal government, while the 14th applies to the states. The first section of the 14th Amendment has two explicit components which are relevant: the "due process" and the "equal protection" clauses. Although the 5th Amendment lacks explicit reference to "equal protection," the Supreme Court has interpreted it to include the same equal protection and due process requirements as are provided in the 14th Amendment.[10]

The "due process" clause provides: "No State shall deprive any person of life . . . without due process of law."[11] Understanding the way the human life amendment affects the "due process" clause will answer the question of what the amendment will restrain the government from doing.

The "equal protection" clause provides: "No State . . . shall deny to any person, within its jurisdiction, the equal protection of the laws."[12] There is precise phrasing in Section 1 of the Garn Amendment. "With respect to the right to life, the word 'person,' as used in this article and in the Fifth and Fourteenth articles of amendment to the Constitution of the United States, applies to all human beings. . . ."[13] It means that the amendment will affect only equal protection of the *lives* of persons—not, for example, of their liberty or property. While the "due process" clause prevents the government *from doing* things which deprive a person of life, the "equal protection" clause, at least on its face, obligates the government *to do* things which protect persons: what it does for one class of human beings it must do for every other class of human beings not relevantly different. Understanding the way the amendment affects the "equal protection" clause, therefore, will answer the question of what the human life amendment will require the government to do.

However, here we ought to take note of an important caveat. To say that the amendment restrains the government from doing something or requires it to do something is to say no more than that the courts can and will issue judgments and injunctions to that effect when their jurisdiction has been properly invoked by persons with "standing" to sue. That means that some aggrieved person must be able to bring suit (or to raise the issue in a proceeding brought against him); that there must be an actual—not a hypothetical—"case or controversy";[14] that someone must be affected by that controversy in a manner which accords "standing" to invoke the constitutional question;[15] and that the remedy for the grievance must be of the sort which a court can effect.

The courts can function most easily in enforcing the "due process" clause. When the government undertakes to do something adverse to someone through one of its organs (such as a public hospital), or through its law enforcement arm or judicial process, that person has standing to go into court and ask the judiciary to issue an injunction ordering that governmental action to cease. In the area of constitutional law, a court's powers are clearest when it acts to forbid impending governmental action by striking a law or enjoining a public official from doing something.

The situation is less clear cut with the equal protection clause. A court has power to strike laws, in whole or in part, but not to add them.[16] Whatever power it has to make positive demands is contingent on its power to strike or forbid something. For example, a court may not directly compel a state to provide specific amenities in its prisons; it must say that if those amenities are not provided by a set date the state may no longer incarcerate prisoners in those institutions.[17]

Furthermore, the equal protection clause has never been interpreted to mean that the government may make no distinction at all. When no suspect class is involved (and no one contends that the human life amendment would make all human beings, simply by virtue of their humanity, members of a suspect class), the government may justify any distinction it draws merely by showing that it has a legitimate interest which is rationally related to the distinction challenged.[18] We shall see the significance of this as we examine each of the applications of the amendment to the areas of *in vitro* fertilization, infanticide, euthanasia, and fetal experimentation.

The final section of the Garn Amendment provides to the Congress and the states "the power to enforce this article by appropriate legislation within their respective jurisdictions."[19] While the other aspects of the amendment may be described as power granted to the courts to enforce its principles even against legislatures, this aspect may be described as power granted to the legislatures to implement and enforce the principles of the amendment even against the courts. This may well be the most significant aspect of the amendment; for it was the courts, rather than the legislatures,[20] that necessitated adoption of the amendment in order to protect human life. The Garn Amendment palpably reverses *Roe v. Wade* by returning the power to the legislatures to protect all human beings. Building upon measures like those declared unconstitutional in the *Roe* and *Doe* cases of 1973, Congress and the states will be able to rely on the amendment to prevent infanticide and euthanasia and to place life-observant restrictions on *in vitro* fertilization and fetal experimentation. The amendment will not, however, by its mere adoption, punish anything or anybody.[21]

In vitro fertilization is best known for the production of Louise Joy Brown by Drs. Edwards and Steptoe in England[22] and for the application for funding of *in vitro* fertilization experiments by Dr. Pierre Soupart of Vanderbilt University in Tennessee,[23] which triggered the "Report of the Ethical Advisory Board."[24] The first was an example of *in vitro* fertilization with embryo transfer; the second was a proposal for *in vitro* fertilization without embryo transfer.

In vitro fertilization without embryo transfer involves the creation of children for use solely as guinea pigs. They are created with the intent that, after being the subjects of experimentation, they die.[25] How would the human life amendment restrain the government with regard to such a practice?

First, we would expect the courts to rule that under the amendment any program that plans or entails the death of the children created, whether through direct action by the scientists or by failure to make any attempt to implant, could not be conducted in government facilities or with the support of government funds. Any government involvement would be clear participation in depriving human beings of life without due process of law and would be subject to court injunction in an action brought by one who could obtain appointment as guardian *ad litem* for children produced by *in vitro* fertilization. The complexities of proof cannot be ignored, for it would have to be shown in any guardian *ad litem* proceeding that the children were then in existence before the suit could effectively be brought.[26] While the case of *Flast v. Cohen*[27] and its progeny[28] might be helpful here, it must be admitted that without the good faith of the government in upholding the letter and spirit of the human life amendment through executive and legislative policy, the quest for redress may produce more procedural mazes than substantive resolutions.

What will the amendment, through the equal protection clause, require the government to do? In reality, nothing. Statutory construction of existing laws might be affected until (and unless) a state or the Congress enacted legislation specifically dealing with *in vitro* fertilization.[29] For example, it would be compatible with the amendment to construe child neglect and negligent homicide laws to cover children conceived *in vitro.* Distinctions between a failure to implant and other forms of child neglect and negligence could be upheld, nevertheless, in view of the problems surrounding any requirement that anyone submit to implantation of an embryo.

The most evident and least problematic effect of the human life amendment would be in answering the third question, that of what the amendment will empower the government to do. Plainly, the government has a compelling interest in protecting the holders of a fundamental right in preservation of the subject matter of that right. Section 2 of the Garn Amendment,[30] when coupled with the enforcement provisions of Section 3, assures the authority of the government to ban private action which threatens the lives of human beings.

In furtherance of its compelling interest in the lives of the human beings created by *in vitro* fertilization, presumably the government could not only forbid direct infliction of harm on the *ex utero in vitro* embryo and make the failure to implant criminal neglect, but it could also establish a system of regulations designed to ensure that no human beings are created by *in vitro* fertilization without a credible assurance that they will be implanted—thus precluding entirely, as a legal matter, *in vitro* fertilization without embryo transfer.

What of *in vitro* fertilization *with* embryo transfer? The common practice of creating several embryos with intent to select only one for implantation[31] could be made subject to the same legal sanctions as *in vitro* fertilization without embryo transfer, and government funding or other involvement in it would be subject to the same invalidation. When *in vitro* fertilization is performed with the intent of embryo transfer in every case, it does not seem that the amendment would restrain the government from performing, funding, or otherwise assisting this, nor would it compel the government to act against it. Indeed, *in vitro* fertilization with embryo transfer in every case would seem to be included as an aspect of the fundamental right to procreation[32] for those persons who cannot otherwise bear children and, at least in such cases, would seem to be constitutionally protected. If there were reasonable grounds for supposing that the procedure was more dangerous to the embryo than *in vivo* fertilization, however, the government could, if it chose, regulate or even forbid it to prevent serious danger to the lives of embryos.[33].

Infanticide, especially of the severely handicapped newborn, is a widespread phenomenon in America.[34] Although it is still illegal throughout the country,[35] the killing of children who fall short of elitist quality standards is supported and advocated by a number of physicians.[36] How would the human life amendment restrain the government from participation in this practice?

Several alternative rationales are typically offered for infanticide. The starkest is the claim that, either because of prematurity or handicap, the newborn is not a person.[37] The amendment would clearly prohibit government participation in such practice. Were the government to ground participation in euthanasia—including withdrawal of necessary treatment when it had a duty of care toward the infant concerned (as in a public hospital)—on an explicit assertion that the infant was not a person, a guardian *ad litem* for an infant or class of infants could obtain an injunction against the government infanticide. To carry sordid governmental support for infanticide to its Kafkaesque ultimate, the government might argue that the infant would not wish to live and might invoke substitute judgment[38] to claim that it was speaking for, as well as in the best interests of, the child. Insofar as the human life amendment crystallizes an ethos which eliminates quality-of-life analysis, the courts would be obliged to enjoin this governmental claim as well. Otherwise, notwithstanding the Garn Amendment's language, judges might still not feel precluded from accepting the substituted judgment argument or from creating an autonomy-based "right to die."

To what extent would the amendment require the government to act against private action constituting infanticide? By reversing *Roe,* the Garn Amendment establishes a life-supportive ethos which may induce prosecutors to act against infanticide in the same manner as against any other homicide. Of course, prosecutorial and judicial discretion would be neither greater nor less than heretofore, but the very repudiation of the *Roe v. Wade* rule by the amendment would destroy any judicial shield for infanticide and renew a sense of institutional and societal obligation grounded in the primacy of protecting all human life.

In the final analysis, the strongest defense the human life amendment provides against infanticide is in its answer to the question of what it will empower the government to do. It will provide a constitutional foundation for laws against infanticide which will withstand constitutional attack. As noted earlier, it will preclude successful argument in court that young or handicapped infants are "nonpersons." Since there can be no question of a voluntary and informed decision to die on the part of the infant, the autonomy issue could arise only through an argument grounded on substituted judgment. But the state has historically been the judge, through its laws, of who speaks for children and the incompetent.[39] If the state puts its weight on the side of life, and that weight is reinforced by the compelling interest government can claim, under the amendment, in protecting the infant's life, it will surely prevail against any claim by a third party, unsanctioned by the state, that the child would, if able, exercise a choice for death.

What of fetal experimentation?[40] Again, the amendment would wield its significant role as spur and sanction for governmental action prohibiting the practice. By affirming the fetal life right, the amendment surrounds the unborn child with the same protections and immunities from exploitation that all other persons have had traditionally. By repudiating *Roe* and renewing the Constitution's commitment to life, the amendment will end the "hunt, destroy, and experiment" syndrome that has turned some scientific researchers from protectors of human life into exploiters of human life. It should also be noted that in a key respect fetal experimentation presents a much simpler problem than *in vitro* fertilization. No court has so far recognized the existence of a fundamental right to perform experiments generally,[41] and courts have uniformly upheld anti–fetal experimentation statutes even after *Roe v. Wade.*[42] Experimentation on the fetus has no relationship to the judicially proclaimed fundamental right to privacy from which the Supreme Court's rulings on abortion stemmed.[43] After passage of a human life amendment, as before, legislatures could legitimately ban the practice. But after passage, the government would be forbidden from funding or facilitating experiments on the fetus that would entail death or grave risk to life, as it is not now forbidden to do. Moreover, governmental standards that govern experimentation on other classes of human beings would have to be applied to unborn children as well in order to pass muster under the "equal protection" clause: the fetus could not be experimented upon in a manner that would be forbidden if practiced upon an infant.

This brings us to euthanasia. Euthanasia may be active or passive, voluntary or involuntary. Euthanasia is currently a homicide—a murder—even if done on request and with consent.[44] No constitutional amendment is necessary; but the human life amendment would help educate and sensitize the people to that legal fact.

The strongest legal check dealt to euthanasia by the amendment would, as with infanticide, lie in what it empowers the government to do. With the exception of care of the competent adult who voluntarily chooses to refuse medical treatment, the situation is identical to that of infanticide. Constitutional challenges to antieuthanasia laws based on the nonpersonhood of the senile or handicapped would be doomed to failure, and those based upon an alleged autonomy right to "substituted judgment" by a third party for the choice of death would be overcome by the government's compelling power to determine who speaks for the incompetent.

The human life amendment will not forestall or overcome all of the dangers which right-to-life advocates see in infanticide, euthanasia, fetal experimentation, and *in vitro* fertilization. But it will surely confirm unshakably the right and ability of Congress and the state legislatures to outlaw infanticide, prevent exploitive experimentation on the unborn, prevent involuntary euthanasia from becoming legal, and stop the direct or negligent destruction of embryonic children conceived through *in vitro* fertilization. Above all, it will forever enshrine in our Constitution, as a beacon and pledge to all, the too-oft-ignored or embattled principle of universal human equality in the assertion and recognition of fundamental human rights.

Appendix

THE HUMAN LIFE BILL

SECTION 1. (a) The Congress finds that the life of each human being begins at conception.

(b) The Congress further finds that the fourteenth amendment to the Constitution of the United States protects all human beings.

SECTION 2. Upon the basis of these findings, and in the exercise of the powers of Congress, including its power under section 5 of the fourteenth amendment to the Constitution of the United States, the Congress hereby recognizes that for the purpose of enforcing the obligation of the States under the fourteenth amendment not to deprive persons of life without due process of law, each human life exists from conception, without regard to race, sex, age, health, defect, or condition of dependency, and for this purpose "person" includes all human beings.

SECTION 3. Congress further recognizes that each State has a compelling interest, independent of the status of unborn children under the fourteenth amendment, in protecting the lives of those within the State's jurisdiction whom the State rationally regards as human beings.

SECTION 4. Notwithstanding any other provision of law, no inferior Federal court ordained and established by Congress under article III of the Constitution of the United States shall have jurisdiction to issue any restraining order, temporary or permanent injunction, or declaratory judgment in any case involving or arising from any State law or municipal ordinance that (1) protects the rights of human persons between conception and birth, or (2) prohibits, limits, or regulates (a) the performance of abortions or (b) the provision at public expense of funds, facilities, personnel, or other assistance for the performance of abortions: Provided, That nothing in this section shall deprive the Supreme Court of the United States of the authority to render appropriate relief in any case.

SECTION 5. Any party may appeal to the Supreme Court of the United States from an interlocutory or final judgment, decree, or order of any court of the United States regarding the enforcement of this Act, or of any State law or municipal ordinance that protects the rights of human beings between conception and birth, or

---

S. 26, 98th Cong., 1st Sess., 129 CONG. REC. S95 (daily ed. Jan. 26, 1983).

which adjudicates the constitutionality of this Act, or of any such law or ordinance. The Supreme Court shall advance on its docket and expedite the disposition of any such appeal.

SECTION 6. If any provision of this Act or the application thereof to any person or circumstance is judicially determined to be invalid, the validity of the remainder of the Act and the application of such provision to other persons and circumstances shall not be affected by such determination.

NOTES

Chapter One Examination of Proposals for a Human Life Amendment

1. 410 U.S. 113 (1973).

2. 410 U.S. 179 (1973).

3. 410 U.S. at 153. The constitutional right of privacy was first recognized in Griswold v. Connecticut, 381 U.S. 479 (1965). *See* L. WARDLE, THE ABORTION PRIVACY DOCTRINE (1980), for the most comprehensive examination of Roe v. Wade and its progeny so far published.

4. 410 U.S. at 156–58.

5. *Id.* at 138–41.

6. *Id.* at 158–59.

7. *Id.* at 163–64.

8. *Id.* at 159–63.

9. *Id.* at 163–64.

10. *See* Endangered Species Conservation Act of 1969, 16 U.S.C. §§ 668aa to 668cc-5.

11. Roe v. Wade, 410 U.S. 113, 221 (1973).

12. *Id.* at 174.

13. A. COX, THE ROLE OF THE SUPREME COURT IN AMERICAN GOVERNMENT 113–14 (1976).

14. Ely, *The Wages of Crying Wolf: A Comment on Roe v. Wade,* 82 YALE L. J. 920, 947 (1973).

15. A. BICHEL, THE MORALITY OF CONSENT 23 (1975).

16. Rice, *The Dred Scott Case of the Twentieth Century,* 10 HOUS. L. REV. 1059 (1973).

17. Epstein, *Substantive Due Process by Any Other Name,* 1973 SUP. CT. REV. 159.

18. Byrn, *An American Tragedy: The Supreme Court on Abortion,* 41 FORDHAM L. REV. 807, 813 (1973) [hereinafter cited as Byrn I].

19. Wellington, *American Law Rules and Constitutional Double Standards,* 83 YALE L. J. 221 (1973).

20. J. NOONAN, A PRIVATE CHOICE 189 (1979).

21. *See* SENATE COMM. ON JUDICIARY, HUMAN LIFE FEDERALISM AMENDMENT, S. REP. NO. 97-465, 97th Cong., 2d Sess. 24-35 (1982) [hereinafter cited as 1982 Senate Report].

22. *See* Tribe, *The Supreme Court, 1972 Term—Forward Toward a Model of Roles in the Due Process of Life and Law,* 87 HARV. L. REV. 1 (1973); Heymann & Barzelay, *The Forest and the Trees: Roe v. Wade and Its Critics,* 53 B.U.L. REV. 765 (1973).

23. *Hearings on the Legal Ramifications of Human Life Amendment, Before the Subcommittee on the Constitution of the Senate Committee on the Judiciary,* 98th Cong., 1st Sess. (February 28, 1983) (statement of Senator Orrin G. Hatch) [hereinafter cited as 1983 Senate Hearings].

24. Ely, *supra* note 14, at 926.

25. 103 S. Ct. 2481 (1983).

26. *Id.* at 2495.

27. *Id.*

28. *See id.* at 2492 n.11.

29. *See id.* at 2495–96.

30. *See id.* at 2502 n.38.

31. *Id.* at 2506.

32. *Id.* at 2491.

33. *See* Petruso, *The Experience of Abortion,* 140 AMERICA 510 (1979).

34. City of Akron v. Akron Center for Reproductive Health, 103 S. Ct. 2481, 2501–03 (1983).

35. *Id.* at 2501.

36. *Id.* at 2500.

37. 410 U.S. at 159.

38. Akron Ordinance No. 160–1978 § 1870.06(3).

39. 103 S. Ct. at 2500.

40. *See id.* at 2487 n.1.

41. *Id.* at 2505.

42. *Id.* at 2509.

43. *Id.* at 2508.

44. For the first time since 1973, there appears to be a realistic prospect that the U.S. Supreme Court, with changes in the Court's personnel, might consider reversal of *Roe v. Wade.* Of the six Justices who voted to reaffirm *Roe v. Wade,* five are seventy-four or older. The dissenters, however, are on the younger end of the spectrum with O'Connor and Rehnquist still in their fifties. The next president, elected in 1984, is likely to make several Supreme Court appointments. The reelection of President Reagan, who has taken a strong public right-to-life position, could result in a shift in favor of reversal. *See* Reagan, *Abortion and the Conscience of the Nation,* 9 HUM. LIFE REV. 7 (1983), for an example of President Reagan's strong commitment on this issue.

45. Chisholm v. Georgia, 2 U.S. 419 (1793).

46. 60 U.S. 393 (1857).

47. Pollock v. Farmer's Loan and Trust Co., 157 U.S. 429 (1895); 158 U.S. 601 (1895).

48. Oregon v. Mitchell, 400 U.S. 112 (1970).

49. Hammer v. Dagenhart, 247 U.S. 251 (1918).

50. Baker v. Carr, 369 U.S. 186 (1962).

51. *Hearings on Proposed Constitutional Amendments on Abortion Before the Subcomm. on Civil and Const. Rights of the House Comm. on the Judiciary,* 94th Cong., 2nd Sess., PROPOSED CONSTITUTIONAL AMENDMENTS ON ABORTION, pt. 1, at 65 (1976) (testimony of John T. Noonan) [hereinafter cited as 1976 House Hearings].

52. For a thorough discussion of the balancing tests see Linscott v. Miller Falls Co., 440 F.2d 14 (1st Cir. 1971).

53. Katzenback v. McClung, 379 U.S. 194 (1964).

54. 428 U.S. 52 (1976).

55. Pierce v. Society of Sisters, 268 U.S. 510 (1925); Wisconsin v. Yoder, 406 U.S. 205 (1972).

56. Planned Parenthood v. Danforth, 428 U.S. 52, 75 (1976).

57. 351 F. Supp. 224 (D. Conn. 1972).

58. *See* cases cited *supra* note 55.

59. 310 F. Supp. 293 (E.D. Wisc. 1970).

60. *See* Committee to Defend Reproductive Rights v. Myers, 172 Cal. Rptr. 866, 625 P.2d 779 (1981), where the California Supreme Court declared that the woman's right to privacy is "clearly among the most intimate and fundamental of all constitutional rights."

61. 42 N.J. 421, 201 A.2d 537 (1964).

62. *See also* Application of President of Georgetown University Hospital, 331 F.2d 1000 (D.C. Cir. 1964).

63. Kramer v. Union Free School District, 395 U.S. 621 (1969); Shapiro v. Thompson, 394 U.S. 618 (1969).

64. *See* S. 1741, known as the Human Life Bill, which includes a section (Section 3) declaring that a state has a compelling interest to protect unborn life. S. 26, 98th Cong., 1st Sess., 129 Cong. Rec. S95 (daily ed. Jan. 26, 1983). For the full text of the Human Life Bill, *see infra,* app.

65. 410 U.S. at 163–64.

66. Cheaney v. State, 259 Ind. 138, 285 N.E.2d 265 (1972).

67. Steinberg v. Brown, 321 F. Supp. 741 (N.D. Ohio 1970).

68. *See* cases cited at Roe v. Wade, 410 U.S. 113, 154 (1973).

69. Young Women's Christian Association v. Kugler, 342 F. Supp. 1048 (D.N.J. 1972); Babbitz v. McCann, 310 F. Supp. 293 (E.D. Wisc. 1970); Doe v. Scott, 321 F. Supp. 1385 (N.D. Ill. 1971).

70. Babbitz v. McCann, 310 F. Supp. 293 (E.D. Wisc. 1970); Doe v. Scott, 321 F. Supp. 1385 (N.D. Ill. 1971); Abele v. Markle, 342 F. Supp. 800 (D. Conn. 1972).

71. Doe v. Scott, 321 F. Supp. 1385 (N.D. Ill. 1971).

72. Babbitz v. McCann, 310 F. Supp. 293 (E.D. Wisc. 1970); Abele v. Markle, 342 F. Supp. 800 (D. Conn. 1972).

73. 172 Cal. Rptr. 866, 625 P.2d 779 (1981).

74. *See* Byrn v. New York City Health & Hosp. Corp., 38 App. Div. 2d 316, 329 N.Y.S.2d 722 (2d Dep't), *aff'd on other grounds,* 31 N.Y.2d 194, 286 N.E.2d 887, 335 N.Y.S.2d 390 (1972) [hereinafter cited as Byrn v. New York City Health & Hosp. Corp.].

75. United States v. Vuitch, 402 U.S. 62, 71–72 (1971).

76. Doe v. Bolton, 410 U.S. 179, 192 (1973).

77. Preamble to World Health Organization Constitution in Toward Mankind's Better Health 21 (1963).

78. Zbaraz v. Quern, No. 77 C4522 (N.D. Ill., Memo. Opin. June 13, 1978).

79. McRae v. Califano, No. 76-C-1804 (E.D.N.Y. Transcript, August 3, 1977, pp. 99–101) (Testimony of Dr. Jane Hodgson).

80. Zbaraz, *Abortion and the Supreme Court: A Physician's Fight for Medical Equality,* 4 SEXUAL MED. TODAY 43 (1980).

81. *Hearings on Bills Proposing a Constitutional Amendment With Respect to Abortion Before the Subcommittee on the Constitution of the Senate Committee on the Judiciary,* 97th Cong. 1st Sess., in 1 CONSTITUTIONAL AMENDMENTS RELATING TO ABORTION (1981), at 158–59 (testimony of Irwin M. Cushner) [hereinafter cited as 1981 Senate Hearings].

82. 410 U.S. at 150.

83. Hilgers & O'Hare, *Abortion Related Maternal Mortality: An Indepth Analysis,* in NEW PERSPECTIVES ON HUMAN ABORTION 89 (T. Hilgers, D. Horan & D. Mall eds. 1981).

84. *Id.*

85. *Id.* at 90.

86. Logrillo, *Effect of Induced Abortion on Subsequent Reproductive Function,* NATIONAL INSTITUTE OF CHILD HEALTH AND HUMAN DEVELOPMENT, NO1-HD-6-2802 (April 18, 1980).

87. Levin, *Association of Abortion with Subsequent Pregnancy Loss,* 243 J. A.M.A. 2495 (1980).

88. H.L. v. Matheson, 450 U.S. 398, 411 (1981).

89. Cates, *Late Effects of Induced Abortion. Hypothesis or Knowledge?,* 22 J. REPRODUCTIVE MED. 207 (1979).

90. Women meet the test established by the Supreme Court in Levy v. Louisiana, 391 U.S. 68, 70 (1978), for the determination of personhood: "They are humans, live, and have their beings. They are clearly 'persons' within the meaning of the Equal Protection Clause of the Fourteenth Amendment."

91. People v. Belous, 80 Cal. Rptr. 354, 458 P.2d 194 (1969).

92. George, *Current Abortion Laws: Proposals and Movement for Reform,* 17 CASE W. RES. L. REV. 371 (1965).

93. Commonwealth v. Wheeler, 315 Mass. 394, 53 N.E.2d 4 (1944); State v. Brandenburg, 137 N.J.L. 124, 58 A.2d 709 (1948): *See also* Johnson v. People, 33 Colo. 224, 80 P. 133 (1905), which interprets an ambiguous state statute to include an exception for the procurement of a miscarriage to save the life of the mother.

94. State v. Siciliano, 21 N.J. 249, 121 A.2d 490, 495 (1956). *See also* Dougherty v. People, 1 Colo. 514 (1872).

95. People v. Barksdale, 105 Cal. Rptr. 1, 503 P.2d 257 (1972). *See also* Crossen v. Attorney Gen., 344 F. Supp. 587 (E.D. Ky. 1972), where the District Court declared that "it is only where the woman's life is in certain and imminent danger that the State may not deny her the right to decide to have an abortion."

96. *Hearings on S.J. Res. 119 and S.J. Res. 130 Before the Subcomm. on Const. of the Senate Comm. on the Judiciary,* 93d Cong., 2d Sess., in ABORTION, pt. 1, at 563 (1974) (testimony of Hon. James A. Burke) [hereinafter cited as 1974 Senate Hearings].

97. J. NOONAN, THE MORALITY OF ABORTION 230 (1970).

98. *See* Byrn I, *supra* note 18, at 801, 853–54 (1973).

99. J. HALL, GENERAL PRINCIPLES OF CRIMINAL LAW 426 (2d ed. 1965).

100. *See, e.g.,* State v. Moore, 25 Iowa 128 (1868); People v. Sessions, 56 Mich. 594, 26 N.W. 301 (1886); Gleitman v. Cosgrave, 49 N.J. 22, 22 A.3d 1411 (1967); Trent v. State, 15 Ala. App. 485, 73 So. 834 (1917).

101. *Contra* Byrn v. New York City Health & Hosp. Corp., *supra* note 74.

102. Commonwealth v. Brunelle, 341 Mass. 675, 171 N.E.2d 850 (1961); Rex v. Bourne, [1938] 1 K.B. 615; 49 GEO. L.J. 521 (1961).

103. State v. Dunklebarger, 206 Ia. 971, 221 N.W. 592 (1928); *see also* Henrie v. Derryberry, 358 F. Supp. 719 (N.D. Okla. 1973).

104. *See* Quay, *Justifiable Abortion—Medical and Legal Foundation,* 49 GEO. L.J. 173 (1960).

105. Civil Rights Cases, 109 U.S. 3, 20 (1883).

106. Jones v. Mayer Co., 392 U.S. 409, 438 (1968).

107. Bell v. Hood, 327 U.S. 678 (1946); Bivens v. Six Unknown Named Agents of the Bureau of Narcotics, 403 U.S. 388 (1971).

108. Butz v. Economou, 438 U.S. 478, 504 (1978).

109. Davis v. Passman, 442 U.S. 228 (1979).

110. *See* Bopp, *Report of NRLC Human Life Amendment Committee,* National Right to Life News, Jan. 27, 1981, at 5, col. 1.

111. Destro, *Abortion and the Constitution: The Need for a Life Protective Amendment,* 63 CALIF. L. REV. 1250, 1320 (1975).

112. Byrn, *A Human Life Amendment: What Would It Mean?* 1 HUM. LIFE REV. 50 (1975) [hereinafter cited as Byrn II].

113. Letter from John T. Noonan, Jr., to Joseph P. Witherspoon (Nov. 10, 1980).

114. 129 CONG. REC. S 498 (daily ed. Jan. 26, 1983) (remarks of Senator Hatch). On March 10, 1982, the Senate Judiciary Committee had endorsed the amendment by a vote of 10 to 7. Additionally, the National Right to Life Committee, on December 12, 1981, had endorsed the amendment as the first step in a two-amendment strategy with the NRLC Amendment as the second and ultimate amendment.

115. Statement of Hon. G. William Whitehurst, 1976 House Hearings, *supra* note 51, at 366.

116. *Id.* at 367.

117. 121 CONG. REC. 31106 (1975) (remarks of Congresswoman Sullivan).

118. *Id. See also* statement of John T. Noonan, 1976 House Hearings, *supra* note 51, at 65-82; statement of David W. Louisell, 1976 House Hearings, *supra* note 51, at 163-67.

119. 129 CONG. REC. S 496 (daily ed. Jan. 26, 1983) (remarks of Senator Hatch).

120. *Id.* at 498.

121. *Id.* at 499.

122. 1982 Senate Report, *supra* note 21, at 54.

123. *Id.* at 55.

124. *Id.* at 57.

125. *Id.* at 58.

126. *Id.* at 59.

127. Rosenberg, *Effect of Proposed Constitutional Amendment on Supreme Court's Abortion Decisions,* LIBR. OF CONGRESS 5 (1975).

128. *Id.* at 6.

129. *See* J. BAKER, THE HATCH AMENDMENT 6–10 (1982).

130. 410 U.S. at 153.

131. *Id.* at 154.

132. Doe v. Bolton, 410 U.S. 179, 189 (1973).

133. 432 U.S. 464 (1977).

134. *Id.* at 473–74.

135. BAKER, *supra* note 129, at 6.

136. *See* Statement of Lynn D. Wardle, 1981 Senate Hearings, *supra* note 81, at 657; Statement of Victor G. Rosenblum, *id.* at 856.

137. Statement of Victor G. Rosenblum, 1981 Senate Hearings, *supra* note 81, at 657.

138. Statement of Lynn D. Wardle, 1981 Senate Hearings, *supra* note 81, at 657.

139. 1982 Senate Report, *supra* note 21, at 55.

140. Plenary is defined as full, entire, complete, absolute, perfect, and unqualified. BLACK'S LAW DICTIONARY 1313 (4th ed. 1968).

141. *See* McCormick & Co. v. Brown, 286 U.S. 123, 144–45 (1932); Everard's Breweries v. Day, 265 U.S. 545, 558–59 (1924); United States v. Lanza, 260 U.S. 377, 380–85 (1922); National Prohibition Cases, 253 U.S. 350, 387 (1920).

142. United States v. Lanza, 260 U.S. 377, 381–82 (1922).

143. Statement of Victor G. Rosenblum, 1981 Senate Hearings, *supra* note 81, at 862.

144. *See* statement of Lynn D. Wardle, 1981 Senate Hearings, *supra* note 81, at 660.

145. U.S. CONST., art. VI, cl. 2.

146. 1982 Senate Report, *supra* note 21, at 59.

147. *See* testimony of Victor G. Rosenblum, 1981 Senate Hearings, *supra* note 81, at 850–52.

148. Bopp, *Are There Changes Necessary in the Hatch Federalism Amendment?,* National Right to Life News, Apr. 8, 1982, at 8, col. 1.

149. *Id.*

150. E. HUGHES, OBSTETRIC-GYNECOLOGIC TERMINOLOGY 414 (1972).

151. *See, e.g.,* People v. Ramsey, 83 Cal. App.2d 707, 189 P.2d 802, 808 (1948).

152. Conn. v. Wood, 302 Mass. 265, 19 N.E.2d 320, 325 (1939).

153. McClure v. State, 214 Ark. 159, 215 S.W.2d 524, 526 (1948).

154. Hall v. People, 119 Colo. 141, 201 P.2d 382 (1948).

155. *See* BAKER, *supra* note 129, at 12–17.

156. Statement of Victor G. Rosenblum, 1981 Senate Hearings, *supra* note 81, at 868.

157. 1982 Senate Report, *supra* note 21, at 56, where the committee defines the word *abortion* "to include those actions which intend the destruction of the human embryo or fetus" and defines those individuals to be protected as "all individual organisms of the species *Homo sapiens* from the onset of fertilization until live birth or its equivalent, without regard to the stage or locus of development, inside or outside the mother's body."

158. Byrn II, *supra* note 112, at 51–52.

159. People v. Belous, 80 Cal. Rptr. 354, 458 P.2d 194 (1969); Moe v. Secretary of Admin. and Fin., 417 N.E.2d 387 (Mass. 1981). *See also* Doe v. Bridgeton Hosp. Ass'n, 71 N.J. 478, 366 A.2d 641 (1976).

160. Rice, *Overruling Roe v. Wade: An Analysis of the Proposed Constitutional Amendments,* 15 B.C. INDUSTRIAL & COMMERCIAL L. REV. 307, 322 (1973).

161. Statement of Dennis J. Horan, 1981 Senate Hearings, *supra* note 81, at 762.

162. As a result, these proposals have been criticized for putting the right to life of the unborn "at the perpetual mercy of shifting legislative majorities and makes it dependent upon the outcome of bitter political campaigns." Byrn II, *supra* note 112, at 53.

163. NRLC has endorsed the Hatch Federalism Amendment, *supra* note 114, as the first amendment and the NRLC Amendment, *infra,* as the second amendment. *See* National Right to Life News, Dec. 21, 1981, at 3, col. 1.

164. For the Senate debate and vote on the Hatch-Eagleton Amendment, *see* 129 CONG. REC. 9076–9170 (daily ed. June 28, 1983) and 129 CONG. REC. 9249–9311 (daily ed. June 28, 1983).

165. Statement of Senator Thomas F. Eagleton, 1983 Senate Hearings, *supra* note 23 (Feb. 28, 1983).

166. St. Louis Globe-Democrat, Oct. 4, 1982, at 1, col. 4.

167. Statement of Senator Thomas F. Eagleton, 1983 Senate Hearings, *supra* note 23 (Feb. 28, 1983).

168. Chicago Sun-Times, Mar. 25, 1983, at 25, col. 3.

169. 410 U.S. 113 (1973).

170. 410 U.S. 179 (1973).

171. Statement of Senator Thomas F. Eagleton, 1983 Senate Hearings, *supra* note 23 (Feb. 28, 1983).

172. *See* testimony of Lawrence Tribe, 1983 Senate Hearings, *supra* note 23 (Feb. 28, 1983) and testimony of Robert Packwood, *id.*

173. Statement of Lynn D. Wardle, *id.*

174. *Id.*

175. SENATE COMM. ON JUDICIARY, HUMAN LIFE FEDERALISM AMENDMENT, S. REP. No. 98–149, 98th Cong., 1st Sess. at 55–56.

176. 1983 Senate Hearings, *supra* note 23 (March 7, 1983).

177. Statement of Dennis J. Horan, *id.*

178. Statement of Victor Rosenblum, *id.*

179. *Id.*

180. *Id.*

181. *Id.*

182. Section 5 of the 14th Amendment states: "The Congress shall have power to enforce, by appropriate legislation, the provisions of this article." U.S. CONST. amend. XIV, § 5.

183. For testimony concerning such an approach, see *Hearing on S. 158 Before the Subcommittee on Separation of Powers of the Senate Committee of the Judiciary,* 97th Cong., 1st Sess., THE HUMAN LIFE BILL, vol. 1 [hereinafter referred to as 1981 HLB Hearings]. For the full text of the Human Life Bill, see *infra,* app.

184. The issue of the constitutionality of a human life bill is beyond the scope of this chapter.

185. Statement of Professor Joseph P. Witherspoon, 1981 HLB Hearings, *supra* note 183, at 704–05.

186. *See generally* Noonan, *A Difficulty that Haunts the Pro-life Movement* (unpublished memorandum, January 1983).

187. U.S. CONST. art. I, § 8, cl. 3.

188. Congress has wide power to regulate interstate commerce, even if the impact of an activity on interstate commerce is small or merely potential or only hypothetical. *See, e.g.,* United States v. Braasch, 505 F.2d 138 (7th Cir. 1974), *cert. denied,* 421 U.S. 910 (1975).

189. Feminist Women's Health Center, Inc. v. Mohammad, 586 F.2d 530 (5th Cir. 1978), *cert. denied,* 444 U.S. 924 (1979).

190. McCulloch v. Maryland, 4 U.S. 316 (1819).

191. 18 U.S.C. § 1961.

192. *Id.* at § 1961 (1).

193. 23 U.S.C. § 154 (a)(1).

194. *Id.* at § 141.

195. Drafted by Robert M. Byrn, Fordham Univ. Law School and Joseph P. Witherspoon, Univ. of Texas Law School. Testimony of Joseph P. Witherspoon, 1976 House Hearings, *supra* note 51 at 27.

196. 120 CONG. REC. 399 (1974) (remarks of Congressman Hogan).

197. 119 CONG. REC. 22226 (1973) (remarks of Senator Helms, senatorial sponsor of the Hogan Amendment).

198. 119 CONG. REC. 17541 (1973) (remarks of Senator Buckley).

199. *Id.*

200. *See* H. STORER, CRIMINAL ABORTION IN AMERICA 10, 100, 107 (1860) ("[T]he foetus (is) already, and from the outset, a human being, alive, however early its *stage of development* and existing independently of its mother. . . . it is not rational to suppose . . . that life . . . dates from any other epoch than conception. . . . medical men, in all obstetric matters, are the physical guardians of women and their offspring. . . . [Protection of the unborn is required] at every stage of gestation.").
See also Miller, *Address (of President of American Medical Association at 1860 Annual Meeting)*, 13 TRANSACTIONS AM. MED. A., 58–59 (June 1860) ("[F]rom the moment of conception, a new being is engendered, in whose constitution, microscopic though its parts may be, lies unfolded the substratum in which inheres

potentially all that pertains to man.... *In every stage of its development,* it is as much an independent being as are its parents. With such enlightenment as this, what virtuous woman ... would be accessory to so foul a deed as the destruction of her offspring.").

201. 60 U.S. 393 (1856).

202. A. Avins, The Reconstruction Amendments' Debates 274, 36–38 (1967).

203. 119 Cong. Rec. 1754 (1973) (remarks of Senator Buckley).

204. *Id. See also* remarks of Senator James Buckley, 1974 Senate Hearings, *supra* note 96, at 29–77.

205. Statement of Senator Jesse Helms, 1974 Senate Hearings, *supra* note 96, pt. 4, at 97. Senator Helms, who had previously cosponsored the Hogan Amendment, introduced the Helms Amendment at the end of the 1974 Senate Hearings on the grounds that he has had an "opportunity to refine (his) thoughts" and reflect "upon the differing criticism" of other amendments. He felt that this amendment is "a great improvement over every other proposal." Statement of Senator Jesse Helms, 1974 Senate Hearings, *supra* note 96, pt. 4, at 96–97. On April 28, 1976, Senator Helms, by parliamentary maneuver, was able to bring to the floor the Helms Amendment, then S.J. Res. 178, in order to force a vote thereon by the entire Senate. Senator Birch Bayh, however, moved to table the amendment, which was agreed to by a vote of 47 to 40.

206. *Id. See also* Rice, *supra* note 160, at 324–25.

207. Statement of Senator Jesse Helms, 1974 Senate Hearings, *supra* note 96, pt. 4, at 98.

208. 122 Cong. Rec. 6457 (1976) (remarks of Senator Helms). *See also* Rice, *supra* note 160, at 326–28.

209. *See* discussion on due process rights of unborn in Noonan, *supra* note 97, at 254–58.

210. Patsone v. Pennsylvania, 232 U.S. 138 (1913).

211. Truax v. Raich, 239 U.S. 33 (1915). *See also* Tigner v. Texas, 310 U.S. 141 (1940).

212. Skinner v. State of Oklahoma, 316 U.S. 535 (1942).

213. *See* discussion in Noonan, *supra* note 97, at 250–51; Rice, *supra* note 160, at 330–40.

214. Truax v. Corrigan, 257 U.S. 312, 333 (1921).

215. 365 U.S. 715 (1960).

216. 387 U.S. 369 (1967).

217. Stern, *Abortion: Reform and the Law,* 59 J. Crim. L. 84, 86 (1968).

218. George, *supra* note 92, at 381.

219. Noonan considered the penalty under prior restrictive abortion statutes to be adequate. Noonan, *supra* note 97, at 247.

220. Testimony of Lawrence H. Tribe, 1974 Senate Hearings, *supra* note 96, pt. 3, at 350–52. *Contra* Statement of John T. Noonan, 1976 House Hearings, *supra* note 51, at 81–82.

221. 410 U.S. at 156–57.

222. *See* United States v. Marin Rock & Asphalt Co., 296 F. Supp. 1213 (C.D. Cal. 1969).

223. Boys Markets, Inc. v. Retail Clerk's Union, 398 U.S. 235 (1970).

224. 410 U.S. at 63–64.

225. 120 CONG. REC. 399 (1974) (remarks of Congressman Hogan).

226. 410 U.S. at 161.

227. Grobstein, *External Human Fertilization,* 240 SCI. AM. 57, 67 (1974).

228. Statement of Jesse Helms, 1974 Senate Hearings, *supra* note 96, at 95.

229. *Id.*

230. *Id.* at 94–95; 120 CONG. REC. 17093 (1974) (remarks of Congressman Roncallo).

231. Rice, *supra* note 160, at 328–29.

232. 120 CONG. REC. 17093 (1974) (remarks of Congressman Roncallo).

233. Authored by Charles Rice of the University of Notre Dame Law School. Rice, *supra* note 160, at 341.

234. 120 CONG. REC. 17093 (1974) (remarks of Congressman Roncallo).

235. *Id. See also* Rice, *supra* note 160, at 340–41.

236. 120 CONG. REC. 17094 (1974) (remarks of Congressman Roncallo).

237. *See* Rice, *supra* note 160, at 329, 340–41.

238. E. HUGHES, OBSTETRIC-GYNECOLOGIC TERMINOLOGY 414 (1972).

239. Packer & Campbell, *Therapeutic Abortion: A Problem in Law and Medicine,* 11 STAN. L. REV. 417, 418 (1959).

240. Authored by Charles Rice of Notre Dame Law School.

241. 127 CONG. REC. S570 (daily ed. Jan. 2, 1981) (remarks of Senator Helms).

242. *Id.* at S574–75.

243. *Id.* at S575.

244. *Id.* at S576.

245. Only the Garn and NRLC amendments would permit the states the option of whether or not to allow maternal lifesaving abortions.

246. *See* cases cited, *supra* note 93.

247. Commonwealth v. Brunelle, *supra* note 102.

248. Rex v. Bourne, [1938] 1 K.B. 615.

249. State v. Dunklebarger, 206 1a. 971, 221 N.W. 592 (1928). Compare the Garn and NRLC amendments, which would permit only a law allowing "medical procedures required to prevent the death of the mother" or "either the pregnant woman or her unborn offspring."

250. People v. Belous, 80 Cal. Rptr. 354, 458 P.2d 194 (1969); State v. Barquet, 262 So.2d 431 (Fla. 1972).

251. Rice, *What About the NRLC Drafting Committee,* Wanderer, Feb. 5, 1981, at 1, col. 1.

252. Drafted by Joseph P. Witherspoon of University of Texas Law School. Testimony of Joseph P. Witherspoon, 1976 House Hearings, *supra* note 51, at 27.

253. Other amendments have been introduced in Congress that would allow for additional exceptions. Congressman McKay, for instance, introduced H.J. RES. 606 in the 95th Congress, which would allow for abortion (1) in the case of rape, and (2) in order to prevent permanent and incapacitating impairment of the mother's health. 123 CONG. REC. 31380 (1977) (remarks of Congressman McKay). Any expansion of the circumstances where abortion would be permitted would reduce the protection offered by the amendment to the unborn. Additionally, such exceptions are not necessary. *See infra* chs. 6 and 9. Additionally, Henle (*infra* ch. 4) argues that an appropriate formulation of an exception clause would be: "Provided, however, that nothing in this article shall prohibit a law permitting, as a last resort, an abortion in order to preserve a value as valuable as human life itself." This formulation beggars the question, since the Supreme Court in *Roe v. Wade* found that it could not determine whether or not unborn life is human life, and, regardless, the Court can be expected to determine that a woman's freedom to decide whether or not to have an abortion is a value equal to life.

254. By permitting, but not requiring, the states to allow maternal lifesaving abortions, the Garn and NRLC amendments should be acceptable to those who adhere to the Catholic doctrine of double effect. *See* Rice, *supra* note 160, at 329.

255. Testimony of Joseph P. Witherspoon, 1976 House Hearings, *supra* note 51, at 28–30.

256. There is precedent for an explicit exception in a constitutional provision. In the 13th Amendment, slavery or involuntary servitude was prohibited "except as a punishment for crime whereof the party shall have been duly convicted." U.S. CONST. amend. XIII, § 1. While imprisonment had not previously been considered slavery or involuntary servitude, the draftsmen of the 13th Amendment wanted to make clear the intended effect of the amendment. The draftsmen of the Garn and NRLC amendments have a similar intent.

257. The editor chaired this committee with committee members Charles Rice, Robert Byrn, Joseph Witherspoon, and Mathew Bulfin.

258. Bopp, *supra* note 110.

259. Byrn, *Majority Report on Section 3 of the Proposed Human Life Amendment,* National Right to Life News, Jan. 27, 1981, at 7, col. 1.

260. Rice, *Separate Report to National Right to Life Committee,* National Right to Life News, Jan. 27, 1981, at 10, col. 1.

261. National Right to Life News, Oct. 13, 1981, at 1, col. 1.

262. Bopp, *On a Human Life Amendment,* in THE ZERO PEOPLE 231 (1983).

Chapter Two The Effects of a Human Life Amendment on Federal and State Law

1. 410 U.S. 113 (1973).

2. *Hearing on S.J. Res. 119 and S.J. Res. 130 Before the Subcomm. on Const. of the Senate Judiciary Comm.,* 93rd Cong., 2nd Sess., ABORTION, pt. III, at 252 (1974) (statement of John Ely) (hereinafter cited as 1974 Senate Hearings).

3. 410 U.S. at 153.

4. *See* Colautti v. Franklin, 439 U.S. 379, 400–01 (1979).

5. 410 U.S. 179 (1973).

6. *See generally* J. MOHR, ABORTION IN AMERICA, THE ORIGINS AND EVOLUTION OF NATIONAL POLICY, 1800–1900 (1978).

7. Epstein, *Substantive Due Process by Any Other Name: The Abortion Cases,* 1973 SUP. CT. REV. 159, 179.

8. The rabid dissents of Justices Blackmun and Marshall in the 1977 abortion funding cases are shocking examples of this.

9. *See generally* L. WARDLE, THE ABORTION PRIVACY DOCTRINE: A COMPENDIUM AND CRITIQUE OF FEDERAL COURT ABORTION CASES 303–08 (1981).

10. *See generally* Korematsu v. United States, 323 U.S. 214 (1944); Hirabayashi v. United States, 320 U.S. 81 (1943).

11. Henshaw, Forrest, Sullivan & Tietze, *Abortion Service in the United States: 1979 and 1980,* 14 FAM. PLAN. PERSP.

12. C. RICE, FIFTY QUESTIONS ON ABORTION 1 (1979).

13. Henshaw, Forest, Sullivan & Tietze, *Abortion in the United States, 1978–1979,* 13 FAM. PLAN. PERSP. 17, 18, Tables 10 & 11 (1981).

14. *Id.* at 7, Table 1.

15. *Id.* at 17, 18.

16. Akron v. Akron Center for Reproductive Health, Inc., 103 S. Ct. 2481 (1983); Planned Parenthood Ass'n v. Ashcroft, 103 S. Ct. 2517 (1983); Simopolous v. Virginia, 103 S. Ct. 2532 (1983).

17. THE FEDERALIST No. 49 (J. Madison).

18. R. LEE, A LAWYER LOOKS AT THE CONSTITUTION 22, 30 (1981).

19. *See* L. WARDLE & M. WOOD, A LAWYER LOOKS AT ABORTION 189–204 (1982).

20. *Hearings on Proposed Constitutional Amendments on Abortion Before the Subcommittee on Civil and Constitutional Rights of the Committee on the Judiciary of the House of Representatives on Proposed Constitutional Amendments on Abortion,* 94th Cong., 2d Sess., PROPOSED CONSTITUTIONAL AMENDMENTS ON ABORTION, Part I, at 166 (1976) (statements of Professor David W. Louisell) [hereinafter cited as 1976 House Hearings].

21. Marbury v. Madison, 5 U.S. (1 Cranch) 137, 177 (1803).

22. *See generally* Fletcher v. Peck, 10 U.S. (6 Cranch) 87 (1810); McCullouch v. Maryland 17 U.S. (4 Wheat.) 316, (1819). *See also* Martin v. Hunter's Lessee, 14 U.S. (1 Wheat.) 384 (1816).

23. For example, the 21st Amendment not only directly repealed the 18th Amendment but operated to partially abrogate the equal protection and due process clauses of the 14th Amendment and the interstate commerce clause of Article I of the Constitution. *See generally* Crabb, *State Power over Liquor under the Twenty First Amendment,* 12 U. DET. L.J. 11 (1948).

24. Marbury v. Madison, 5 U.S. (1 Cranch) 177, 178 (1803).

25. 1976 House Hearings, *supra* note 20, at 166.

26. D. BELL, RACE RACISM AND AMERICAN LAW 33–38 (2d ed. 1980).

27. *See* L. WARDLE & M. WOOD, *supra* note 19, at 189–205, 211–23.

28. *See supra* ch. 1.

29. Gerster, *What Is the Best H.L.A. Wording?* National Right to Life News, Jan. 12, 1981, at 1, 7.

30. Rice, *Overruling Roe v. Wade: An Analysis of the Proposed Human Life Amendments,* 15 B. C. Industrial & Commercial L. Rev. 307, 340 (1974) ("It should not be supposed that any form of amendment is sacrosanct.").

31. Civil Rights Cases, 109 U.S. 3, 11 (1883) ("Civil rights such as are guaranteed by the Constitution against state aggression, cannot be impaired by the wrongful acts of individuals, unsupported by State authority. . . . The wrongful act of an individual, unsupported by any such authority, is simply a private wrong.").

32. 428 U.S. 52 (1976).

33. 444 U.S. 277, 281 (1980).

34. Discussing the nonpersonhood of the unborn, Justice Blackmun referred to a prior case in which an abortion statute had been liberally construed and noted: "[W]e there would not have indulged in statutory interpretation favorable to abortion in specified circumstances if the necessary consequence was the termination of life entitled to Fourteenth Amendment protection." Roe v. Wade, 410 U.S. 113, 159 (1973). Professor Rice relies on this passage to support his conclusion that a personhood amendment would reach private abortion. Rice, *supra* note 30, at 330, 331. But I do not think that this dictum supports that conclusion. The language quoted comes from the section of *Roe* in which Justice Blackmun is explaining why the unborn are not persons for purposes of the 14th Amendment. Thus, the gist of the quoted passage is only that the Court's prior decision assumed that the unborn were not persons. It is not necessary for purposes of the argument Justice Blackmun was making to further suggest, as Professor Rice does, that if the unborn were persons private abortion would be proscribed under the 5th and 14th amendments.

35. 410 U.S. at 156, 157.

36. Statement of John Ely, 1974 Senate Hearings, *supra* note 2, at 256.

37. Statement of Laurence Tribe, 1974 Senate Hearings, *supra* note 2, at 347.

> But if anything is clear about the abortion controversy, it seems to me one thing is. That no amount of constitutional redefinition of fetuses as persons can alter the biological reality that they are persons of a rather special sort—persons that in the early phase of their development cannot survive without using the body of someone else.
>
> And that, of course, is the source of the entire constitutional controversy surrounding abortion. It was the Court's conclusion that the dependence of the fetus on the woman prior to viability—prior to the time the fetus could survive independently—makes it not only reasonable, but mandatory, that the ultimate choice whether or not to continue the pregnancy should be the woman's. And in no way does that conclusion rest on an argument about the personhood of the fetus. That is, one could easily conclude, with these amendments, that the fetus is a human being, a full person from the moment of conception, and still say that to deny such a person protection from the woman's choice until the point of viability is a reasonable policy, entirely consistent with due process and equal protection.

See also statement of John Ely, 1974 Senate Hearings, *supra* note 2, at 250, 253.

38. Statement of Laurence Tribe, 1974 Senate Hearings, *supra* note 2, at 347.

39. U.S. Const. amend. XIII [1865].

> SECTION 1. Neither slavery nor involuntary servitude, except as a punishment for crime whereof the party shall have been duly convicted, shall exist within the United States, or any place subject to their jurisdiction.
>
> SECTION 2. Congress shall have the power to enforce this article by appropriate legislation.

40. U.S. Const. amend. XVIII [1919].

> SECTION 1. After one year from the ratification of this article the manufacture, sale, or transportation of intoxicating liquors within, the importation thereof into, or the exportation thereof from the United States and all territory subject to the jurisdiction thereof for beverage purposes is hereby prohibited.

SECTION 2. The Congress and the several States shall have concurrent power to enforce this article by appropriate legislation.
SECTION 3. This article shall be inoperative unless it shall have been ratified as an amendment to the Constitution by the legislatures of the several States, as provided in the Constitution, within seven years from the date of the submission hereof to the States by the Congress.

41. 109 U.S. 3, 20 (1883).

42. CONGRESSIONAL RESEARCH SERVICE, THE CONSTITUTION OF THE UNITED STATES: AN INTERPRETATION 1290–91 (1973).

43. Alma Society, Inc. v. Mellon, 601 F.2d 1225, 1237 (2d Cir. 1979).

44. D. BELL, *supra* note 27, at 33.

45. 253 U.S. 350, 386 (1920). *See further infra* note 50.

46. 258 U.S. 403 (1922).

47. *Id.* at 407–08.

48. *Id.* at 408.

49. J. NOWAK, R. ROTUNDA & J. YOUNG, CONSTITUTIONAL LAW 389 (1978).

50. In several cases dealing with the 18th Amendment, the Supreme Court elucidated what the "concurrent power" provision meant with respect to the concurrent authority of the states and Congress to enforce prohibition.

1. Enforcement acts of Congress and/or the states did not have to be approved by the other to be effective, but were effective within the territorial limits of the respective sovereign. Thus, an act could be violative of and prosecuted under both federal and state law without violating the double jeopardy clause.

2. States could enact legislation regulating dealing with liquor even if it was stricter or more lenient than the federal law, the National Prohibition Act.

3. However, to be sustainable under the 18th Amendment, such legislation would have to be *directed toward the enforcement* of the constitutional prohibition.

4. If the federal or state legislature authorized or sanctioned what the sections prohibited, it would be invalid. *See* National Prohibition Cases, 253 U.S. 350 (1920); United States v. Lanza, 260 U.S. 377 (1922); Everard's Breweries v. Day, 265 U.S. 545 (1924); Donnelly v. United States, 276 U.S. 506 (1928); McCormick Co. v. Brown, 286 U.S. 131 (1932). *See also* Vigliotti v. Commonwealth, 258 U.S. 403 (1922), and *supra* notes 46–48 and accompanying text.

51. S.J. Res. 110, 97th Cong., 1st Sess. (1981).

52. Human Life Federalism Amendment, S. Rep. No. 97-465, 97th Cong., 2d Sess. 6 (1982).

53. *Id.* at 1, 2.

54. *Id.* at 7.

55. National Right to Life News, Sept. 30, 1982, at 1.

56. *See supra* text accompanying notes 45–50.

57. S. Rep. No. 97-465, *supra* note 52, at 57.

58. *Id.* at 59.

59. *Id.* at 54.

60. S.J. Res. 3, 98th Cong., 2d Sess. (1983).

61. S. Rep. No. 98-148, 98th Cong., 2d Sess. 57 (1983).

62. S. Rep. No. 98-149, 98th Cong., 2d Sess. 1–6 (1983).

63. CONG. Q. WEEKLY REP. (1983).

64. L. WARDLE & M. WOOD, *supra* note 19, at 202; *see also* S. Rep. No. 98-148, *supra* note 61, at 57.

65. S.J. Res. 137, 97th Cong., 1st Sess. (1981).

66. H.R.J. Res. 380, 97th Cong., 1st Sess. (1981).

67. *Id.*

68. Pilpel, *The Fetus as a Person: Possible Legal Consequences of the Hogan-Helms Amendment,* 6 FAM. PLAN. PERSP., 6–7 (1974).

69. Statement of Harriet F. Pilpel, 1976 House Hearings, *supra* note 20, at 176, 153.

70. *Id.* at 179.

71. New York Times, Feb. 15, 1981, at 8.

72. Copelon, *Danger—A "Human Life" Amendment Is on the Way,* Ms., Feb., 1981, at 46.

73. *Id.*

74. *Id.* at 72.

75. REPRODUCTIVE FREEDOM PROJECT, ACLU FOUNDATION; THE SO-CALLED "HUMAN LIFE" AMENDMENT, THE MOST CRITICAL THREAT TO OUR RIGHT TO PRIVACY 8 (1981) [hereinafter cited as REPRODUCTIVE FREEDOM PROJECT].

76. *Id.* at 12.

77. UNITED STATES COMMISSION ON CIVIL RIGHTS, CONSTITUTIONAL ASPECTS OF THE RIGHT TO LIMIT CHILD BEARING 92 (April 1975) [hereinafter cited as U.S.C.C.R. Report].

78. *Id.* at 90.

79. *Id.* at 27–76.

80. Statement of Arthur S. Flemming, 1976 House Hearings, *supra* note 20, at 141.

81. Pilpel, *supra* note 68, at 7.

82. Chicago Sunday Sun-Times, Feb. 15, 1981, at 7. *See also NARAL Rebuked for Distortions by Washington Star,* National Right to Life News, Jan. 27, 1981, at 5.

83. BLACK'S LAW DICTIONARY 906 (4th ed. 1968).

84. *Hearings on S.J. Res. 6, S.J. Res. 10 and 11, and S.J. Res. 91 Before the Subcomm. on Const. of the Comm. on the Judiciary of the United States Senate,* 94th Cong., 1st Sess., ABORTION, Part IV, at 106, 109 (1975) (statement of Robert M. Byrn).

85. 5 R. POWELL, POWELL ON REAL PROPERTY 728 (1979).

86. *Id.* at 115.

87. *Id.* at 728 nn. 17 & 18.

88. UNIFORM PROBATE CODE § 32-108.

89. 3 R. POWELL, POWELL ON REAL PROPERTY 187 (1979).

90. W. PROSSER, LAW OF TORTS 336 (1971).

91. *Id.* at 337.

92. *Id.;* C. DALE, POTENTIAL IMPLICATIONS OF S. 158 FOR THE LEGAL RIGHTS OF THE UNBORN IN TRADITIONAL AREAS OF TORT, PROPERTY, AND CRIMINAL LAW, 3 n.18 (April 21, 1981) (printed by Congressional Research Service). ("What is especially interesting to me as a teacher of torts for the past several years is that tort law has recently been and is today far more supportive of the sanctity of life than is the Supreme Court's present position on abortion.") 1976 House Hearings, *supra* note 20, at 195, 196 (statement by Professor Victor Rosenblum).

93. RESTATEMENT (SECOND) OF TORTS § 869 (1979).

94. W. PROSSER, *supra* note 90, at 338.

95. *See, e.g.,* U.S.C.C.R. Report, *supra* note 77, at 90; REPRODUCTIVE FREEDOM PROJECT, *supra* note 75, at 16.

96. *See, e.g.,* Pilpel, *supra* note 68, at 6, 7; REPRODUCTIVE FREEDOM PROJECT, *supra* note 75, at 16.

97. W. PROSSER, *supra* note 90, at 336.

98. In the case of In Re Unborn Baby Smith, J923725 (1981), the California Supreme Court declared moot a petition for a writ of habeas corpus filed on behalf of a psychotic, mentally retarded, vagrant, pregnant mother who was ordered detained in a secure facility—possibly a psychiatric hospital—until the birth of her child. The unborn child was viable and expert testimony established that the mother's conduct presented a real and substantial threat to the life of the child *in utero.* Similar orders have been issued in similar cases involving psychotic or drug-abusing expectant mothers whose extreme conduct presents clear and present threat to the life or health of their viable unborn children. *See* LEGAL RESPONSE: CHILD ADVOCATE & PROTECTION, Spring 1981, at 4. *See further* Jefferson v. Griffin Spaulding County Hospital Authority, 247 Ga. 86, 274 S.E.2d 457 (1981), in which the court ordered a mother objecting on religious grounds to submit to cesarean section necessary to save the life of the unborn child. *See also* Raleigh-Fitkin Memorial Hosp. v. Anderson, 42 N.J. 421, 201 A.2d 537 (1964).

99. W. PROSSER, *supra* note 90, at 866–67 (1971); R. PERKINS, PERKINS ON CRIMINAL LAW 987 (1969).

100. Statement of Professor Robert M. Byrn, 1974 Senate Hearings, *supra* note 2, at 106, 111–15.

101. *Id.* at 223.

102. *See generally* Roe v. Wade, 410 U.S. 113, 151n. 49.

Chapter Three The Unborn as Person

1. *Cf.* I. KANT, FOUNDATIONS OF THE METAPHYSICS OF MORALS 47 (L. W. Beck trans. 1959) (The categorical imperative: "Act so that you treat humanity, whether in your own person or in that of another, always as an end and never as a means only.").

2. ARISTOTLE, METAPHYSICS V, 1015a 13–15.

3. *See, e.g.,* Suarez, *Disputationes Metaphysicae,* 25 OPERA OMNIA 558 (C. Berton ed. 1856–77).

4. For Hume on personal identity, *see* D. HUME, TREATISE OF HUMAN NATURE, bk. 1, pt. 1, § 6 (1896).

5. *See also* Wade, *Potentiality in the Abortion Discussion,* 29 REV. METAPHYSICS 239 (1975) [hereinafter cited as *Wade*]. The points that, (1) contrary to common belief, John Locke never denied the existence of substance, and that (2) Immanuel Kant reduced it to a mental category, which is required for the unity of experience, mean that in any case we are obliged to think with substance if we are going to think at all. *Id.* at 247–48.

6. 64 J. MIGNE, PATROLOGIA LATINA 1343 (1862).

7. *See* ST. THOMAS AQUINAS, SUMMA THEOLOGIAE, I, 29, 3, ad 4 [hereinafter cited as SUMMA]; ST. THOMAS AQUINAS, DE POTENTIA, q. 9, a. 2, ad 10 [hereinafter cited as DE POTENTIA]; *Id.* at a. 3, ad 4 et 5.

8. On Ibn Gabirol as the source of the medieval doctrine of the plurality of forms, *see* G. THÉRY, *L'augustinisme médiéval et le problème de la forme substantielle,* in ACTA HEBDOMADAE AUGUSTINIANAE-THOMISTICAE 140 (1931).

9. *See* PLATO, REPUBLIC, IV, 436AC.

10. *See* SUMMA, *supra* note 7, at I, 76, 3; DE POTENTIA, *supra* note 7, at q. 3, a. 9, ad 9; ST. THOMAS AQUINAS, DE SPIRITUALIBUS CREATURIS, a. 3.

11. SUMMA, *supra* note 7, at I, 76, 3, ad 3; *id.,* 118, 2, ad 2.

12. For some of the embryological observations which led to this conclusion, *see* ARISTOTLE, HISTORY OF ANIMALS VII, 5836 13–24.

13. *See* J. ROSTAND, HUMANLY POSSIBLE, A BIOLOGIST'S NOTES ON THE FUTURE OF MANKIND (1973). Shading off slightly in this connection, Rostand, a French biologist, speaks of a continuing "chemical" or "biological" personality.

> I have emphasized the part played by the chemical personality of the original cell in the genesis of the person. This chemical personality is maintained through all the cellular divisions that take place in the organism, beginning with the ovum, and is thus found in each of the billions of cells that compose the individual. Peter's blood corpuscles, the cells of his epidermis and glands, the fibers of his muscles, and the neurons of his brain differ, by their nucleic acids from Paul's blood corpuscles, epidermal and glandular cells, muscle fibers, and neurons. Peter and Paul are themselves—and unique—in even the least of their elements. Furthermore, this identity will be preserved all through their lives, despite the renewal of tissues (some of which are replaced very often), senile decline, changes of appearance, illnesses, accidents, medical treatments, and even blood transfusions. From conception to death, the biological personality is constant, invariable; we all remain faithful to ourselves to the end.

Id. at 47.

14. *Cf., e.g.,* W. HAMILTON & H. MOSSMAN, HUMAN EMBRYOLOGY 1 (4th ed. 1972) ("The zygote, which has been formed by the fusion of a male and female gamete is a single celled organism."); S. LURIA, 36 LECTURES IN BIOLOGY 146 (1975) ("The zygote is the starting cell of the new individual."). Both texts are among those cited by Dr. Micheline M. Matthews-Roth in recent Senate hearings on the question of when human life begins. *Proposed Human Life Bill: Hearings on S158 Before the Subcomm. on Separation of Powers of the Senate Comm. on the Judiciary,* 97th Cong., 1st Sess. (1981) (statement of Dr. Micheline M. Matthews-Roth). Dr. Matthews-Roth's testimony contains one of the best listings I have seen of current biological authorities on the subject of the beginning of human life. Her own conclusion is: "[I]t is scientifically correct to say that an individual human life begins at conception, when egg and sperm join to form the zygote, and that this developing human always is a member of our species in all stages of its life." *Id.* It is interesting to note that her testimony was totally in agreement with that of the majority of expert witnesses appearing before the Senate Subcommittee and that when it was opposed, as for instance by Leon Rosenberg, it was on semireligious and philosophical grounds. *Id.* (statement of Leon Rosenberg). Thus, Professor Rosenberg, not denying the facts of conception and the reality of the fetus, but stepping out of the role of scientist, introduced what can only be described as a quasi-religious or a metaphysical distinction between this fetus (which he, misusing an Aristotelian metaphysical notion, would call "potentially" human) and a further *je ne sais pas quoi* (I do not know what) called "actual human life."

15. *Cf.* K. MOORE, THE DEVELOPING HUMAN: CLINICALLY ORIENTED EMBRYOLOGY 1 (2nd ed. 1977) ("Each of us started life as a cell called a zygote."); M. GILBERT, BIOGRAPHY OF THE UNBORN, *cited in* R. RUGH & L. SHETTLES, FROM CONCEPTION TO BIRTH: THE DRAMA OF LIFE'S BEGINNINGS 17 (1971) ("Life begins for each of us at an unfelt, unknown, and unhonored instant when a minute wriggling sperm plunges headlong into a mature ovum or egg.").

16. *See* Tooley, *Abortion and Infanticide,* 2 PHIL. PUB. AFF. 37 (1972); Tooley, *Infanticide: A Philosophical Perspective,* 2 ENCYCLOPEDIA OF BIOETHICS 742 (1978).

17. *See* Engelhardt, *The Ontology of Abortion,* 84 ETHICS 217 (1974). Engelhardt has summarized his thesis in one paragraph.

> The question of abortion turns primarily upon the status of the fetus. I argue that in considering human life one must distinguish between human biological life and human personal life. Moreover, there are, so I contend, two senses of persons. The first denotes self-conscious, moral agents. The second denotes instances of human life which can and must play active, social roles. Neither of these characterizations can be made to apply to fetuses, in particular to non-viable fetuses. Since our obligations are solely to persons, there is, therefore, no one wronged in abortion, in particular the abortion of non-viable fetuses.

Engelhardt, Abstract, 1974 PHILOSOPHER'S INDEX 787. Somewhat similar is the view of Bernard David, which is cited in Switzer, *When Human Life Begins,* VOGUE, Sept. 1981, at 604.

18. Donceel, *Abortion: Mediate and Immediate Animation,* 5 CONTINUUM 167 (1967); Donceel, *Causality and Evolution,* 39 NEW SCHOLASTICISM 295 (1965); Donceel, *Immediate Animation and Delayed Hominization,* 31 THEOLOGICAL STUD. 76 (1970); Donceel, *Why Is Abortion Wrong?,* AMERICA, Aug. 16, 1975, at 65.

19. Diamond, *Abortion, Animation, and Biological Hominization,* 36 THEOLOGICAL STUD. 305 (1975).

20. *See* E. HAECKEL, THE RIDDLE OF THE UNIVERSE 81 (J. McCabe trans. 1900). It is notable that at one point Diamond has referred to "the Haeckel theory" as "illuminative." Diamond, *supra* note 19, at 321.

21. L. AREY, DEVELOPMENTAL ANATOMY: A TEXTBOOK AND LABORATORY MANUAL OF EMBRYOLOGY 7 (1965); G. CORNER, OURSELVES UNBORN: AN EMBRYOLOGIST'S ESSAY ON MAN 8, 67 (1944); Medawar, *Embryology,* in THE HARPER DICTIONARY OF MODERN THOUGHT 200 (A. Bullock & O. Stallybrass eds. 1977).

22. *Cf.* Engelhardt, *supra* note 17, at 225 ("[I]t is easier to construe the situation as development from biological properties *with a consequent essential and substantial change* in the significance of the bearer of the properties.") (emphasis added).

23. Note the statement of Dr. Hymie Gordon:

> [F]rom the moment of fertilization, when the deoxyribose nucleic acids from the spermatozoon and the ovum come together to form the zygote, the pattern of the individual's constitutional development is irrevocably determined; his future health, his future intellectual potential, even his future criminal proclivities are all dependent on the sequence of the purine and pyrimidine bases in the original set of DNA molecules of the unicellular individual. True, environmental influences both during the intra-uterine period and after birth modify the individual's constitution and continue to do so right until his death, but it is at the moment of conception that the individual's capacity to respond to these exogenous influences is established.

Heffernan, *The Early Biography of Everyman,* in ABORTION AND SOCIAL JUSTICE 5 (T. Hilgers & D. Horan, eds. 1972).

24. M. BUBER, I AND THOU (R. Smith trans. 2d ed. 1958).

25. G. MARCEL, THE MYSTERY OF BEING (G. Fraser and R. Hague eds. 1960).

26. J. Macmurray, The Form of the Personal (2 vols., 1957, 1961).

27. *See* Wade, *supra* note 5, at 251.

28. Joyce, *Personhood and the Conception Event,* 52 New Scholasticism 106 (1978).

29. Wade has put his intellectual finger upon a central feature of nature in this context when he suggests

> that the natural tendency to think and to choose is basic to the being of the fetus, and the biological tendencies (the ones most clearly active in the genotype) are only specifications of the radical tendency to become a thinking being. Only by the specification of a body and a brain can this fetus ever become the actually thinking being its nature tends to be. Consequently, it is not metaphorical to say that the fetus is in this sense personal: its whole natural thrust is to become a functioning person. And this is true of all the stages of its existence and continues even after it has partially attained personhood (as is the case with me and you), constantly striving to become more fully a person. Aristotle stated it this way: "All men by nature desire to know."

Wade, *supra* note 5, at 254–55. Without actually saying it, Wade here is touching upon the note of internal finality marked by Aristotle's well-known characterization of essence or nature as "what a thing was to be." Aristotle, Posterior Analytics, I, 22, 826 38; Aristotle, De Anima, III, 6, 4306 28; Aristotle, Metaphysics, VII, 3, 10286 34. Consider also the following:

> When we ask the question—What is this thing?—the complete answer is the statement of its definition, or that which the nature tends to fulfill. For example, if the thing in question is a man, the answer is: He is a rational animal. The definition thus expresses what a thing is, its *whatness* or the *what a thing was to be.* The past tense of the verb (*was*) does not express past time. It expresses absolutely the direction of the tendency of a being's nature.

A. Maurer, On Being and Essence by St. Thomas Aquinas 27 (1949).

Chapter Four Morality and Virtue in a Pluralistic Society

1. But even in these societies cultural heroes arise and social eruptions occur. Something like this seems to have happened in Hawaii prior to the coming of Europeans and, perhaps, on Easter Island.

2. Redfield, *Anthropology's Contribution to the Understanding of Man,* 32 Anthropology Q. 16 (1959).

3. In this chapter I am assuming a doctrine of natural law.

4. D. Bidney, Anthropology Today 694 (A. Krober ed., 1953). *See also* Redfield, *The Universally Human & the Cultural Variable,* 10 J. Gen. Educ. 150–60 (1957).

5. For the interplay between natural law and human determinism, see Fuller, *Reason and Fiat in Case Law,* 59 Harv. L. Rev. 377–95 (1946). I believe he makes "fiat" too arbitrary and voluntaristic.

6. Of course, infanticide is against the natural law, but it was not normative ethics that stopped the practice.

7. Henle, *Positive Pluralism vs. Positive Secularism,* Catholic League for Religious and Civil Rights Newsletter, Jan. 1980 (Supp.).

8. Henle, *American Principles and Religious Schools,* 3 St. Louis U.L.J. 237–51 (1955).

9. The publication of the National Organization for Women (NOW) consistently lists the right to choose abortion as one of the "reproductive" rights of women. If there were a right to choose abortion, it would have to be called a "destructive" right since it would destroy what has already been reproduced.

10. I believe this is true even though there are legal cases that espouse a jurisprudential position contrary to both natural justice and our own main legal and moral tradition. For a survey of cases see J. Noonan, A Private Choice 13–19 (1979).

11. Roe v. Wade, 410 U.S. 113, 157 (1973).

12. *See* Testimony of Micheline M. Mathews-Roth, M.D., *Hearings on S. 159 Before the Subcomm. on Separation of Powers of the Senate Comm. on the Judiciary,* 97th Cong., 1st Sess., THE HUMAN LIFE BILL, at 13 (1981), for a comprehensive examination of the position of major medical textbooks on this issue.

13. NOONAN, *supra* note 10, at 52.

14. ST. THOMAS AQUINAS, SUMMA THEOLOGIAE I–II, q. 96, *a* 2, *c,* ad. 1, *q.* 95, *a* 3.

15. See list of religious positions in B. NATHANSON, ABORTING AMERICA 294–303 (1979).

16. By "possible" I refer to possible varying provisions in the enforcing laws in the several states.

17. I am assuming that the state laws would be more specific than the amendment.

Chapter Five The Familial Context of Induced Abortion

1. *The Battle over Abortion,* TIME, Apr. 6, 1981, at 20.

2. Riga, *The Supreme Court's View of Marriage and the Family: Tradition or Transition,* 18 J. FAM. L. 310 (1980).

3. Crutchfield, *Medical Treatment for Minor Children: The Roles of Parents, the State, the Child, and the Supreme Court of the United States,* 30 FAM. REL. 165 (1981).

4. J. DEMPSEY, THE FAMILY AND PUBLIC POLICY 71 (1981).

5. Garn & Oliphant, *Abortion and the American Family: A Note on a Court Long Overdue,* 6 HUM. LIFE REV. 16 (1980).

6. CENTERS FOR DISEASE CONTROL, ABORTION SURVEILLANCE, ANNUAL SUMMARY 1979–1980, 66 (1983).

7. Forrest, Teitze & Sullivan, *Abortion in the United States, 1976–1977,* 10 FAM. PLAN. PERSP. 271 (1978).

8. Krannich, *Abortion in the United States: Past, Present, and Future Trends,* 29 FAM. REL. 365 (1980).

9. Alan Guttmacher Institute, *Continued Increase in Teen Sex, Pregnancy,* 12 FAM. THERAPY NEWS 13 (1981).

10. Senate Labor and Human Resources Committee, March 31, 1981 (testimony of James Ford).

11. Ebaugh & Haney, *Shifts in Abortion Attitudes: 1972–1978,* 42 J. MARITAL & FAM. THERAPY 491 (1980).

12. D. YANKELOVICH, NEW RULES (1980).

13. C. LASCH, THE CULTURE OF NARCISSISM (1981).

14. Roe v. Wade, 410 U.S. 113 (1973).

15. U.S. DEP'T OF HEALTH, EDUC. & WELFARE, CENTER FOR DISEASE CONTROL, ABORTION SURVEILLANCE ANNUAL SUMMARY, 1978 (1980).

16. R. HILL, FAMILIES UNDER STRESS (1949).

17. Planned Parenthood v. Danforth, 428 U.S. 52 (1976).

18. For a legal review, see Brief of Amicus Curiae, Committee to Defend Reproductive Rights v. Meyers, 29 Cal. 3d 252, 625 P.2d 779, 172 Cal. Rptr. 866 (1979). For reviews in the family literature, see Hill, *Status of Family Research, 1900–70,* in THE STATUS OF CHILDREN, YOUTH, AND FAMILIES (J. Calhoun ed. 1980); Klein & Hill, *Determinants of Family Problem Solving Effectiveness,* 2 CONTEMPORARY THEORIES ABOUT THE FAMILY 493 (W. Burr, R. Hill, F. Nye & I. Reiss eds. 1979); Sussman, *Family,* in ENCYCLOPEDIA OF SOCIAL WORK (J. Turner 17th ed. 1977); E. SHORTER, THE MAKING OF THE MODERN FAMILY (1975); FAMILY PROBLEM SOLVING (J. Aldous, T. Condon, P. Hill, M. Strauss & I. Tallman eds. 1971).

19. Eliot, *Handling Family Strains and Shocks,* in FAMILY MARRIAGE AND PARENTHOOD (H. Becker and R. Hill 2d ed. 1955).

20. W. WALLER, THE FAMILY: A DYNAMIC INTERPRETATION (R. Hill rev. ed. 1951).

21. Cotroneo & Krasner, *A Study of Abortion and Problems in Decisionmaking,* 3 J. MARRIAGE & FAM. COUNSELING 69 (1977).

22. Rosen, Teenage Pregnancy and Parental Involvement: Changing Trends (1977) (paper to Annual Meeting of Society for the Study of Social Problems).

23. R. WILSON, PROBLEM PREGNANCY AND ABORTION COUNSELING (1973).

24. C. CHILMAN, ADOLESCENT SEXUALITY IN A CHANGING AMERICAN SOCIETY (1978).

25. Halpern, Cauale, Gant & Bellamy, *A Systems-Crisis Approach to Family Treatment,* J. MARITAL & FAM. THERAPY, April, 1979, at 87.

26. Manderscheid, Silbergeld & Dager, *Alienation: A Response to Stress,* 5 J. CYBERNETICS 91 (1975).

27. P. BLOS, THE ADOLESCENT PASSAGE (1979).

28. Gedan, *Abortion Counseling with Adolescents,* in ABORTION: THE EMOTIONAL IMPLICATIONS 102 (R. Kalmar ed. 1977).

29. SEX INFORMATION AND EDUCATION COUNCIL OF THE U.S., TEENAGE PREGNANCY: PREVENTION AND TREATMENT (1971).

30. Sarrel, *Teenage Pregnancy,* 16 PEDIATRICS CLINICS N. AM. 121 (1969).

31. Aguirre, *Repeat Induced Abortion: Single, Married, and Divorced Women,* 12 J. BIOSOCIAL SCI. 275 (1980).

32. Braen, *The School Age Pregnant Girl,* 10 CLINICAL CHILD PSYCHIATRIC NEWSLETTER 17 (1971).

33. Foster, *Pregnancy among School Age Girls—A Local Evaluation of a National Problem,* 11 PUB. WELFARE 73 (1972).

34. Ademak, *Abortion, Personal Freedom and Public Policy,* 23 FAM. COORDINATOR 411 (1974).

35. Cobliner, Schulman & Romney, *The Termination of Adolescent Out-of-Wedlock Pregnancies and the Prospects for Their Primary Prevention,* 115 AM. J. OBSTETRICS & GYNECOLOGY 432 (1973).

36. C. CHILMAN, *supra* note 24, at 302.

37. CHILD WELFARE LEAGUE OF AM., PREVENTION OF ADOLESCENT PREGNANCY 18 (1974) (Consortium on Early Childbearing and Childrearing).

38. Fox, *The Family's Role in Adolescent Sexual Behavior,* in TEENAGE PREGNANCY IN A FAMILY CONTEXT 124 (T. Ooms ed. 1981).

39. Furstenberg, *Implicating the Family: Teenage Parenthood and Kinship Involvement,* in TEENAGE PREGNANCY IN A FAMILY CONTEXT 162 (T. Ooms ed. 1981).

40. *Id.* at 373.

41. J. CONGER, CONTEMPORARY ISSUES IN ADOLESCENT DEVELOPMENT (1975).

42. Honig, *What We Need to Know to Help the Teenage Parent,* 27 FAM. COORDINATOR 113 (1978).

43. Inazu & Fox, *Maternal Influence on the Sexual Behavior of Teen-age Daughters,* 1 J. FAM. ISSUES 81 (1980).

44. Fox & Inazu, The Effects of Mother-Daughter Communication on Daughter's Sexual and Contraceptive Knowledge and Behavior (1979) (presented to Annual Meeting of Population A. Am.); Chilman, *Some Psychological Aspects of Female Sexuality,* 23 FAM. COORDINATOR 123 (1974); Kantner & Zelnik, *Sexual Experiences of Young Unmarried Women in the United States,* 4 FAM. PLAN. PERSP. 9 (1972).

45. Miller & Simon, *Adolescent Sexual Behavior: Context and Change,* 22 SOC. PROBS. 58 (1974).

46. Jessor & Jessor, *Maternal Ideology and Adolescent Problem Behavior,* 10 DEVELOPMENTAL PSYCHOLOGY 246 (1974).

47. J. CARD, LONG-TERM CONSEQUENCES FOR CHILDREN BORN TO ADOLESCENT PARENTS (1978).

48. Presser, Some Consequences of Adolescent Pregnancies (1975) (presented to Conference of National Institute of Child Health and Human Development).

49. Fox, *supra* note 38, at 112–13.

50. Inazu & Fox, *supra* note 43, at 98–99.

51. E. ROBERTS, D. KLINE & J. GAGNON, FAMILY LIFE AND SEXUAL LEARNING (1978).

52. Rosen, *Adolescent Pregnancy Decision Making: Are Parents Important?,* 15 ADOLESCENCE 43 (1980).

53. Rueveni, *Family Network Intervention: Mobilizing Support for Families in Crisis,* 6 INT'L J. FAM. COUNSELING 77 (1977).

54. Umbarger & White, *Redefining the Problem: Individual Symptoms and Family System,* 6 INT'L J. FAM. COUNSELING 19 (1978).

55. Milling, *The Men Who Wait,* WOMAN'S LIFE, April 1975, at 48.

56. Shostak, *Abortion as Fatherhood Lost: Problems and Reforms,* 28 FAM. COORDINATOR 569 (1979).

57. Jaffee, *What Abortion Counselors Want from Their Clients,* 28 SOC. PROBS. 112 (1978).

58. K. LUKER, TAKING CHANCES (1975).

59. Luscutoff & Elms, *Advice in the Abortion Decision,* 30 J. COUNSELING PSYCHOLOGY 140 (1975).

60. J. Smetana, Personal and Moral Concepts: A Study of Women's Reasoning and Decision Making about Abortion (1978) (unpublished doctoral dissertation, University of California, Santa Cruz).

61. T. ZORABEDIAN, THE VIEW FROM OUR SIDE (1975).

62. L. FRANCKE, THE AMBIVALENCE OF ABORTION (1978).

63. Francke, *Abortion and Men,* Esquire, September 1978, at 58.

64. Rothstein, *Adolescent Males, Fatherhood, and Abortion,* 7 J. Youth & Adolescence 203 (1978).

65. Shostak, *supra* note 56, at 574.

66. Levy, *Abortion and Dissenting Parents: A Dialogue,* 90 Ethics 162 (1980).

67. Shostak, *supra* note 56, at 574.

68. Osborn & Silkey, *Husbands' Attitudes towards Abortion and Canadian Abortion Law,* 12 J. Biosocial Sci. 21 (1960).

69. Blackwood & Blackwood, *What are the Father's Rights in Abortion?,* 3 J. Legal Med. 20 (1975).

70. *See* Weber v. Aetna Casualty and Surety Co., 406 U.S. 164 (1972).

71. Illsey & Hale, *Psychosocial Research in Abortion: Selected Issues,* in Abortion in Psychosocial Perspective 11 (H. David ed. 1978); Walter, *Psychologic and Emotional Consequences of Elective Abortion: A Review,* in Abortion: The Emotional Implications 24 (R. Kalmar ed. 1974).

72. Liebman & Zimmer, *The Psychological Sequelae of Abortion: Fact and Fallacy,* in The Psychological Aspects of Abortion 127, 151 (D. Mall and W. Watts eds. 1979).

73. Illsey & Hale, *supra* note 71, at 12.

74. V. Logrillo, P. Quickenton, G. Therriault & M. Ellrott, Effect of Induced Abortion on Subsequent Reproductive Function (April 18, 1980) (final report, National Institute of Child Health and Human Development).

75. Sim, *Abortion and the Psychiatrist,* 2 Brit. Med. J. 145 (1963).

76. White, *Induced Abortions: A Survey of Their Psychiatric Implications, Complications, and Indications,* 24 Tex. Rep. Biology & Med. 531 (1966).

77. Pare & Raven, *Follow-up of Patients Referred for Termination of Pregnancy,* Lancet, March 28, 1970, at 635.

78. A. Colman & L. Colman, Pregnancy (1971).

79. Calef, *The Hostility of Parents to Children: Some Notes on Infertility, Child Abuse, and Abortions,* 1 Int'l J. Psychoanalytic Psychotherapy 79 (1972).

80. Bracken & Suigar, *Factors Associated with Delay in Seeking Induced Abortions,* 113 Am. J. Obstetrics & Gynecology 301 (1972).

81. Osofsky & Osofsky, *The Psychological Reaction of Patients to Legalized Abortions,* 42 Am. J. Orthopsychiatry 48 (1972).

82. Perez-Reyes & Falk, *Follow-up after Therapeutic Abortion in Early Adolescence,* 28 Archives of Gen. Psychiatry 120 (1973).

83. Kaltreider, *Psychological Factors in Mid-trimester Abortions,* 4 Psychology & Med. 129 (1973).

84. Ewing & Rouse, *Therapeutic Abortions and a Prior Psychiatric History,* 130 Am. J. Psychology 37 (1973).

85. Hutcherson, *The Self Concept of Women at the Time of Elective Abortion,* 33 Dissertation Abstracts Int'l 5493 (1973).

86. Lawrence, *Anxiety-Adjustment and Other Personality Factors in Teen-age Patients before and after Abortion,* in Proc. 81st Ann. Convention Am. Psychology A. 413 (1973).

87. Barglow & Weinstein, *Therapeutic Abortion during Adolescence: Psychiatric Observations,* 4 J. YOUTH & ADOLESCENCE 331 (1973).

88. Martin, *Psychological Problems of Abortion for the Unwed Teenage Girl,* 88 GENETIC PSYCHOLOGY MONOGRAPHS 23 (1973).

89. Moore-Caver, The International Inventory on Information on Induced Abortion (1974) (Int'l Inst. for Stud. Human Reproduction).

90. Bracken, Hachamovitch & Grossman, *The Decision to Abort and Psychological Sequelae,* 158 J. NERVOUS AND MENTAL DISEASE 154 (1974).

91. Blumberg, Golbus & Hanson, *The Psychological Sequelae of Abortion Performed for Genetic Indication,* 122 AM. J. OBSTETRICS & GYNECOLOGY 215 (1975).

92. Adler, *Emotional Responses of Women Following Therapeutic Abortion,* 5 AM. J. ORTHOPSYCHIATRY 446 (1975).

93. Evans, Selstad & Welcher, *Teenagers: Fertility Control Behavior and Attitudes before and after Abortion, Childbearing or Negative Pregnancy Test,* 8 FAM. PLAN. PERSP. 192 (1976).

94. Lipper & Feigenbaum, *Obsessive-Compulsive Neurosis after Viewing the Fetus during Therapeutic Abortion,* 30 AM. J. PSYCHOTHERAPY 666 (1976).

95. Greenglass, *Therapeutic Abortion and Psychiatric Disturbance in Canadian Women,* 21 CAN. PSYCHIATRIC A. J. 45 (1976).

96. Jacobsen, Perris & Espvall, *Personality Patterns in Induced Abortion,* in ABORTION: THE EMOTIONAL IMPLICATIONS (R. Kalmar ed. 1977).

97. I. Kent, Emotional Sequelae of Therapeutic Abortion (September 1977) (unpublished manuscript).

98. Burkle, *A Developmental Approach to Post Partum Abortion Depression,* 218 PRACTITIONER 217 (1977).

99. Bracken, *A Causal Model of Psychosomatic Reactions to Vacuum Aspiration,* 13 SOC. PSYCHIATRY 135 (1978).

100. Blumenfield, *Psychological Factors Involved in Request for Elective Abortion,* 39 J. CLINICAL PSYCHOLOGY 17 (1978).

101. Spaulding & Cavenar, *Psychoses following Therapeutic Abortion,* 135 AM. J. PSYCHIATRY 364 (1978).

102. Cavenar, Maltbie & Sullivan, *Psychiatric Sequelae of Therapeutic Abortion,* 39 N.C. MED. J. 101 (1978).

103. Cavenar, *Aftermath of Abortion: Anniversary Depressions and Abdominal Pain,* 42 BULL. MENNINGER CLINIC 433 (1978).

104. Brewer, *Induced Abortions after Feeling Fetal Movement: Its Causes and Emotional Consequences,* 10 J. BIOLOGICAL AND SOC. SCI. 203 (1978).

105. Fisher, *Abortion: Pain or Pleasure?,* in PSYCHOLOGICAL ASPECTS OF ABORTION 39 (D. Mall & W. Watts eds. 1979).

106. Shusterman, *Predicting the Psychological Consequences of Abortion,* 13A SOC. SCI. AND MED. 683 (1979).

107. Cavenar, Maltbie & Sullivan, *supra* note 102.

108. Liebman & Zimmer, *supra* note 72.

109. Zelnik & Kantner, *Attitudes of American Teenagers towards Abortion,* 7 FAM. PLAN. PERSP. 89 (1975). *See also* Tietze, Foreword to ABORTION IN PSYCHOSOCIAL PERSPECTIVE (H. David ed. 1978).

110. Watson & Rue, *Problem Pregnancies: Analyzing the Counselor's Role,* SHARING, Spring 1974, at 15.

111. Kent, *supra* note 97, at 12.

112. Granberg & Granberg, *Abortion Attitudes, 1965–1980: Trends and Determinants,* 12 FAM. PLAN. PERSP. 251 (1980).

113. Rothman, *Sterilizing the Poor,* 14 SOCIETY 36 (1977).

114. J. MILLER, TOWARD A NEW PSYCHOLOGY OF WOMEN (1976); M. SKOWRONSKI, ABORTION AND ALTERNATIVES (1977).

115. Oliver & Dewhurst, *Six Generations of Ill-used Children in a Huntington's Pedigree,* 45 POSTGRADUATE MED. J. 757 (1969).

116. Lebensohn, *Legal Abortion as a Positive Mental Health Measure in Family Planning,* 14 COMPREHENSIVE PSYCHIATRY 95 (1973).

117. A. MANDER & A. RUSH, FEMINISM AS THERAPY (1974).

118. Lowry, *Abortion as a Preventive for Abused Children,* 8 PSYCHIATRIC OPINION 19 (1970).

119. Tietze, *Repeat Abortions—Why More?,* 10 FAM. PLAN. PERSP. 286 (1978).

120. H. LENNARD & A. BERNSTEIN, PATTERNS IN HUMAN INTERACTION 180 (1970).

121. *Id.* at 181.

122. M. Strauss, Husbands and Wives as Victims and Aggressors in Marital Violence (1980) (unpublished manuscript).

123. Mall, *Abortion and the Cognitive Foundation of Dehumanization,* in PSYCHOLOGICAL ASPECTS OF ABORTION 139 (D. Mall ed. 1979).

124. Ney, *Relationship between Abortion and Child Abuse,* 24 CAN. J. PSYCHIATRY 610 (1979).

125. Calef, *supra* note 79.

126. Kumar & Robson, *Previous Induced Abortion and Antenatal Depression in Primiparae: Preliminary Report of a Survey of Mental Health in Pregnancy,* 8 J. PSYCHOLOGICAL MED. 711 (1978).

127. Granberg & Granberg, *supra* note 112.

128. Shusterman, *supra* note 106, at 685.

129. *Id.* at 686.

130. Bracken, *supra* note 99.

131. D. YANKELOVICH, *supra* note 12, at 239.

Chapter Six Medical Treatment for Pregnant Women

1. Roe v. Wade, 410 U.S. 113 (1973); Doe v. Bolton, 410 U.S. 179 (1973).

2. Roe v. Wade, 410 U.S. at 116.

3. *Id.* at 131.

4. *Id.* at 134.

5. *Id.* at 19.

6. *Id.* at 137.

7. *Id.* at 149.

8. *Id.* note 44, at 149.

9. *Id.* at 150.

10. This is before any of the state laws were liberalized except Colorado, and the total number of deaths is less than half the number of homicides in St. Louis in the same year.

11. Joseph P. Kennedy, Jr., Foundation, The Terrible Choice: The Abortion Dilemma (1968).

12. Roe v. Wade, 410 U.S. at 159.

13. *New Ethics for Medicine in Society,* 113 Calif. Med. 67 (1970).

14. Duff & Campbell, *Moral and Ethical Dilemmas in the Special-Care Nursery,* 289 New Eng. J. Med. 890 (1973).

15. Reproductive Freedom Project, ACLU Found., The So-called "Human Life" Amendment—the Most Critical Threat to Our Right to Privacy (1981).

16. *Id.* at 1.

17. Woods & Cavanagh, *Hemorrhage in Early Pregnancy,* in Obstetric Emergencies (D. Cavanagh, R. Woods & T. O'Conner eds. 1978) [hereinafter cited as Obstetric Emergencies].

18. Grimes, Cates & Selilo, *Fatal Septic Abortion in the United States, 1975–1977,* 57 Am. J. Obstetrics & Gynecology 739 (1981).

19. N. Eastman & L. Hellman, Williams Obstetrics 550 (12th ed. 1961).

20. National Center for Health Statistics, Department of Health, Education and Welfare, *Final Mortality Statistics, 1975,* in 25 Monthly Vital Statistics Rep. 3 (Suppl. Feb. 11, 1977).

21. E. Hughes, Obstetric-Gynecologic Terminology 414 (1972).

22. Lautes, Cunningham & Whalley, *Management of Pregnancy-Induced Hypertension in Nullipara,* 48 Am. J. Obstetrics & Gynecology 253 (1976).

23. Cavanagh & Woods, *Hemorrhage in Late Pregnancy,* in Obstetric Emergencies, *supra* note 21.

24. Sandberg, *Abortion,* in 2 Comprehensive Textbook of Psychiatry (H. Kaplan, A. Freedman & B. Sadock eds. 1980).

25. Hall, *Therapeutic Abortion, Sterilization and Contraception,* 91 Am. J. Obstetrics & Gynecology 518 (1965).

26. Precis, *An Update in Obstetrics and Gynecology,* Am. Coll. Obstetrics & Gynecology 116 (1981).

27. Hardin, *Cyclophosphamide Treatment of Lymphoma during Third Trimester of Pregnancy,* 39 Am. J. Obstetrics & Gynecology 850 (1972).

28. Shin, *Adverse Effect of Pregnancy on Melanoma,* 37 Cancer 181 (1976).

29. Green, Harris & Massey, *Cancer of the Colon during Pregnancy,* 46 Obstetrics & Gynecology 480 (1975).

30. NATIONAL CENTER FOR HEALTH STATISTICS, DEP'T HEALTH, EDUC. & WELFARE, *Final Mortality Statistics, 1977,* in 28 MONTHLY VITAL STATISTICS REP. 3 (Supp. May 11, 1979).

31. CENTER FOR DISEASE CONTROL, 28 MORBIDITY AND MORTALITY WEEKLY REP. 1 (Feb. 2, 1979).

32. *See* Horan, *Fertility Control, infra* ch. 8.

33. Derman, *Early Diagnosis of Pregnancy—A Symposium,* 26 J. REPRODUCTIVE MED. 149 (1981).

34. Hilgers, *Reproduction: Three Issues for the Moral Theologian,* 38 THEOL. STUD. 136 (1977).

35. *See* Tyrer, *When Does Life Begin?,* SEXUAL MED. TODAY 30 (July 1981).

36. Hall, *supra* note 25.

37. *Id.*

Chapter Seven The Medical Aspects of Birth Control

1. Kletz, *The Risk Equations: What Risks Should We Run?,* 73 NEW SCIENTIST 320 (1977).

2. Miller, *Fetal Loss after Implantation,* 2 LANCET 554 (1980).

3. Harlap & Shiono, *Alcohol, Smoking and Incidence of Spontaneous Abortion in First and Second Trimester,* 2 LANCET 173, 176 (1980).

4. Guerrero & Rojas, *Spontaneous Abortion and Aging of Human Ova and Spermatozoa,* 293 NEW ENG. J. MED. 573 (1975).

5. Jongbloet, *Down's Syndrome and Religious Groups,* 2 LANCET 1310 (1978).

6. Jick, *Vaginal Spermicides and Congenital Disorders,* 245 J. A.M.A. 1329 (1981).

7. Orr & Elstein, *Luteinizing Hormone Levels in Plasma and Urine in Women during Normal Menstrual Cycles and in Women Taking Combined Contraceptives or Chlormadinone Acetate,* 43 J. ENDOCRINOLOGY 617 (1969).

8. ROYAL COLLEGE OF GEN. PRACTITIONERS, ORAL CONTRACEPTIVES AND HEALTH: AN INTERIM REPORT FROM THE ORAL CONTRACEPTION STUDY OF THE ROYAL COLLEGE OF GENERAL PRACTITIONERS 100 (1974).

9. McGuire, *Effect of Low Dose Contraceptives Containing Norethindrone and Ethinyl on Serum Levels of Progesterone and Pituitary Gonadotropins,* 2 CONTRACEPTION 329 (1975).

10. Moghissi & Syner, *Studies on the Mechanism of Action of Continuous Microdose Quingestanol Acetate,* 26 FERTILITY AND STERILITY 818 (1975).

11. U.S. DEP'T OF HEALTH, EDUC. & WELFARE, FOOD AND DRUG ADMINISTRATION, MEDICAL DEVICE AND DRUG ADVISORY COMMITTEE ON OBSTETRICS AND GYNECOLOGY, SECOND REPORT ON INTRAUTERINE CONTRACEPTIVE DEVICES 102 (1978) [hereinafter cited as REPORT ON INTRAUTERINE DEVICES].

12. Beling, Cederqvist & Fuchs, *Demonstrations of Gonadotropin during the Second Half of the Cycle in Women Using Intrauterine Contraception,* 125 AM. J. OBSTETRICS & GYNECOLOGY 855 (1976).

13. Klein & Mishell, *Absence of Circulating Chorionic Gonadotropin in Wearers of Intrauterine Contraceptive Devices,* 129 AM. J. OBSTETRICS & GYNECOLOGY 626 (1977); Sharpe, *Absence of HCG-like Activity in the Blood of Women Fitted with Intra-uterine Contraceptive Devices,* 45 J. CLIN. ENDOCRINOLOGY & METABOLISM 496 (1977); Custo, Carenza & Pala, *Levels of HCG in Subjects Using the Progestasert®* Intrauterine Progesterone Systems, 21 CONTRACEPTION 311 (1980).

14. Morgenstern, *Observations on Spermatozoa in the Human Uterus and Oviducts in the Chronic Presence of Intrauterine Devices,* 96 Am. J. Obstetrics & Gynecology 114 (1966); El-Habashi, *Effect of Lippes Loop on Sperm Recovery from Human Fallopian Tubes,* 22 Contraception 549 (1980).

15. Report on Intrauterine Devices, *supra* note 11.

16. Aref & Hafez, *Postcoital Contraception: Physiological and Clinical Parameters,* 32 Obstetrical & Gynecological Surv. 417 (1977).

Chapter Eight Fertility Control

1. 410 U.S. 113 (1973).

2. 318 U.S. 479 (1965).

3. 405 U.S. 438 (1972).

4. 410 U.S. 113 (1973).

5. 410 U.S. 179 (1973).

6. *See, e.g.,* Bivens v. Six Unknown Named Agents of the Bureau of Narcotics, 403 U.S. 388 (1971).

7. *See, e.g.,* David v. Passman, 442 U.S. 228 (1979).

8. Section 3 of the Garn Amendment is substantially similar in effect in this regard to Section 4 of the NRLC Amendment.

9. Section 1 of the NRLC Amendment would not affect the analysis since it deals only with the balancing of constitutional rights when the unborn's right to life is implicated. The right to contraceptives does not implicate the unborn's right to life since it acts before the creation of the unborn child.

Chapter Nine Pregnancy Due to Rape and Incest

1. Whether it dawns on them right away or more slowly, the possibility of pregnancy clearly is one of the top concerns of rape victims. Most typically, the adult rape victims in the study said pregnancy was a big concern. . . . Some victims were visibly shaken at the thought of a pregnancy from the rape.

L. Holmstrom & A. Burgess, The Victim of Rape: Institutional Reactions 84 (1978).

2. S. Brownmiller, Against Our Will: Men, Women and Rape 210 (1975).

3. *See* Model Penal Code § 207.11, Comment p. 155 (Tent. Draft No. 9, 1959).

4. A 1974 poll commissioned by the National Committee for a Human Life Amendment showed 74 percent support for a rape exception. A 1978 Gallup poll showed majority support for a rape exception. These statistics are reported in various memoranda of the National Committee for a Human Life Amendment.

5. *See, e.g.,* Gustafson, *A Protestant Ethical Approach,* in The Morality of Abortion 107 (J. Noonan ed. 1970); Williams, *The Sacred Condominium, id.* at 164–67.

6. As a result of responses received from female medical students, McGuire and Stern concluded that "the general tendency in female responses was . . . to overestimate the incidence [of pregnancy]." Similar dynamics [ignorance, fear, and exaggeration] probably account for an escalation of estimates of the frequency of pregnancy resulting from sexual assault.

Mahkorn and Dolan, *Sexual Assault and Pregnancy,* in New Perspectives on Human Abortion 188 (T. Hilgers, D. Horan & D. Mall eds. 1981).

7. R. GARDNER, ABORTION: THE PERSONAL DILEMMA 168–69 (1972).

8. A pamphlet published by the U.S. Department of Justice, the Law Enforcement Assistance Administration, and the National Institute of Law Enforcement and Criminal Justice recommends the "morning-after" pill within seventy-two hours of the attack, menstrual extraction later, then abortion or carrying to term after one missed period. FORCIBLE RAPE: MEDICAL AND LEGAL INFORMATION (Oct. 1977).

9. *See* comments of Senator Brooke during Labor/HEW Appropriations Bill Conference Committee Meeting Sept. 15, 1976, estimating ten thousand rape-induced pregnancies per year in the U.S.

10. N. LEE, THE SEARCH FOR AN ABORTIONIST 149 (1969).

11. Registrar General's *Statistical Review of England and Wales for 1969* (London 1971, H.M.S.O.), cited in GARDNER, *supra* note 7, at 169 n. 10.

12. B. WILLKE AND J. WILLKE, HANDBOOK ON ABORTION 40 (1979).

13. Diamond, *ISMS Symposium on Medical Implications of the Current Abortion Law in Illinois,* 131 ILL. MED. J. 677–80 (1967).

14. Hayman, *Sexual Assault on Women and Children in the District of Columbia,* 83 PUB. HEALTH REP. 1021–28 (1968).

15. Makhorn & Dolan, *supra* note 6, at 187–88. *See also* Fujita & Wagner, *Referendum 20—Abortion Reform in Washington State,* in THE ABORTION EXPERIENCE: PSYCHOLOGICAL AND MEDICAL IMPACTS (H. Osofsky & J. Osofsky eds. 1973).

16. REPORT OF THE ROYAL COMMISSION OF INQUIRY INTO CONTRACEPTION, STERILIZATION AND ABORTION (New Zealand, 1977).

17. Tietze, *Probability of Pregnancy Resulting from a Single Unprotected Coitus,* 11 FERTILITY & STERILITY 485–88 (1960).

18. Mahkorn & Dolan, *supra* note 6, at 189.

19. Hellgers, U.S.C.C. Abortion Conference, Washington, D.C., October 1967, cited in Mecklenburg, *The Indications for Induced Abortion: A Physician's Perspective,* in ABORTION AND SOCIAL JUSTICE 49 (T. Hilgers & D. Horan eds. 1972). *See also* D. GRANFIELD, THE ABORTION DECISION 112 (1969).

20. Mahkorn & Dolan, *supra* note 6, at 189.

21. *Id.* at 188.

22. Mecklenburg, *supra* note 19, at 50.

23. Maloof, *The Consequences of Incest: Giving and Taking Life,* in THE PSYCHOLOGICAL ASPECTS OF ABORTION 74 (D. Mall & R. Watts eds. 1974). [Hereinafter cited as *Maloof*].

24. *Id.*

25. *Id.*

26. *Id.*

27. *Id.* at 74–75.

28. *Id.* at 75.

29. *See* Comment, *Abortion Laws: A Constitutional Right to Abortion,* 49 N.C.L. REV. 487 (1971). A typical statute would have been CAL. PENAL CODE §§ 274–75 (1949). For a compilation of the antiabortion laws of all fifty states prior to 1961, see Quay, *Justifiable Abortion—Medical and Legal Foundations,* 49 GEO. L.J. 173, 395 (1961).

30. [1938] 1 K.B. 615.

31. *Therapeutic Abortion and the Law,* 2 BRIT. MED. J. 226 (1938), cited in G. GRISEZ, ABORTION: THE MYTHS, THE REALITIES, AND THE ARGUMENTS 222 n.175 (1970).

32. MODEL PENAL CODE § 230.3 et seq. (1962).

33. MODEL PENAL CODE § 207.11 (Tent. Draft No. 9, 1959) at p. 154.

34. *Id.*

35. Arkansas, California, Colorado, Delaware, Kansas, New Mexico, North Carolina, Oregon, South Carolina, and Virginia.

36. Georgia, Maryland, and Mississippi.

37. Alaska, Hawaii, New York, and Washington.

38. *See, e.g.,* Comment, *Certification of Rape under the Colorado Abortion Statute,* 42 U. COLO. L. REV. 12 (1970).

39. George, *Current Abortion Laws: Proposals and Movements for Reform,* in ABORTION AND THE LAW 28 (D. Smith ed. 1967).

40. Here the term "surgical" would include chemical abortions performed by physicians on established pregnancies as in the use of saline or prostaglandin instillation.

41. *See, e.g.,* Ely, *The Wages of Crying Wolf: A Comment on Roe v. Wade,* 82 YALE L.J. 720 (1973).

42. J. NOONAN, A PRIVATE CHOICE: ABORTION IN AMERICA IN THE SEVENTIES 182 (1979).

43. Destro, *Abortion and the Constitution: The Need for a Life-Protective Amendment,* 63 CALIF. L. REV. 1250, 1324–25 n.359 (1975).

44. B. NATHANSON, ABORTING AMERICA 239 (1979).

45. Packer & Gampell, *Therapeutic Abortion: A Problem in Law & Medicine,* 11 STAN. L. REV. 417, 435–44 (1959).

46. Overstreet, *Abortion and Obstetrics—The Means of Determining the Legitimacy of Requests for Abortion,* 2 ABORTION IN A CHANGING WORLD 74 (J. Hall ed. 1970).

47. *Id.* at 81.

48. *Id.* at 81–82.

49. Margolin, *Rape: The Facts,* 3 WOMEN: A JOURNAL OF LIBERATION 20–21, cited in Sagarin, *Forcible Rape and the Problem of the Rights of the Accused,* in FORCIBLE RAPE: THE CRIME, THE VICTIM AND THE OFFENDER 155 (D. Chappell ed. 1977).

50. Comments of Dr. Carl Olstrom in MED. WORLD NEWS, Feb. 4, 1967, reported in *Rape and Incest Exception Not Needed and Unwarranted,* by the National Committee for a Human Life Amendment.

51. K. MEISELMAN, INCEST: A PSYCHOLOGICAL STUDY OF CAUSES AND EFFECTS WITH TREATMENT RECOMMENDATIONS 335 (1979).

52. This is borne out by the data. "Studies of incestuous pregnancies have invariably revealed that more pregnancies are allowed to go to term than are aborted." Maloof, *supra* note 23, at 84. Of course, these figures are not all the product of a fear of disclosure. Oftentimes the pregnant daughter resists abortion despite the wishes of the parents. *Id.* at 84–85.

53. *See supra* notes 23–28 and accompanying text.

54. Maloof, *supra* note 23, at 75.

55. The "scarlet letter syndrome" is effectively discussed and criticized in Mahkorn & Dolan, *supra* note 6, at 192.

56. On responses to rape pregnancies, see Mahkorn, *Pregnancy and Sexual Assault,* in THE PSYCHOLOGICAL ASPECTS OF ABORTION 53 (D. Mall and R. Watts eds. 1979). On incest pregnancies, see Maloof, *supra* note 23, at 73. *See also* Meiselman, *supra* note 51, at 331 passim.

57. There are other crisis responses to rape pregnancy prevention—for example, preventative D&C and menstrual extraction. These are so infrequently used or recommended that full treatment is unwarranted here. But, to the extent that they would operate after a confirmation of pregnancy, they would fall under my discussion of surgical abortion. To the extent that they operate before pregnancy can be confirmed, they would be treated similar to DES.

58. AMA DRUG EVALUATIONS 701–02 (4th ed. 1980).

59. *See, e.g.,* Aref & Hafez, *Postcoital Contraceptives,* in HUMAN REPRODUCTION: CONCEPTION AND CONTRACEPTION 747 (E. Hafez ed. 1980).

60. *Id.* at 751.

61. *Id.*

62. J. LONG, THE ESSENTIAL GUIDE TO PRESCRIPTION DRUGS 222 (rev. ed. 1980).

63. Hayman, *supra* note 14.

64. *See, e.g.,* People v. Collins, 80 Cal. App. 2d 526, 182 P.2d 585 (1947), *cert. denied,* 335 U.S. 831 (1948); People v. Stuart, 168 Cal. App. 2d 62, 335 P.2d 192 (1959); and People v. Murphy, 60 Cal. App. 2d 762, 141 P.2d 755 (1943). *See generally* Quay, *supra* note 29, at 447–526.

Chapter Ten Infanticide, Euthanasia, In Vitro Fertilization, and Fetal Experimentation

1. H.J. Res. 261, 93rd Cong., 1st Sess., 119 CONG. REC. 2589 (1973) (Hogan Amendment).

2. 410 U.S. 113 (1973).

3. *See* Bopp, *Examination of Proposals for a Human Life Amendment, infra* ch. 1.

4. *Cf. A New Ethic for Medicine and Society,* 13 Cal. Med. 67 (1970). Section 2 of the NRLC Amendment is substantially similar.

5. *See infra* ch. 1 for the text of the Garn Amendment. Section 2 of the Garn Amendment is substantially similar to Section 3 of the NRLC Amendment.

6. *Id.* at §§ 1, 2.

7. Olmstead v. United States, 277 U.S. 438, 485 (1928).

8. U.S. CONST. amends. I–X.

9. U.S. CONST. amend. XIII.

10. Buckley v. Valeo, 424 U.S. 1, 93 (1976); Bolling v. Sharpe, 347 U.S. 497, 499–500 (1954).

11. U.S. CONST. amend. XIV, § 1.

12. *Id.*

13. *See supra* ch. 1. This portion of Section 2 of the NRLC Amendment is identical.

14. Flast v. Cohen, 392 U.S. 83, 94–95, 101 (1968); Joint Anti-Fascist Refugee Committee v. McGrath, 341 U.S. 123, 149–50 (1951).

15. Baker v. Carr, 369 U.S. 186, 204 (1962).

16. *See* McCarkle v. United States, 559 F.2d 1258 (4th Cir. 1977).

17. *See, e.g.,* Holt v. Hutto, 363 F. Supp. 194, 217 (E.D. Ark. 1973), *aff'd,* 548 F.2d 740 (8th Cir. 1977), *aff'd sub. nom.* Hutto v. Finney, 437 U.S. 678 (1978).

18. San Antonio School District v. Rodriguez, 411 U.S. 1 (1973).

19. Garn Amendment, Section 3, *supra* ch. 1. Section 4 of the NRLC Amendment is similar in effect.

20. *See* Roe v. Wade, 410 U.S. 113, 174 (Rehnquist, J., dissenting).

21. *See* Horan, *Fertility Control, supra* ch. 8.

22. Steptoe & Edwards, *Birth after the Reimplantation of a Human Embryo,* 2 LANCET 366 (1978).

23. Soupart, Cytogenetics of Human Preimplantation Embryos (June 1, 1977) (National Institute of Child Health & Human Development Grant Application No. HD08837-04).

24. DEP. HEALTH, EDUC., WELFARE, PROTECTION OF HUMAN SUBJECTS; HEW SUPPORT OF HUMAN IN VITRO FERTILIZATION AND EMBRYO TRANSFER: REPORT OF THE ETHICAL ADVISORY BOARD, 44 Fed. Reg. 35033 (June 18, 1979).

25. *Id.* at 34040.

26. *Cf.* Memorandum and Order on Motions Re Intervention and Class Certification, Women's Services, P. C. v. Douglas, No. CV 80-0-349 (D. Neb. March 25, 1981).

27. Flast v. Cohen, 392 U.S. 83 (1968).

28. *See, e.g.,* application to taxpayers intervening to defend prohibition on funding abortions, McCrae v. Matthews, 421 F. Supp. 533 (S.D.N.Y. 1976).

29. *See* United States v. Quarles, 350 U.S. 11 (1955); 2A. SANDS, STATUTES AND STATUTORY CONSTRUCTION § 56.04 (4th ed. 1973).

30. Garn Amendment, Section 2, *supra* ch. 1. Section 3 of the NRLC Amendment is similar in effect.

31. REPORT OF THE ETHICAL ADVISORY BOARD, *supra* note 24, at 35015.

32. *See* Skinner v. Oklahoma, 315 U.S. 535, 541 (1942).

33. This authority would come under the general police power of the government, for which *see* New York *ex rel.* Lieberman v. Van De Carr, 199 U.S. 552 (1905); Jacobson v. Massachusetts, 197 U.S. 11 (1905).

34. *See* Koop, *Ethical and Surgical Considerations in the Care of the Newborn with Congenital Abnormalities,* in INFANTICIDE AND THE HANDICAPPED NEWBORN 89–106 (D. J. Horan & M. Delahoyde eds. 1982).

35. Robertson, *Involuntary Euthanasia of Defective Newborns: A Legal Analysis,* 27 STAN. L. REV. 213 (1975), reprinted in DEATH, DYING AND EUTHANASIA 139 (D. Horan & D. Mall eds. 1977).

36. Shaw, Randolph & Manard, *Ethical Issues in Pediatric Surgery: A National Survey of Pediatricians and Pediatric Surgeons,* 60 PEDIATRICS 588 (1977); Duff & Campbell, *Moral and Ethical Dilemmas in the Special Care Nursery,* 288 NEW ENG. J. MED. 890 (1973), *reprinted in* HORAN & MALL, *supra* note 35, at 91.

37. Thomas, *Potential for Personhood: A Measure of Life,* 2 BIOETHICS Q. 164, 179–80 (1980).

38. *Cf. In re* Quinlan, 70 N.J. 10, 355 A.2d 647 (1976).

39. ILL. REV. STAT. ch. 110½, §§ 11-1 et seq. (1978); ILL. REV. STAT. ch. 110½, §§11a-1 et seq. (Supp. 1981).

40. *See generally, Fetal Research,* 22 VILL. L. REV. 297 (1977); NATIONAL COMMISSION FOR THE PROTECTION OF HUMAN SUBJECTS OF BIOMEDICAL AND BEHAVIORAL RESEARCH, *Report and Recommendations: Research on the Fetus* (DHEW Pub. No. (OS) 76-127, 1975), 40 Fed. Reg. 33,530 (1975).

41. *See* Wynn v. Scott, 449 F. Supp. 1302, 1322 (N.D. Ill. 1978) (three-judge court) *aff'd sub nom.* Wynn v. Carey, 599 F.2d 193 (7th Cir. 1979). *But cf.* Comment, *Considerations in the Regulation of Biological Research,* 126 U. PA. L. REV. 1420, 1427–35 (1978); Davidson, *First Amendment Protection for Biomedical Research,* 19 ARIZ. L. REV. 893, 899 (1977).

42. Margaret S. v. Edwards, 488 F. Supp. 181, 219–21 (E.D. La. 1980); Wynn v. Scott, 449 F. Supp. 1302, 1322 (N.D. Ill. 1978), *aff'd sub nom.* Wynn v. Carey, 599 F.2d 193 (7th Cir. 1979); Wolfe v. Schroering, 388 F. Supp. 631, 638 (W.D. Ky. 1974) *aff'd in part, rev'd in part* 541 F.2d 523 (6th Cir. 1976).

43. Horan, *Fetal Experimentation and Federal Regulation,* 22 VILL. L. REV. 325, 342 (1977).

44. Kamisar, *Some Non-Religious Views against Proposed "Mercy-Killing" Legislation,* 42 MINN. L. REV. 969 n.9 (1958), *reprinted in* HORAN & MALL, *supra* note 35, at 406, 407 n.9.

INDEX